๛ A Baby? . . . Maybe

Also by Elizabeth M. Whelan

Boy or Girl? The Sex Selection Technique That Makes All Others Obsolete

Preventing Cancer: What You Can Do to Cut Your Risks by Up to 50 Percent

Eat OK—Feel OK!: Food Facts and Your Health (with Fredrick J. Stare, M.D.)

The Pregnancy Experience: The Psychology of Expectant Parenthood

Sex and Sensibility: A New Look at Being a Woman

Making Sense out of Sex: A New Look at Being a Man (with Stephen T. Whelan, M.D)

Panic in the Pantry: Food Facts, Fads and Fallacies (with Fredrick J. Stare, M.D.)

Human Reproduction and Family Planning: A Programmed Text (with Michael C. Quadland, M.P.H.)

7-18-88

A BABY?
. . . MAYBE

A Guide To Making
The Most Fateful Decision
Of Your Life

Revised Edition

Dr. Elizabeth M. Whelan

The Bobbs-Merrill Company, Inc.
INDIANAPOLIS NEW YORK

In Chapter Five, the first greeting card poem is used by permission of Norcross, Inc., West Chester, Pennsylvania, Copyrighted—All Rights Reserved.
The second and third poems are copyright © Gibson Greeting Cards, Inc. Used with permission.
The remaining four poems are copyright © 1975 Hallmark Cards, Inc. Used by permission.
The excerpt from the poem "On Children" is reprinted from *The Prophet*, by Kahlil Gibran, with permission of the publisher, Alfred A. Knopf, Inc. Copyright 1923 by Kahlil Gibran; renewal copyright 1951 by Administrators C.T.A. of Kahlil Gibran Estate, and Mary G. Gibran.
The excerpt from "The Road Not Taken" from *The Poetry of Robert Frost* edited by Edward Connery Lathem. Copyright 1916, © 1969 by Holt, Rinehart and Winston, Inc. Copyright 1944 by Robert Frost. Reprinted by permission of Holt, Rinehart and Winston, Publishers.
Material in Chapter Nine on the cost of having a baby originally appeared in *Glamour*, November 1974, under the title, "How Much It Costs to Have a Baby Today." Copyright © 1974 by The Conde Nast Publications, Inc.
Planned Parenthood's "Seven Wrong Reasons for Having a Baby" are reprinted by kind permission of Planned Parenthood-World Population.

Published by The Bobbs-Merrill Company, Inc.
Indianapolis   New York

First printing

Library of Congress Cataloging in Publication Data

Whelan, Elizabeth M
  A baby? . . . Maybe.

  1. Family—United States. 2. Parenthood.
3. Childlessness. 4. Family size. I. Title.
HQ536.W5 1980   301.42'6   79-55437
ISBN 0-672-52628-X
ISBN 0-672-52629-8 pbk.

Designed by Ingrid Beckman
Manufactured in the United States of America

To my parents
To my parents-in-law

Contents

Acknowledgments

The conception, gestation, and delivery of this book involved a large number of individuals whose professional interests, descriptions of their personal life situations, and attitudes toward childbearing proved invaluable in my research into the if, when, and how many of parenthood. I am unable to thank formally each of the more than three hundred people who made a contribution to this work, but I would like to identify a few of those who were particularly helpful.

Professor Erik H. Erikson; Dr. Isaac Asimov; Dr. Henry Greenbaum, Clinical Associate Professor of Psychiatry at New York University School of Medicine; Dr. Robert E. Gould, Professor of Psychiatry at New York Medical College; Dr. Charles H. Debrovner, Associate Professor of Obstetrics and Gynecology at New York University School of Medicine; Dr. Joanna Ehre of the Postgraduate Center for Mental Health; Dr. Allan Rosenfield, Director of the Center for Population Sciences at Columbia University; Dr. Robert Lapham and Dr. Anna Quandt of the Technical Assistance Division of The Population Council; Dr. Donald M. Kaplan, President of the New York Society for Freudian Psychologists; Dr. Peter Wernick of Cornell University; Dr. Susan Bram of the Foundation for Child Development; Dr. William F. Nickel of the Cornell University Medical College and The New York Hospital; Dr. Judith Goldberg, research statistician at the Health Insurance Plan of New York; Dr. Paula Kanarek, Assistant Professor of Epidemiology and Biostatistics at the University of Washington School of Public Health; Dr. Geraldine Oliva, staff physician at Planned Parenthood of San Francisco; Miss Naomi Weiss, Director of the Family Planning Council of New York City; Dr. Rodrigo Guerrero of the University of Valle in Cali, Colombia; Dr. Janet Wittes of Hunter College; Dr.

Robert Wittes of New York Memorial Hospital; Robin Elliott, Director of Information and Education for Planned Parenthood—World Population; Mrs. Arlene Nash of the Child Welfare League of America; Dr. Joseph T. Miller, Board of Directors, Association for the Advancement of Health Education; and Dr. Saul Kapel—all offered professional and personal commentary on the subject of parenthood.

I am also indebted to Marion Goldin, Morley Safer, and Mike Wallace of CBS News; Lynn Caine, Margaret Drabble, Amy Gross, Gael Greene, Ellen Peck, Rosalyn and Mike Cherry, Elaine and Mort Norman, Marilyn and Ivan Mendelsohn, Susan Perricone, Carole Goldman, Betty Higgins, Lee Hersch, Lance and Deirdre Wilson, Britt Colbert, Corky Stoller, Linda Paul, John and Barbara Diesem, Barbara Schacher, Judith Lesser, Ralph and Jeri Olsen, Desmond O'Hagan, Bob Moriarty, Lana and Bob Feinschreiber, Ruth and Edward Lukashok, Martha Chapple Steel, Hallie Sether, Jane Moore, Edna Arena, Kay Ryan, Frieda Dodenhoff, Dorothy Jehle, Sally Felzen, Barry Bartle, Minnie Goldberg, Judy Coonley, Annette and Charles Knechtel, Nancye and Bob Mittendorff, Linda Stone, Gloria Solomon, Nancy Ampel, Dorothy Paul, Lenore and James Parker, Libby and Paul Fitzgerald, Maureen Mittler, Marcy and Carl Erikson, Meredith McSherry, Barbara Blee, Leslie Abramson, Cathy Abramson, Ann Partlow, Gael O'Rourke, Sharon Baum, Emily Eisen, Jan Gilmore, Jack L. Messman, Mary Ann Somerville, Marilynn Leader, Gary Pedigo, Carol Daniel, Katherine Deere, Marie Casey, Connie Christophel, Gayle Hall, Barbara Brown, Hadley Watson, Marion and Joseph Murphy, and Stephen and Virginia Whelan.

I would like to express my gratitude to the staffs of the New York Academy of Medicine; Cornell University Medical College; Planned Parenthood—World Population; and the New York Public libraries for their assistance in locating the great quantity of reference material that was vital to the preparation of this manuscript.

Finally, a special acknowledgment to four people whose efforts were uniquely valuable. Marilyn Bartle not only typed this manuscript, but she also offered extensive comments on each of the earlier drafts. Stefanie Tashjian-Woodbridge, my editor, took a personal interest in this book while it was still only a literary gleam in my eye. June Miller offered considerable assistance in the preparation of this revised edition. And my husband, Steve, played the ongoing role of friendly critic and helped me formulate and evaluate each of the premises on which the book is based.

Preface

I wish everyone, men as well as women, would read this fine book before making what really *is* the most fateful decision of their lives.

We are living in an era when, more than ever before, we have the freedom to choose and the ability to plan the direction our lives will take. We have a healthy respect for individuality, recognizing that there simply is no virtue in sameness. We know now that we do not have to do like one another to respect one another. In all aspects of our lives, acknowledging and maintaining our individuality is an important part of self-acceptance and self-adequacy. But when it comes to making the decision about whether or not to bring a child into the world, a respect for individuality and free, independent, and intelligent choices is particularly critical.

A Baby? . . . *Maybe* offers you a unique opportunity to experience vicariously some of the joys and psychological costs of parenthood; it presents a framework for evaluating your own personal motivations for having or not having children; and it summarizes the latest facts about such practical issues as pregnancy and maternal age, genetic counseling, sex predetermination techniques, and adoption procedures.

It is a splendid work written with sensitivity, humor, intelligence, and compassion. In these pages you'll find an ideal combination: a crucial subject, skilled and entertaining writing, love for the human condition, and solid expertise. *A Baby?* . . . *Maybe* raises many questions and provides some answers. It will help you toward the final answer—which can be found only within yourself.

—THEODORE ISAAC RUBIN, M.D.

Introduction

Quandary. Perplexity. Dilemma. Indecision. My husband and I could not make up our minds about whether or not to become parents.

Uncertainty was new to us. Faced with the usual sorts of decisions couples must make, we had always proceeded straightforwardly. We collected the necessary information and evaluated it. I said what I thought. He said what he thought. We discussed it, decided, and acted. It was really quite simple.

The baby issue was different. The obvious finality, the permanence, the irreversibility of such a decision had us totally bewildered and even a little frightened. In our search for an answer we looked for books that might help. There were none. We talked to a few friends and relatives to learn their reasons for having, or not having, children—only to discover that if there were reasons at all, they simply didn't apply very well to us. At best they provided only partial insight toward working out our dilemma.

What I really needed, of course, was a baby-motivation-analysis machine I could plug myself into to find out once and for all if my inclination toward parenthood fell in the high, medium, low, or replace-battery range. But without such a device I had to settle for conjugal summit conferences, a great deal of self-analysis, and a period of intensive, systematic research. The results of that personal inquiry were presented in the original version of *A Baby? . . . Maybe*.

In the five years that have passed since I put together the first edition of *A Baby? . . . Maybe,* changes have begun to occur in the social culture of our country. More and more women—and men—are finally realizing that some people are cut out to be parents and others are not. Gradually the *option* of parenthood is becoming an acceptable fact.

1

Somewhere between the traditional babies-without-question and the National Organization for Nonparenthood's* stance of no-babies-at-all lie the calmer seas of freedom-of-choice. I say calm*er*; by no means do I wish to imply the waters are necessarily *calm*. The multitude of factors inherent in such an emotional issue do not tend to foster tranquility. Necessarily, one must first acknowledge that the choice exists; that it creates indecision among many would-be parents; and that there is no single "right" or "wrong" answer.

Such acknowledgment does not come easily. The pressures imposed on almost every female from the days of infancy are based on the assumption that she will one day become a mother, like it or not. These suppositions, so thoroughly woven into a young woman's cultural upbringing, are hard to shake. For generations one did not question; one simply had babies.

So at this juncture, I must note that although the issue confused *both* of us, the quandary got to me more than to my husband. We realized it was a joint decision. But I experienced more of the pressure and raised more of the questions than he did. And, of course, it would be *my* life-style that would undergo the greater number of changes. For this reason, I will focus on my own feelings; but don't assume that decisions on parenthood are only female ones. Most decidedly, they are not.

I'm fairly well organized and rational (only later did it occur to me that this might have been a major cause of my problem). I had made many major life decisions already—educational commitments, career choice, and marriage. But every time I raised a question about parenthood and started to consider some of the changes it would bring to our lives, I was stymied. Trying to analyze a thought about parenthood was like trying to enjoy cotton candy: it's gone before you can swallow it. I kept asking myself, "How did we end up in this situation?"

I think I would better understand our ambivalence if we had had miserable family lives and mean, uncaring, difficult parents. But we didn't. We both emerged from family lives we could look back on fondly, with a pretty good ratio of smiles to winces. Our parents enjoyed their children. So, we couldn't look to what a sociologist might call a "poor model relationship." And no, neither of us had a radical streak or a pervasive desire to scorn something because it was expected of us. As a matter of fact, we respect traditions as well as

*In the text I refer to this organization as the National Organization for Non-Parents (NON). Actually, since the first edition of this book, NON has changed its name to the National Alliance for Optional Parenthood (NAOP).

people. For instance, I've always done what was expected of me. I performed well in school; I learned how to swim, sail, and play tennis; and I married the "right" man at Saint Patrick's Cathedral. I was completing the traditional jumping rope rhyme: "First comes love, then comes marriage, then comes Beth with a baby carriage." Or so I expected.

Nor can the quandary be traced to my getting less than my share of the subtle and not-so-subtle motherhood indoctrination. "Take care of your dollies. Tuck them nicely in their carriages." "You should never go swimming during your period or you won't be able to have a baby." "Let me pick that up! You may hurt yourself and never be able to be a mother." (I also remember throwing my favorite doll out of a fast-moving car, swimming during forbidden times, and constantly rearranging the heavy furniture in my college dorm room.)

Naturally, the pressure mounted with marriage. As soon as the engagement was announced, my mother wondered aloud, "Do you think you can find an apartment with an extra room?" (Wink.) "Will you be working part time?" Driving home from a bridal shower, she remarked, "Well, I hope you won't wait *too* long. You're no spring chicken, you know. A smart girl will use what Mother Nature gave her before Father Time takes it away." I suggested that perhaps we could move the schedule ahead somewhat—say, have her first grandchild delivered six months after the wedding. Of course she was horrified. I wonder now which she would have considered worse: a child coming too early, or one not coming at all.

My mother was hardly the only source of pressure. My mother-in-law offered what, in retrospect, was probably the sagest advice: "Don't wait too long to have children, or you might get too used to being just the two of you." And various well-meaning relatives informed me that motherhood was "simply divine" and that "you should have a baby as soon as possible and get it over with," a contradiction that I found very puzzling.

The irony was that all the social and parental pressure was unnecessary; we fully intended to have children. On our honeymoon, we even discussed the timing: one would be born after about two or three years and another about two years after that. For me, there was no question about having more than two. My graduate training included the study of demography. At that point I would have had 2.179 children if it had been possible.

The pressure became really intense about two years after we were married—right about the time that I began to work out of an office in my home. "Now you have the ideal arrangement for combining motherhood and a career," my friends informed me, "so what are you waiting for?"

My parents and in-laws became even more interested: "You've been married a long time now. When are you going to get down to business?" When my husband called home that June to wish his dad a happy Father's Day, the response was, "Too bad I can't wish you the same." And one of my concerned aunts sent me a novelty light which, when you plugged it in, blinked *Tonight's the night.* She added that it was most effective when you "just forget everything; he won't know the difference and then it will be too late."

My mother informed me that she couldn't resist a half-price sale on maternity dress patterns and was now in possession of three. We could handle most of these comments in a lighthearted and straightforward manner ("we're just not ready yet"). But in some circumstances it was a bit more awkward—and sometimes it even hurt.

For instance, when my first book was accepted for publication, I was wildly excited. After telling my husband, I called my mother, opening with a loud and enthusiastic, "GUESS WHAT!" What followed can only be described as a pregnant pause. Of course my mother was pleased with my literary success—but she was obviously disappointed. In the future I was more selective about my exclamations.

One of our main problems was that after our two-year postponement period, it occurred to us that we were happy the way we were. We enjoyed our work, even when it meant long hours. And we enjoyed our vacations. Would a baby fit into our way of life? Could we afford a child? Was I willing to turn the main focus of my attention away from my career? And most important, *were we parent types? Did we like children?*

Well, that depends. Sometimes when coming home on the Fifth Avenue bus from the New York Academy of Medicine, I would see the most gorgeous children sitting with their gloved mothers. They were well scrubbed (both the children and the mothers) and impeccably dressed. They seemed to be very polite, and I'm sure that when they asked their mothers to tell them a story, the mothers enthusiastically complied. They were the sort of children you see in a Saks Fifth Avenue catalog, and if I could I might have ordered one. Saks is very nice about returns.

But I saw other situations, too: harassed parents whose infants were screaming for no identifiable reason; embarrassed parents who tried to explain to you why their daughter pushed every elevator button between one and six, while you were just thankful she wasn't tall enough to push all the others; sad parents who were disappointed because their child did not choose to go to college; discouraged parents who said, "I just can't take it anymore."

Am I the parent type? I sometimes think about a woman physician with whom I once worked. She would often bring the youngest of her six children to the office. This particular child's favorite pastime was inserting metal objects into electric sockets. "No, Billy, you shouldn't do that," the doctor would calmly remonstrate while I quietly choked. Could I learn to be as relaxed as she was about a child's constant activity?

I looked around my apartment and wondered how long a child and our belongings would survive together. The figurines on the étagère would probably be first to go. The low-level bookcases next. The rear corner of our den, which could understandably be confused with a Con Edison annex, accommodated calculators, typewriters, hair dryers, radios, lamps, clocks, electric pencil sharpeners, and a mini-television. Wouldn't *that* be an inviting place to play!

I really didn't know if I had the patience and composure to be a parent. I clearly saw some potential disadvantages of parenthood. But if these negative issues were all that I saw, I would just have decided not to have children. There was more, however: my profamily orientation, and, more important, the collage of feelings that I can only classify as *the unknown factor*. A gut feeling that I "should" have at least one child. A feeling that varied with intensity and probably reached its peak during a certain insurance company's commercial—the one telling that "the future is now." One of their ads was particularly anxiety provoking. It showed a happy young couple walking down the aisle, and within six quick scenes in ten seconds, they're in rocking chairs. "Time is running out and you'd better act fast" was the message that hit me, and the lyrics of the song that begins "Did you ever have to make up your mind?" again began to haunt me. I was thirty, and I began to feel like a rocket, complete with my own countdown.

It's easy to say that this feeling was socially engendered, that I was brainwashed, and that when the pressure was on I couldn't shake my proparenthood condition. Yet I think my feelings involved more than current social pressure and past social indoctrination. Two opposing forces—my doubts about assuming the parenthood role and my gut feeling that I would miss a major life experience by not having a child—were vying for a big prize: the rest of my life.

At times when I have had an acute case of indecision, my remedy has been some time off and a steady diet of information. Facts, I would say to myself; that's what we need to make decisions. But the baby books I found assumed I already had a baby. And the pregnancy books assumed I was already pregnant. Then I read *The Baby Trap* (Ellen Peck), *The Case Against Having Children* (Anna and Arnold Silverman), *Mother's Day Is Over* (Shirley Radl), and a few other how-not-to and why-not-to-guides. I even joined the local chapter of the National Organization for Non-Parents (NON) in an effort to learn more about their side of the parenthood arguments. I got the feeling that parenthood was a dread disease. Unite against cancer! Unite against parenthood!

I called Planned Parenthood and asked if they had any counseling services for couples who were pondering parenthood. The woman who answered the phone could only tell me that I could get contraceptive services at any of the ten clinics in my area. When I repeated my question, she was thrown into a spin; she connected me with her superior, who recommended that I contact a counselor at an adoption agency. The day after I called Planned Parenthood I was traveling on the subway and saw their sign—SEVEN DUMB REASONS FOR HAVING A BABY. But I knew the wrong reasons. I wanted to hear some right reasons. I wanted information on both sides of the issue so that I could break through my own personal impasse.

When I couldn't find the help I needed to make an intelligent decision, I decided to conduct an official investigation, looking closely at some of the psychological and practical factors that might influence the decision to have a child—or not. I had a head start, since my graduate school courses had included the psychological and sociological determinants of fertility and contraceptive use. I pursued the subject by reading hundreds more medical, psychological, and sociological articles.

I talked with dozens of "experts" in the field. I interviewed more than two hundred men and women: those who were single, married, widowed, and divorced; those who, like my husband and me, were undecided; those who were confirmed nonparents or confirmed parents. I talked with couples who were well past their childbearing years, and I asked them to look back and evaluate their decisions to have or not have children. And to round out my research, I turned to some people in novels, plays, and nonfiction to see if their thoughts and actions could provide some additional insight on the parenthood question. Literature is, after all, one of the great repositories of human experience and wisdom.

I cannot claim to have gathered a scientifically representative sample of American couples. Louis Harris would not approve. And I must confess that I did not do one chi-square test. But I did get human responses from a vast range of people. Some were friends, friends of friends, friends of friends of friends. I stopped people in the park, in elevators, in prenatal and well-baby clinics, in subways and stores, and at cocktail parties. (At cocktail parties I got a before-martini and after-martini version of the same answer.) I tried to get different people with different life-styles—and I put it all together to make this book.

To whom are these pages directed? To both men and women. Of all ages. And all marital statuses. To anyone who is seriously considering whether or not to have children. Although the primary focus of each chapter is on the decision to have a *first* child, many of the issues apply equally to decisions about later children.

I first offer an overview of the whole parenthood question, focusing on the various reasons for having children and the specific joys of parenthood. Next I look at nonparenthood—the characteristics of the decision-making process and the advantages and disadvantages of not having children. Then I try to bring it all together by introducing some parents and nonparents who made their decisions years ago and can now look back and evaluate the consequences.

Finally, I discuss some major questions about pregnancy planning—the relationship of maternal age to pregnancy outcome, genetic counseling, sex predetermination, and the financial aspects of having a child. After all, you need some practical information to ensure intelligent planning.

And when you *do* make up your mind—either way—you can consult the Appendix, which carries some questions and answers on subjects of interest to both prospective parents and prospective nonparents.

Meanwhile, you'll meet a number of the couples I had the opportunity to speak with. Some young men and women will tell you how they arrived at their decisions (or in some cases, their nondecisions); those who have made and acted on their decisions will describe some of their feelings. Maybe you'll see a little bit of yourself in these couples. From what I've told you, perhaps you will see a little bit of me, too.

I can tell you one thing right away: all of us have some nonparent and parent elements in us. There are no neat categories. I feel that you, as I did, can get a balanced picture by considering both sides of the question. Perhaps you'll be able to see how your own nonparent and parent elements mesh. And that's at least half the battle.

In *Optional Parenthood Today,* the publication of the recently formed National Alliance for Optional Parenthood, Executive Director Carole Baker writes:

> [T]here is one right of children that, in my opinion, is the most basic right of all. That is, the right to be born into a family that has made a firm commitment of time, love, energy, and financial resources to that child. Let us not forget that adults have rights too. They have the right to choose *not* to make such a commitment to another person. They have the right to choose a life-style compatible with their own individual values, goals, and needs . . . . And, if they choose a direction other than parenthood, they have the right to be accepted and respected for that choice.

A Baby? . . . Maybe says: *think* about the if, when, and how many of parenthood. It does not try to sell you on any one option. It does not provide universal answers. It offers facts, relates experiences, raises questions, and points at the various directions in which you could travel. Above all, it emphasizes the need to *know yourself* before you make *any* major life decision, particularly when that decision involves the possibility of bringing a new life into the world. I attempt to offer you a framework for deciding. And then, as it should be, it's up to you.

—ELIZABETH M. WHELAN
New York City

"I was a-trembling because I'd got to decide forever betwixt two things, and I knowed it. I studied for a minute, sort of holding my breath . . . . "

—Mark Twain, *Adventures of Huckleberry Finn*

"General propositions do not decide concrete cases. The decision will depend on a judgment or intuition more subtle than any articulate major premise."

—Justice Oliver Wendell Holmes, Jr.

❧ 1 ❧

The Parenthood Puzzle

Where Do You Stand on the Baby Question?

What's the nature of *your* personal parenthood puzzle? Perhaps, like my husband and me, the two of you just can't make up your minds, just can't settle it one way or the other and feel satisfied with your decision. Or maybe one of you wants to and the other doesn't, at least not right now. Maybe for you it isn't a question of none or one, but two or three. If you're single, you could be pondering the pros and cons of going it alone. And, of course, there remains the possibility that you are the lucky type: you've always known you did or did not want children. In that case, maybe your only question is "when?"—or how to ensure "never."

If you're confused about the maybe of having a baby, be assured that you're not alone. A lot of other people are confused with you. These days it's becoming more and more common to raise questions about this all-important issue. And some questions don't give rise to answers before they've given rise to more questions. Even if you're fairly sure you've made up your mind, you're likely to rehash *why* you decided one way or the other.

We have recently emerged from the "Don't ask—just do it" stage. We are, if you will, pioneers, on the threshold of a new age, where a decision about having children is acknowledged for what it is: the most consequential decision of your life. Books for new parents are just beginning to comment on the importance of thoughtful, individualized decision making. Dr. Lee Salk in *Preparing for Parenthood* recommends that "we . . . encourage our young people to consider alternatives to parenthood early enough so that they can plan for them. If . . . they still choose to be parents, they will have chosen positively, not passively." Again, this is the thinking of the future, not the past. You're still bound to encounter many people who insist that you *not* ask questions and *not* try to evaluate your own potential for parenthood. Let me give you an example.

"How do you think a couple today should go about deciding if they should be parents?" I asked a father of four teenagers as I watched him reassemble a broken bike in his garage. He seemed more interested in his work than in my question, but he was listening, so I went on. "How do you think a man and woman today should go about planning and budgeting for their first baby and making sure they are ready to be parents?"

He dropped his pliers, turned around, and stared at me. "Planning? Budgeting? You've got to be kidding. You can't talk about a baby the way you'd talk about a European vacation. Some things in life just shouldn't be thought out!" His tone left no doubt that he was not only incredulous, but annoyed. He pronounced each word very deliberately, trying to control his temper.

Then he shook his head as if he were scolding me. "You learn to cope as you go along; that's just the way it was meant to be. I can't think of anything more selfish than budgeting for a baby. Besides, every child brings his own loaf of bread."

I knew I was in dangerous territory, but I persisted. "Today a child costs more than a European vacation and possibly as much as a trip to the moon. And, well, couples *are* thinking about the whole question now. Maybe some men and women just shouldn't have children at all. You know, parenthood no longer is an inevitable part of married life."

Now he was really angry. He didn't even attempt to hide it. He glared at me. "Look, if you've got to ask all those questions, forget it. If you've got to go into the pros and cons and this and that, you're already so far off base, it's hopeless. It's like looking at a yacht. If you have to ask how much it costs, you can't afford it."

He turned his back and started tinkering with the gears control. It was obvious he had nothing else to say to me.

For him, having children was not an option. You did it automatically, and as soon as possible. In terms of years, we're not very far away from the period when this *was* the prevailing point of view. If you look in the pre-1968 issues of the *Reader's Guide to Periodical Literature,* you'll find a subject heading that reads "Childlessness: see 'sterility.' " No one considered the possibility that a couple was childless by choice. Nonparenthood just wasn't an option. Prior to the mid-1960s, couples just had babies and welcomed them with open arms and, if necessary, empty wallets. After having one, two, or three, *then* perhaps parents of the 1940s and 1950s might have asked themselves, "Do we want more?" More often than not, however, children, especially a first child, just happened.

Things have changed. First, we are living in the age of the contraceptive revolution. As recently as two decades ago, 25 percent of American couples used no form of birth control at all, and those who did attempt to plan the size of their families had to choose from a limited number of risky, cumbersome devices. Today 97 percent of the young married couples in the United States are using or plan to use some form of contraception, and the methods available are both highly effective and relatively convenient to use.

Second, also in the mid-1960s, the alternatives to parenthood—particularly for women—became more attractive. It became clear that our lives could take directions that bypass the role of mother and father and still be fulfilling and satisfying. Indeed, in many social circles priorities seem to have shifted. Dual careers for husband and wife often are considered more desirable than the traditional family arrangement where the wife stays home with the children while the husband goes off to conquer the world. Life goals that either exclude parenthood or make the option to have children a particularly expensive one in terms of personal sacrifice seem to have been instilled in many women who reached the childbearing age in the sixties and seventies. Where a couple marrying in the 1940s or 1950s may have been prepared immediately to turn their attention from themselves to another dependent individual, young marrieds of the next generation are more concerned about their own achievements and satisfactions and less willing to make that instant transition.

Third, the late 1960s and the 1970s brought a new acceptance of the free-to-be philosophy. A number of social attitudes changed, becoming less rigid. There was the so-called sexual revolution, described by some as "a strong breeze of honesty that blew away many of the Victorian ideas about the unnaturalness of sex." A new tolerance slowly began to develop toward homosexuality, abortion, birth control for teenagers, and one-parent and one-child families. People began to feel that they could do their own thing without social censure—as long as it didn't interfere with the rights of others.

Fourth, the rise in the general cost of living and the unprecedented expenses of having and raising a child have led couples to think twice before they assume the economic burdens of parenthood. After World War II and during the 1950s, for instance, there was a significant economic boom, a circumstance in which the birthrate flourished; however, the late 1960s and the 1970s saw a full reversal of this trend. Some economists even feel that babies are a type of consumer durable which in times of plenty are affordable and (given that they really *don't* bring their own loaves of bread) in times of difficulty must compete with other priorities on the things-we-need list.

Fifth, for reasons of population pressure, most of us now are deeply concerned about the question of how many, if any, children we should have. National surveys confirm that only a small minority of young American couples approach parenthood with the old-fashioned as-many-as-God-will-send-me attitude. Decisions on childbearing are viewed as having some social, as well as personal, ramifications.

Today that father of four with his just-do-it approach is no longer typically representative. "If there is any doubt, don't!" a mother of two half-grown sons told me. "Bringing a child into the world is a very serious responsibility. An undecided couple can always reverse a negative decision, but not a positive one. Parenthood is forever. In our case, we knew we *wanted* a family; we wanted to enlarge our circle of love. But a couple who does not want children owes apologies to no one. After all, they're doing their part to control the population explosion."

Parenthood has decidedly become an option. But the decision one way or another is understandably complex, given that the upper-age limits on female fertility haven't changed.

In a sense, it was easier in the unplanned past. We have no precedent to follow in making these important decisions. There are no formulas for us to apply. There are many marriage counselors, but preparenthood counselors are still relatively rare. Except in a few select areas of the country where such counseling services do now exist, most couples are pretty much on their own. Even with counseling, the ultimate choice is still a personal one; counselors do not make actual decisions. With the new freedom to choose, we are forced to choose wisely. And that usually means taking a long, hard look inside oneself.

It's a Highly Emotional Issue!

That fuming father of four who described his "don't ask questions; having children is something you can't map out" philosophy is wrong—and right. The don't-hesitate, just-procreate attitude is no longer appropriate. Maybe it never was. But he is right in that, even in the age of the Pill, the topic of having children cannot be approached through a formal family business meeting that meticulously follows *Robert's Rules of Order*, presents flow charts and economic forecasts, evaluates lists of advantages and disadvantages, and concludes with a cost benefit analysis of all viable options. We *do* have more control than ever before over human reproduction. We *can* consider everyday facts in our planning; for instance, the cost of having a child or the best timing for coordinating a career and parenthood. But we must face the fact that actual decisions about having or not having babies are not totally rational ones. *The decision to have a baby is primarily emotional.*

Consider the uniqueness of the question. By comparison, the marriage decision is easier to make. Before you say "I do," you've dated a number of people and thought about the type of person you'd like as a lifelong partner. And after you're married, life doesn't really change drastically. There may be new ways you divide up tasks and responsibilities, but basically you are still your own person and plan your day pretty much the way you want. And although you're probably not aware of it, the day you take the vows, somewhere in your brain's storage compartment is the knowledge that, if necessary, the marriage can be dissolved.

The decision to be a parent is different. The result is unpredictable. You have no idea what this person you may produce will be like. Will she be a cheerful, friendly child or a withdrawn, gloomy one? Will he be clever and intelligent like you or bumbling and absentminded like your Uncle Mortimer? What will she look like? Will he have huge ears like your mother-in-law?

Even if you are a Superparent, you have no guarantee of what the child will be like and how he'll develop. Children have a way of being remarkably independent, and parents have been known to stare in awe at their own offspring, thinking, Could he really be mine? Of course this type of speculation works both ways; the child could either amaze you with success and accomplishments or frustrate you with a rejection of what you see as ideal goals.

Additionally, you don't know in advance what *you* will be like after you become a parent. Will you discover positive attributes you thought you never had? Will you be patient and self-sacrificing and almost moo with contentment? Or will you become a frustrated, irritable zombie?

Parenthood decisions are emotional ones made without benefit of relevant facts. The changes a child brings to a couple's life can be very significant. Children are dependents. And unless you are unusually wealthy, it is you who will be taking care of them. His or her wants will take priority over yours. But probably most sobering of all, children are not returnable. You can have an ex-wife, ex-husband, ex-job, but you cannot have an ex-child. The result of your decision, in other words, is not only unpredictable, it is irrevocable. That is why it's the most fateful decision of your life.

But it is possible to tense up and approach it *too* rationally, too systematically, with too many logistical requirements. At some point after the relevant facts are digested, we have to look inward for the ultimate gut-level, emotional answer (especially if it is yes).

Let's examine this point carefully. We tend to be wary of emotion, traditionally, because it can overwhelm us. But without it we're lost. What's the proper perspective?

In recent years, a minority of individuals has been attempting to ignore or deny the emotional aspects of pregnancy and birth. For instance, I have a friend who is an enthusiastic, outspoken nonparent. She constantly complains to me about the pro-baby forces our society exerts on us, and she bitterly condemns what she refers to as the mystique that surrounds babies and children. "What's the big deal about a baby?" she asks. "We have too many of them anyway. I would hardly consider them a precious commodity today. So why do people still get choked up with tears when they receive a birth announcement? It's just ridiculous."

I strongly feel that this woman and many other young men and women like her are victims of a highly unfortunate side effect of the contraceptive revolution. They have come to take childbearing for granted. They coolly refer to a new human life as a "commodity," one, they add, that we don't need. Militant antiparenthood people seem to want to strip human procreation down to its strictly biological components—and pass off any other attitudes or motivations as a "mystique." They come up with self-righteous polemics about the wrong reasons to have children, and they encourage us to consider the whole parenthood issue on a purely rational level that takes into account the population growth factor in India, the wife's IQ and career potential, and the mutual willingness to take a group of children to the zoo on Saturday morning.

But attitudes and decisions about having children are colored by a whole headful of psychological needs and conflicts. By becoming a parent, for example, you may find that your images of yourself and your mate change—in either a positive or a negative direction. You may see the child as a strong emotional bond that brings you and your spouse even closer than you were in the first place. You probably will find that people react differently toward you and that your relationships with relatives are altered.

On the other hand, in *Of Woman Born*, Adrienne Rich describes what poet Lynn Sukenick refers to as "matraphobia"—the fear of becoming one's mother. For many women, the idea of parenthood recalls to mind thoughts of their own childhood with a mother who led a rather joyless existence in a spotless house, entertained by women's magazines and occasional club meetings, measuring her daughter's success in terms of clean, starched dresses and good grades in school. Understandably, a modern woman absorbed in career, encounter groups, and any number of other activities (perhaps in addition to a husband) may break out in goosebumps at the thought of becoming enmeshed in a similar anti-life style.

Choosing between becoming a parent and remaining child-free directly affects your whole future orientation—the direction in which your energy is focused, and your whole way of life. These are all emotionally charged issues, and they are there, exerting their force, as you sit down to put your own parenthood puzzle together. And at the core of this puzzle is an emotional-psychological factor that is the most critical and pervasive of all. Perhaps it could be called *the moral factor*: the ability to justify to yourself whatever decision you make. The willingness to accept the consequence—both desirable and not so desirable—of either parenthood or nonparenthood. The capacity to feel comfortable with your decision. And, if the resolution is in favor of having a child, the willingness—indeed, eagerness—to assume the responsibility for creating a new life.

Consider another more specific example of an emotional-psychological aspect of pregnancy and our attitudes toward it. The issue of one's ability to conceive or impregnate is a very sensitive one, and, when the matter is successfully resolved, there can be an unconscious or conscious feeling of emotional reinforcement. "I was so thrilled that I could do it," one twenty-eight-year-old woman told me, "and I know my husband was as pleased as could be too. It took us almost eight months to conceive, and after awhile I began to worry. It was really a relief for both of us when the doctor told me my test was positive."

It is not popular these days to talk about conception as a means of confirming sexual identity and physical completeness. But the fact remains that pregnancy can do just this. Even the *diagnosis* of pregnancy, as opposed to the full gestation and delivery experience, may elicit this type of reinforcement about one's physical ability to reproduce.

A graduate school student I talked with recalled her feelings about the abortion she had had two years before: "When I found out I was pregnant and knew there was absolutely no way I would be able to continue it, I was, of course, upset over the prospect of facing the expense and emotional trauma of having an abortion. But I also remember some strangely positive feelings. I was happy to know that I *could* conceive—and there was something almost magical about knowing that I now had the capability of bringing a new life into the world. My fiancé overtly demonstrated pure panic over my condition, but I detected a sincere interest in what was going on inside me. He later told me that he had been secretly fascinated with the idea that I was pregnant, but didn't really know why."

Jane Howard, in her book *A Different Woman*, writes of a similar conversation with a woman who had undergone an abortion. "It was strange when I heard I was pregnant," the woman told her. "In spite of everything, even though I wasn't sure I wanted to have a baby, I was actually happy because at least I knew that it was possible for me to conceive."

Jane Howard adds, "I'd be reassured if I knew that for a fact, too."

This emotional aspect of conception and its frequent tie with a man's or woman's self-concept—or even their concept of each other—was particularly evident among those couples I met who were trying unsuccessfully to have a child. In the first place, many of them did not even want to admit they were having a problem. ("Oh, well, we really haven't been trying that hard or that long. I imagine everything is all right.") In some cases, both the man and the woman would repeatedly stress the fact that the wife had had at least one miscarriage. The miscarriage almost seemed to be a status symbol that separated them from the "poor infertile" couples. ("At least we know I *can* conceive; it's just a matter of retaining the pregnancy.")

Why do some people have to deny the emotional, nonrational aspects of parenthood? Maybe they are unwilling to acknowledge that we don't have 100 percent rational control over this intimate area of life. Or perhaps it's an overreaction to the baby-adoring society and economy in which we have lived for so many years. But there is no way you can walk around with even one eye and ear open and miss the deep emotional feelings associated with babies and children. These feelings and attitudes do exist, and they come into play when we consider having children. This is not to say that all men and women need to have children, that every one of us craves the emotional experience that surrounds parenthood. But to deny these feelings or to label them purely "socially engendered" is to ignore what appears to be a basic part of human nature.

I asked nearly one hundred women how they felt the day they learned they were pregnant with their first child. Probably one of the most significant points I gleaned was that each one of them remembered the exact circumstance in which she got the news—even though in some cases this day occurred over thirty years ago. "Back in those days you didn't find out right away," one grandmother told me. "I remember walking into the doctor's office and seeing him beaming as he said, 'Mrs. Miller, the rabbit died—and it wasn't of a heart attack!' I was just thrilled. I ran home and put up Welcome Home, Daddy signs all over the living room. I felt the same kind of feeling the day my daughter called and told me I was going to be a grandmother. I just broke down and cried."

The militant antiparenthood argument goes something like this: there was a time when death rates were high and babies indeed were precious, both from the point of view of continuing the human race and because of their utility as laborers. But we are far away from those days, and children are no longer precious creatures to whom you become emotionally attached. They are just a burden to both the individual and the planet.

There is a valid rebuttal. Maybe children are *more* precious and *more* emotion-provoking today than ever before. Consider four demographically typical families of the past before you say, "Oh, no, never."

Wolfgang Amadeus Mozart was one of seven children, five of whom died within six months of their birth. He himself was the father of six children, only two of whom lived beyond age six months. Mozart was a survivor of scarlet fever and smallpox, and he died at the age of thirty-five of an unknown cause.

Three of our illustrious presidents and their families demonstrate a similar profile. George Washington married Martha when she was a twenty-six-year-old widow who had already had four children, two of whom had died in infancy; of the two surviving, one died at age seventeen, the other in early adulthood. Thomas Jefferson lost his father at age fourteen; he married his wife, Martha, a twenty-three-year-old widow, who died eleven years later, having given birth to six children, only two of whom lived to maturity. Abraham Lincoln's mother died when she was thirty-five years old and he was nine. She had had three children, one of whom died in infancy, another in her early twenties. Abraham's first love, Anne Rutledge, died at age nineteen—and of the four sons born to Abraham and Mary Todd Lincoln, only one survived to maturity.

Sociologists have documented that in high mortality societies—where there is a high probability that an infant will not survive his first year of life, and if he does, a good chance he won't make it to age twenty—parents have relatively aloof attitudes toward their children. It was just not practical to make an emotional commitment to an infant who ran such a high risk of dying. Dr. David M. Heer of the University of Southern California has stated: "In a society wherein many children will die before reaching the age of five, parents may frequently steel themselves for the possibility of their child's early death by forbidding themselves to develop a strong emotional attachment . . . furthermore, where mortality is high, parents may be loath to make sacrifices for the future success of their children, since the probability of the child's living to maturity is by no means certain."

The feeling of preciousness and deep parent-child bonding was not the same before modern medicine and improved nutrition made infant, childhood, and early adulthood death a relative rarity. Now add to that the prevalence of effective contraceptive use and the increased odds that the child was planned, and you have perfect mystique material: a wanted infant with whom you will probably intimately relate for at least thirty-five years of your life.

For many people there *is* something thrilling about learning that a much-desired pregnancy or birth has occurred. "When I heard that the first girl in my college group was pregnant, I got all teary," explained Virginia, one of the young child-free wives I spoke with. "I knew she'd always wanted children, and I was sincerely thrilled for her."

"I'm highly emotional about all children, not just my own," a young father commented to me as his three young children crawled over him. "I just cannot read magazine or newspaper stories about children being brutalized. I can't understand how anyone could ever mistreat a child. They're so innocent—so helpless. I guess that's why, when I read about a plane or automobile crash, I feel doubly upset when I learn that there were infants or children involved. Youngsters are so unblemished—and they have everything ahead of them!"

Yes, Virginia, there is a mystique about children—but it doesn't mean that everyone needs to or should have a child of his or her own. It just indicates that for many people children are indeed precious—not from the material point of view, but for purely emotional reasons, for themselves. Only the most scientifically rigid people would deny that there is at least a trace of miracle in the whole process. "I can't believe this little human being actually came out of *me!*" one new mother exclaimed for the third time that morning.

"You know, I'm not even religious in the slightest bit. The last time I went to church was when I was twelve years old. But when the doctor first handed me my daughter, and I saw her perfect little body, all I could say was 'Thank you, God.' "

Relax. It's Only the Most Important Decision You'll Ever Make

I really mean that! The statement above doesn't have to be a contradiction. In deciding whether or not to have a child, you'll want to take your time to ask questions, get some answers and reflect on them. Undoubtedly you'll get your share of advice from concerned friends and relatives, and some are sure to tell you "you're going against nature" by even *considering* not having children or stopping after one. Many may be eager to offer their counsel. But most important, you'll want to look inside yourself.

As you do, I suggest you consider the words of Plutarch, the Greek philosopher and historian. They're relevant.

> There are two of the inscriptions at Delphi [an oracle] which are most indispensable to living. These are "Know Thyself " and "Avoid Extremes," for on those two commandments hang all the rest. These two are in harmony and agreement with each other, and the one seems to be made as clear as possible through the other. For in self-knowledge is included the avoidance of extremes and in the latter is included self-knowledge.

Know thyself. It's a statement that has been around a long time. It's been attributed to a variety of writers, including Plato and Socrates, and was picked up by later "greats," such as Cervantes and Thomas Mann. It hasn't worn out in the last two thousand years.

Know thyself. It's a key to the parenthood puzzle. It's a particularly complex key because it usually involves not one person, but two. Know thyselves, then. Know who you are singly and who you are as a couple. Know, for instance, what your strengths and your weaknesses are, what you have to offer, and what a child would simply have to tolerate. Self-awareness is the best, most reliable way to reach the final decision about whether or not you would like to be a parent.

Think about the other part of that ancient advice, about avoiding extremes. Feelings about parenthood and nonparenthood overlap.

So whichever decision you make, expect to have mixed feelings: there are points on both sides. Making up your mind about having a baby would be much easier if you could expect that one day a bell would ring, a smile would come to your face, and you would know for sure that you had the answer. Don't hold out for that day. It won't come. If you really know yourself, it can't come, because, by going to such an extreme, you'd be denying the very ambivalences and conflicts that characterize us as human.

So relax. Think about parenthood. Talk about parenthood. Keep asking questions of yourself and each other. Recognize that you have feelings on both sides of the issue, and accept them. By doing so, you'll come to understand yourself better, and the pieces of your own parenthood puzzle will begin to fall into place. In the words of Oriana Fallaci in *Letter to a Child Never Born:* "To be a mother is not a trade. It's not even a duty. It's only one right among many." You may choose to exercise that right or you may choose to pass.

Should you decide negatively, that does not mean you will be forever removed from the world of children. On a recent Mother's Day, writer Erma Bombeck dedicated her syndicated column to "Nonmothers." Among others, she referred specifically to teachers and caretakers. She could as well have included volunteer helpers in orphanages and children's hospitals. Her point was simply to acknowledge all the Nonmothers for whom no songs are sung, no appropriate cards written, no special days set aside, yet "who touch a child's life in a million ways."

If you decide positively, don't be alarmed if you continue to harbor occasional ambivalent feelings throughout pregnancy and perhaps longer. Such feelings, too, are normal. But you will have the satisfaction of knowing that you have thoroughly examined the options and reached the best probable decision for *you.*

⋖ 2 ⋗

Here Comes the Bribe: Pronatalism, Past and Present

The Procreative Push

One of the first things you should realize is that you are surrounded by proparenthood propaganda, otherwise known as *pronatalism.** Religions. Family traditions. Media. Employers (of husbands). Friends and neighbors. Even your friendly local insurance representative, who may keep asking, "What are your plans?" And let's not forget those eager prospective grandparents. All of them provide the gentle push to ensure that what is natural will occur on schedule.

In terms of historical perspective, the pronatalist spirit in our culture today is nothing new. The forces we are now facing, including our ongoing debate about tax and home mortgage privileges that favor parents, have about the strength of a marshmallow when compared to some of the forces in the past.

Consider some early examples. The Code of Hammurabi, enacted in the eighteenth century B.C. in Babylon, is the first recorded attempt to increase the number of births by outright legislation. Pronatalist policies were enacted in Rome during the

---

*In case you don't have a demographic dictionary handy, *pronatalism* refers to all social policies that encourage us to reproduce ourselves, preferably more than once.

reign of Caesar Augustus somewhere between 18 B.C. and A.D. 9. The *Lex Papia et Poppaea,* for instance, contained various provisions designed to encourage marriage and the raising of children: fathers were given preference in public office according to the number of children they had, and mothers were given the right to wear distinctive clothes and ornaments. In seventeenth-century Spain, men who married early and had large families received partial or full exemptions from taxes, and in France, any of the nobility who had ten or more legitimate children received annual pensions.

Even the official symbol associated with babies and childbirth was one chosen because of its high esteem. The stork itself has long been a highly respected animal and often the subject of religious worship. Aristotle wrote that it was a crime to kill a stork, for it was rumored that this bird had the capacity to protect human beings from such evils as fire, lightning—and sterility. Storks are monogamous creatures (once one loses its mate, it never remates), and historically they have been identified as good birds to know when you wanted a baby. Actually, of course, the stork too often gets the credit for what is more justly attributable to a lark.

The reason for the long, although not uninterrupted, history of pronatalist policies is pretty obvious: if the human race is to survive, the majority of us must have children. On the other hand, particularly in our current demographic complex, *everyone* does not have to have children. The social pressures we live with, however, do not discriminate. They apply to all married individuals who carry around reproductive equipment.

As I mentioned above, proparenthood propaganda comes from a number of sources. It's worth taking a closer look at some of the major pressure points. By recognizing the subtle and not-so-subtle facets of the procreative push, you might have a better chance of coping with them.

I climbed to the fourth floor of a slightly run-down suburban apartment house, rang the bell, and was greeted by a well-rounded, rosy-cheeked woman in a floral housedress. She knew I was coming to ask her some questions about parenthood, and her enthusiasm was evident.

"I was so excited that you wanted me in your book! I have so many stories I can tell you." After about thirty seconds I got the feeling that our visit was going to be the high point of her day.

She led me down a dark hall to the living room and we sat down. "Do you know that I have five wonderful children?" She was beaming about as much as one can beam. "Let me tell you about them—or would you prefer to ask me questions?" I suggested a little of both. For the next half hour she told me the life stories of each of her offspring.

Then I thought I had earned the right to ask a question: "Did you ever think about *why* you had children?" My previous experience with that particular question had led me to expect a blank stare. I was not disappointed.

As she thought about it, she began to look more puzzled. "I'm not quite sure what you mean. Why I had children? Well, what else is there to say except that it's just natural, and my God says that's what marriage is all about."

"Your God?"

She was beginning to eye me with suspicion. "Yes. You see, I'm Catholic. And for Catholics, children are the most important part of marriage."

"How did you learn this?" I asked. "Did someone tell you, or did you just know?"

Now she looked uncomfortable. She shifted in her chair and put her hand on her chin. "Well, it's like this. You're married, so I guess it's all right to talk about these things. When the priest says you are husband and wife, you get . . . well . . . privileges. But part of the deal is that you get the responsibility, too. We knew about that, but, so we wouldn't forget, our priest gave us a book. It told us about, you know, our duties."

After that conversation, I decided to read some of those religious marriage manuals. I started with Father Kelly's *The Catholic Marriage Manual* and was informed that "your primary job is to perform the function of parenthood. . . . Most Catholic husbands and wives realize that a home without children, no matter how luxurious, is not a home in the true sense. . . . The whole success of your marriage depends, therefore, upon your recognition of the fact that its purpose is the bearing and rearing of children."

I moved on to Charles McFadden's book, *Medical Ethics:* "Should both parties actually bestow on each other the right to proper marital intercourse but mutually agree to have only contraceptive relationships with each other, their marrige is valid, but gravely sinful." (Earlier in the book he stated that a marriage contracted with the intent of being childless was invalid and that such a situation was grounds for annulment.)

And then there was Reverend Edwin F. Healy's *Marriage Guidance:*

Every husband and wife should sincerely desire that children be born to them, for children bring to married couples innumerable blessings. Experience teaches that, during the first few months of marriage, the young couple will as a rule overflow with ardent love for each other and will be much enamored of their new life. After about a year the novelty of marriage tends to wear off, and each begins to realize that the other has certain defects—defects which may be quite irritating. The burdens of life together then begin to make themselves felt, and the husband and wife find that their hearts are not so perfectly united as they were during the honeymoon. If at this time a baby is born to them, it will serve as a golden link of love between husband and wife. The child will bind them together more firmly.

Children: a form of God-given glue. Some blushing brides' first introduction to married life came from Father Healy.

If you're Catholic, you have your own special push. But don't assume that because you're not Catholic, you're off the religious hook. The Talmud proclaims that he "who brings no children into the world is like a murderer. . . . A childless person is like dead." Jewish law is explicit in stating that it is the obligation of the individual to marry and propagate the race. A man has performed the biblical precept to "be fruitful and multiply" if he has at least a son and a daughter, but preferably he should have more. As with Catholicism, strict interpretation of Jewish law would require annulment or divorce in the case of voluntary childlessness.

"And the pressure's picking up," one Orthodox Jewish wife told me (at the time, pregnant with her third). "Our rabbi has been telling us each week to have more than two children. I guess he's afraid there aren't going to be enough of us to survive through the next generations if we don't do more than replace ourselves. You know, with what's happening in Israel and all."

You're Protestant? Maybe then your church does take a more moderate stand. With the exception of some of the really fundamentalist groups such as the Hutterites (a sect renowned for its extraordinarily large families), most Protestant codes accept in principle the idea of birth control, and followers are told to make decisions about childbearing "intelligently." Andrew Eickhoff in *A Christian View of Sex and Marriage* writes that "some mothers have no difficulty in bearing and caring for many children; others are unable to cope with the problem of more than one or two." The fact that he does not even mention the possibility of a zero-child family does suggest that some children are expected, and perhaps theologically required. So Protestantism may have its own more subtle form of pronatalism.

But the push comes from more than religious indoctrination. It includes our earliest forms of education, and constant reminders from our friends and parents.

When are we first oriented toward the parenthood role? Some insist it begins in the nursery, with the presentation of the first doll and the early encouragement of mothering and fathering games. They maintain that if little girls were given trucks instead of dolls, they wouldn't have a deep desire for motherhood later on. Maybe. But maybe every one of those little girls would grow up with the fervent desire to be a truck driver.

I'm inclined to focus more on what comes after infancy and early childhood. One of the first things we all got in school was a colorful primer depicting the happy three- or four-child family with a beaming mother who was on a short chain reaching from the refrigerator to the oven to the washing machine. Antinatalists certainly have a right to criticize such romanticized and narrow views of what family life is all about; indeed, groups such as one called Women, on Words and Images, located in Princeton, New Jersey (producers of the booklet *Dick and Jane as Victims*, a content analysis of 150 school readers), have conducted an all-out attack on those textbook publishers who are still pointing in this direction.

In addition to our textbooks, we received subliminal messages from movies and radio and television programs that told us we were merely underdeveloped versions of mothers or fathers, a condition that time would rectify. But in fairness to our parents and to those who wrote our books, that *was* what usually happened. Non-parenthood or a one-child family were not considered viable options, primarily because motherhood was the one and only job description that most women fitted, and contraception was not sufficiently advanced to allow couples to postpone, space, or avoid children.

As I have indicated, the real pressure mounts with the sound of wedding bells. Most religious ceremonies are performed to solemnize the expressed intent to have children. Jovial guests throw rice—a traditional nuptial preventive measure believed to ward off infertility. (In mythology there are reports that evil spirits attend weddings and, out of jealousy, will attack the bridegroom. The rice is to distract these ugly, and evidently hungry, spirits.) Then the wedding toasts begin: "May all your troubles be little ones." "Orange blossoms this year, orange juice next." "We wish you love—we wish you joy—and every year a ten-pound boy." (*Every* year?!)

After the ceremony, parents and friends begin to greet you with looks of fertile expectation. I've met few child-free couples who didn't have some experience with the forces of planned grandpar-enthood. "Both my parents started on us during our wedding reception," a mother of two young boys told me. " We were married five months when I found out I was pregnant, and when I told my mother the news, she gasped, 'Finally!' "

"You won't believe this," confided a radio technician I was interviewing over the roar of the transmitter, "but my mother used to call us every night about eleven. 'What are you *doing*, dear? Are you getting ready for *bed*?' We were polite for the first year of this. We even figured out ways of fielding her not-so-subtle comments. But after a while, it got to be too much. When her late-night call came in a few weeks ago, I put the whole issue on the line and said, 'Look, ma, if you ever do want grandchildren, you'd better stop calling us at this hour.' Now she calls on Sunday mornings, and that's not so great either."

Comments that fall in the not-so-subtle category include the following: "Did I tell you that Bill and his wife and their new baby will be in town? *They've* only been married a year and half!" Or, "*When* is the younger generation coming to?" "Is everything *okay*? Are you *all right*?" "Do you have anything to *tell* me?" "Now that would be a nice room for a baby." And, "Your fox terrier is cute—but I really think you can do better than that."

Sometimes the comments are resigned or introspective: "Well, I guess I'll never be a grandmother." "None of my daughters seem to want children. Did I do something wrong?" There can be threats, and forms of emotional blackmail: "Look. You know I have emphysema. Well, I'm not giving up smoking until you give me a grandchild!" And then maybe some gifts will arrive: baby books, or books with titles like *Sterility and How to Handle It*, blankets, clothing, toys ("for the future"), and even coupons for baby foods—complete with expiration dates.

Writing in *The New York Times Sunday Magazine*, Chip McGrath recounts the story of his mother's anxiety. After he and his wife had been married a few years with no child in sight, his mother bluntly offered a thousand-dollar reward, "boy or girl." The blackmail isn't necessarily just emotional.

A woman I interviewed told of continued explanations to her mother that there just wasn't enough money for a baby yet. "Finally my mom just got tired of hearing it, I guess. She actually came over and replotted our entire budget for the next five years—complete with her idea of raised expectations and inflation estimates. She insisted, right there on paper, we could work it out. Of course, it would have meant no hairdressers or movies for the next three years, but that didn't bother her a bit. I almost threw a tantrum!"

In their desperate attempts to win themselves grandchildren, these parents may have just the opposite effect. "My mother and sister are always inviting me to someone's house so I can see the new baby," a thirty-one-year-old career sociologist complained to me at her midtown Manhattan office. "It's so obvious that they have formed a let's-get-Joan-to-like-babies conspiracy. I really don't have time to look at every new baby my mother meets—and somewhere in the course of saying no to her invitations and her outright requests for grandchildren, I find that I've painted myself into a corner. I really *don't* dislike children, but I've been forced to assume that role. Now I wonder if I can shake it. Even if I did decide to become pregnant now, I'm not sure I could even enjoy it."

Why do so many parents have this great desire to have grandchildren? And why is it such an intense feeling? People have speculated that there is a somewhat sadistic component to their feelings: the we-went-through-it, now-you-should-too attitude. Perhaps it's their way of ensuring that their children, finally and without question, do understand what they themselves "went through" during the child-raising years. But obviously it's more than that. As one would-be grandfather put it, "Children are the investment, grandchildren are the dividends."

There's the prestige factor, too. In my neighborhood I frequently see women in their fifties and sixties sitting in the park comparing photographs ("he's at the top of his fifth-grade class—and a year younger than everyone else, too"), and I get some sense of the emptiness a grandchild-free woman might feel. Even if her daughter or son is having unprecedented career success, that specific emptiness may be there. Perhaps that, in part, accounts for some of the unpleasant behavior a few older women exhibit toward "other people's" grandchildren. How often I step out on my terrace to hear, in the playground below, one of them barking at some young child or other to get off the grass or ride his bicycle elsewhere or stop making so much noise. It is a *children's* playground, after all, and I can't help but wonder at the severity of the wrath that is so often directed at children when the only thing they are guilty of is existing.

It might be easy to pass off these feelings of parents as irrelevant and unnecessary, but if you consider some of the problems faced by aging people in our society, their concerns appear more legitimate. Often older people *do* lead empty lives, and the pressure for having a new-life facet to alleviate that potential loneliness may be very strong. This may be particularly true for an older woman. First, because of the difference in life-span and age at marriage between a male and female, she is more likely to be left alone; and second, with her own childbearing years over, she may feel reassured and revalidated as a woman if she can assume the role of grandmother. In a sense, the birth of grandchildren provides aging parents with an opportunity for some vicarious living, and when this is denied, the prospective grandparents may feel cheated. This doesn't mean you should have a child for their sakes! But if you understand the source of their demands, you may be able to deal with them more effectively and more sympathetically.

There may be yet another viewpoint. One father wrote his child-free daughter-in-law that "the basic concept of marriage is the creation of a family unit. The family unit does not only consist of a husband and wife; children are also a part of this unit, which is the basic cornerstone of society. Anything less than this is a sterile, dead-end approach, and marriage is meaningless." This attitude may not be yours or mine, and I will not elaborate on it here because it is one of those all-time unresolvable questions, really a twofold question: Can a marriage be happy without children, and, What is the point of becoming formally married if you're not going to have children? But prospective grandparents who do think this way may be sincerely concerned about their sons or daughters, and the fulfillment they will be deriving from marriage specifically and from life in general. Maybe, in other words, the pressure from parents is not always completely self-serving.

In addition to parental pressure, you may find yourself coping with the "friendly interest" of your peers. If children are not forthcoming within a "reasonable" time, you may first get some unsolicited advice. Riding home on a crowded rush-hour bus one evening, an ambitious twenty-eight-year-old banking executive told me of one of her experiences. She was half laughing and half annoyed as she began: "A few months ago this girl I hardly know came over to my desk and began marveling about this 'super' doctor who treated Elizabeth Taylor or Sophia Loren or someone. She was very vague and kept going on about how hard it was to get an appointment with him and how she had some contacts if I was interested. It finally occurred to me that she was talking about an infertility specialist. I had to laugh as I said, 'But Marion, I'm on the Pill!' It would be an understatement to say she was confused. She hasn't talked to me lately."

When people learn that you are deliberately avoiding having

children, they may get annoyed and react as a veteran does when he meets a draft dodger. You're not carrying your share of the load. "Just wait until you have children of your own," a matron cackled at me from behind the jewelry counter at Bloomingdale's. "Don't ask me why I'm smiling . . . just wait." You seem to be having too much fun. And that's apparently not right.

To give that evaluation some perspective, recall one of Shakespeare's lines in *Much Ado about Nothing*. Beatrice, in discussing her life situation with Leonato, refers to the curse of old maids and the inevitability that they will be called upon to "lead . . . apes into hell." This line is widely interpreted as the popular belief that spinsters—and for that matter all women on earth who are childless—must pay a price for avoiding the trouble of children.

One thirty-eight-year-old Los Angeles insurance executive told me that he could manage the snide comments and strange looks he got from certain of his friends, but what really worried him was the attitude of the people he worked with. "It's really getting to me. I have the distinct feeling that they hold it against me at work. I know I'd be moving up faster if I had children, and I bet you anything I'd be making more money. The big boys think you're more stable or responsible or something if you've got pictures of the kiddies on your desk. It gets me so goddam mad. But what am I supposed to do about it?"

This problem had obviously been burning him up for a while and he was happy to tell someone about it.

He went on: "The funny part of this is that I see the women in my office getting the shaft for just the opposite reason. When they become mothers, it's held against them. The boss begins to wonder what will happen when the baby gets sick and all that. The kid is a real minus sign there." He shook his head in disgust.

"Well, what do you do about it?" I asked.

He was still shaking his head. "Oh, hell, what can I do? I try to get around it by telling people we're just not ready for children. I try to make them believe that someday we will do what's expected of us. I don't know how long I can get away with that. Honestly, it's occurred to me that they might never make me an officer because of this."

"Do your associates ever actually say something to you about it? Do they send around memos asking how large your brood is?"

He laughed. "Just about. No, they limit themselves to snide remarks and jokes. I get razzed a lot about the quality—and quantity—of our sex life. But my God, do the women ever keep after my wife! Take last week. We were at this party and Judy made a casual statement about how great it was to be out of the smog of the city since she hadn't been feeling well all week and the fresh air was a good change. Right away all eyes looked up. And one of the old hens clucked, 'Well, it's the air—or an heir!' "

In many parts of the country, particularly in the small-to-middling-sized towns of the South and Midwest, entire communities tend to be almost totally family-oriented. Couples are encouraged to marry young and, of course, to immediately begin breeding. And a great many of them do exactly that just to avoid becoming socially isolated, if for no other reason. Local Little League activities are social events for the parents, quite apart from the original purpose for which the organization might have been intended. Without such groups like the PTA and Cub Scouts, the average younger couple finds itself with little to do in the way of community involvement. Even civic and religious groups tend to focus on the products of procreation.

Henry P. David and Raymond L. Johnson of the Transnational Family Research Institute refer to childbearing as "norm-governed behavior." Writing in *Preventive Medicine* they note that even today the childbearing norm alone is often strong enough to override the "temptation" to avoid parenthood. It does indeed seem shameful that in an advanced culture such as ours, some couples continue to feel coerced into keeping up with the Joneses.

The pressures are not necessarily limited to the production of a first baby, either. More likely than not, after the first reaches a suitable age (suitable being determined by whoever is doing the judging), noises begin about the impropriety of raising an only child. Nevertheless, among the prochild pressure groups, an only is still preferable to none at all.

In their population planning study mentioned above, David and Johnson also comment on the shifting American values concerning child-centered family life. As an example they suggest watching a rerun of the film *Gone With The Wind:* "What was accepted as believable character motivation in the 1930s now seems to be a lavish parody of an old-time soap opera. Sudden and profound character transformations and suicidal personal sacrifice are explained and justified by the joyous experiences of being a parent. Rhett Butler instantly gives up his racy cavalier ways to become a doting father, while saintly Melanie Wilkes knowingly risks her life to bear beloved Ashley a second child because 'birth renews life.' " (The two researchers refer to the 1930s, but similar attitudes prevailed well into the forties and fifties.) And then there was Scarlett O'Hara's adamant refusal to have another child since it would interfere too greatly with both her social life and career. She was looked upon as wicked and self-indulgent at the time, but her independence prophesied the beginning of a new trend. It is of additional interest, if not necessarily significant, that in an era when large families were still the mode, both the Butlers and the Wilkeses had only one child.

Traditionally, a child-free couple *has* been a subject of either sorrow or scorn. Sociologist Lee Rainwater in *Family Design* found that deliberately childless women were characterized as "either totally self-involved, childish, neurotic or in poor health." And many articles on child-free living have elicited similar responses. When in 1963 Gael Greene published her now-classic article "A Vote Against Motherhood" in the *Saturday Evening Post,* she noted that the reaction "could not have been greater if my husband had announced that he had just accepted a job spying for the Russians and I was busy running a Communist Party cell in a basement boiler room." Over three thousand letters poured into the editorial department, the great majority of which were negative reactions.

When *Look* senior editor Betty Rollin wrote "Motherhood: Who Needs It?" in 1970, forcefully arguing against the myth that all women must have children, and when in the same year *Redbook* carried Lynnell Michel's piece "Why We Don't Want Children," the mail was also voluminous. Dr. Peter Wernick of Cornell University analyzed these reader letters and noted that they were fairly evenly split with responses covering the gamut from deep empathy to total disgust with the authors. Dr. Wernick observed that many of the negative reactions characterized the child-free individual as "selfish," "frustrated," "immature," "fearful," "insecure," and "shallow." Many letters criticized the magazines for carrying such articles and expressed their fear that the world and those particular publications were going down the drain. (Within a year, as it happened, *Look* did.)

In recent years there has been a new openness about voluntary nonparenthood—and peer pressure in this area does seem to be abating. But, particularly among those over age fifty, there is still a note of suspicion, and perhaps contempt, in reaction to the decision not to have children. I asked a suburban housewife and mother of three young children about her feelings on child-free marriages. "Oh, I'm very liberal," she said. "I think nonparenthood is just fine. If people want to take drugs, have abortions, live like hippies, or not have children, that's up to them. I'm very open-minded, right?"

Beware: The Social Pressure Razor Has Two Edges

So you know one thing about yourself now: you're surrounded by an A-1 pronatalist society, right? Well, yes; but also no. Even those who encourage us to be parents adhere to strict rules about when and how often babies should arrive. And in recent years there has been a growth in the *antiparenthood movement* that has brought with it a social pressure of its own. First consider the rules of the baby game.

Let's start with the obvious. According to the prevailing social norm, babies before marriage or too soon after marriage raise eyebrows. Things are loosening up in this area, but out-of-wedlock and premaritally conceived births are not exactly "in."

Scientist and author Dr. Isaac Asimov points out that childlessness is actually held in great reverence in some situations. It's just great, for instance, for spinsters, nuns, and young girls. As a matter of fact, it is fine given the existence of one condition: childlessness must be accompanied by chastity. It's perfectly all right not to have children as long as you don't have sex. In fact, it might be better that way. In presexual revolution days, it was considered wrong to engage in masturbation, genital-oral contact, homosexuality, and contraceptive-protected sex; that is, any and all forms of sexual expression that excluded the possibility of conception. In some religious groups these proscriptions remain in effect today and, in fact, are still carried in the lawbooks of many states as being downright illegal. Consider, too, that in a few states sex education has met with legal problems. Up until 1979 Tennessee, for example, did not allow any form of sex education, *even at the college level.* Apparently there are those who fear that if too many people find out what causes babies they might stop having so many—or perhaps have none at all. "The last thing you'd want to have is a married couple without children," Dr. Asimov explains. "It would be like getting something for nothing."

Even after marriage the childbearing ground rules don't say "anything goes." For instance, a baby can come too soon. "I wish my daughter had waited awhile—so she could have finished college," a grandmother-to-be lamented as we sat on her porch and watched her husband mow the lawn. "Of course we are looking forward to having a grandchild, but I was not exactly as thrilled as I always thought I would be when I got the news." This woman obviously felt that her daughter showed some indiscretion, but she was going to accept it. That's one reaction to a slightly premature first grandchild. What I found more unbelievable were some of the negative reactions to the second.

"How many grandchildren do you have?" I asked an elegantly dressed woman I met at a New York concert one night. We had been chatting during the intermission, and she seemed particularly friendly. But when she heard the question, her face tightened.

"Well, we have one now—a boy—and we're expecting another." She spoke quickly and then began to fumble for something in her pocketbook. I couldn't understand why she was suddenly uncomfortable. I thought grandparents liked to be asked about grandchildren. So I went on.

"And how old is your grandson?"

She was still looking into the purse. "Well, actually, I'm embarrassed to tell you."

"Oh?"

"He's only eight months old now. I was so shocked when my daughter told me she was pregnant again *so soon*. It's just not *done!*" She looked up at me to see if I shared her mortification and then leaned toward me and whispered, "Couldn't Bob have *held off* a bit? Really, what will people think? I know what they'll think—that my daughter and son-in-law have no self-control!" The lights began to dim, so I don't think she ever saw the look on my face.

She wasn't the only person I met who shared this concern. "I know it's ridiculous," a new father told me between sighs, "but I have to say that the what-will-people-think syndrome did affect the timing of our second child. It's kind of a socially determined decision in a way, kind of a mixture of concern over the possibility that people will think you're a sex maniac and a sincere worry about how you are going to manage two under two."

"How old are your sons?" I asked the woman who runs the bakery in my area. She was stuffing a bag with bagels for me.

"One's twenty-two and the other's nineteen." She also didn't seem as enthusiastic about her children as I had expected.

"And they're both married?"

"No, no. Well, I guess you could say one of them is. But he married outside the religion. So he really isn't fully married, if you know what I mean." I didn't really know but decided to drop it and move on.

"Any grandchildren yet?"

She looked up in horror. "Oh, please! About that I have nightmares! Really!" She put both hands to her face and threw her head back. "Sometimes I wake up in the middle of the night shrieking. I think of my son being a father of that woman's child! You see, she's not Jewish. I pray every day that she is sterile! Maybe then they will break up and my son can have a real marriage and real children."

I nodded. She interpreted it as sympathy and threw in another bagel.

So babies have to be "properly" timed products of the "right" union, and they can't come in unlimited numbers. *Time* magazine reports that an Atlanta couple was harassed by obscene telephone calls after they and their eight children were in a television commercial for a laundry detergent. *New York* magazine noted that Ellen Peck, author of *The Baby Trap*, once approached a rather fertile television cameraman and said, "I'm bothered by your nine children." (He smiled and volunteered that he sometimes was bothered by them too.)

"When I tell people at cocktail parties that I have four children, they stare at me as if I'm a social deviant," the wife of a pediatrician told me. "What's going on? Are there rules now about how many you're allowed? Either I find myself feeling guilty about it—or sometimes I get very defensive, which is worse. *I'm* comfortable with our decision to have four, so why should I be concerned about anyone else?"

Antiparenthood pressure can be as oppressive as the much maligned pronatalism. The pendulum is swinging. Small families and the child-free life are "in" now, and it is those who are having children, particularly those having more than two, who are beginning to get the funny looks.

"It was really annoying," my friend Sally told me one afternoon when she got back from walking her two poodles. "About ten minutes ago when I was out—with my very protruding abdomen in full view—I saw Stewart Mott [the philanthropist and supporter of such causes as Planned Parenthood and NON] riding his bicycle. When he saw my condition, he shot two visual daggers at my middle. I know, maybe I'm reading all of this into it, but I think we've reached the ridiculous stage where people feel guilty about having babies!"

Letty Cottin Pogrebin wrote in *Ms.* magazine about another pregnant girl with similar thoughts: "I've come full circle right back to where my Victorian grandmother was . . . Granny had to hide her condition out of modesty. My belly is embarrassing in 1973 because it labels me as a population exploder or an exploited baby machine."

A number of national organizations, among them Zero Population Growth (ZPG) and the National Organization for Non-Parents, are promoting their antinatalist position by attacking what they term *media pressure*. For instance, ZPG members are upset because an Ivory Snow television advertisement features mom, two boys, and an infant. Three children! They are concerned about the Mary Worth cartoon strip because its creators let a rather liberated female character submit to her husband's unreasonable demand that she quit her job and play housewife and mother. And they are furious with the *National Enquirer* for sponsoring a search for America's oldest father with a child under twelve months of age. I never did find out their reaction to the Emko Contraceptive Foam ad that goes: "Baby—a four-letter word for love." But they like the Atlantic Richfield Company (ARCO) because their commercials have commentaries on the hazards of uncontrolled population growth and represent "enlightened advertising." I wonder, too, how they've managed to cope with the highly successfully television series, "Eight Is Enough." (At the very least they must have yearned to retitle it, "Eight Is at Least Six More Than Enough.")

Ellen Peck, a founder of NON and self-styled leader of the cause of nonparents, told me how annoyed she is by the song in which Paul Anka croons that bearing his child is a marvelous way of showing love for him. Ellen fumed, "Were I sixteen and pregnant, that song could keep me pregnant." (The National Organization for Women [NOW], equally incensed with the words of the song, gave Paul the Keep Her in Her Place Award.) Ellen is very concerned with "The Waltons," daytime TV shows that have a birthrate rivaling that of rabbits, and all those other nostalgia-oriented shows that focus on the joys of large families. She says, "All *they* ever show is the joys of family life. All we ever see is the warm part. Family dinners. Opening packages at Christmas. Even the worst traumas turn out fine. We're not getting the whole story from television." But Ellen did like "All in the Family's" equal time for nonparenthood, and she probably also approved of Bob and Emily's glamorous child-free life on the "Bob Newhart Show."

Even certain factions of the woman's movement—and *Ms.* magazine in particular—are under scrutiny. For instance, one advocate of the antinatalist ideology, Dr. Helen Franzwa of Hunter College, feels that *Ms.* promotes motherhood by taking the position that women should play the role of mother *and* jobholder; while it encourages them to work other roles into their lives, *Ms.* takes it for granted that women will be mothers. She feels that the magazine,

"perhaps unwittingly, puts a great deal of pressure on women.
. . . Apparently *Ms.* has not yet recognized that it is neither in
society's interest nor in the women movement's interest to
encourage every woman to be a mother."

Whether or not the media are pushing parenthood is debatable.
What we should beware of is any tendency to push nonparenthood
or to criticize those who choose to have a third or a fourth child.
Parenthood, for the overwhelming majority of married couples, *is*
an important part of life. It is natural material for advertisements,
news and magazine stories, and songs. Although we now recognize
the importance of being socially responsible about bringing a new
child into an already crowded world, it is still important to
emphasize that *decisions about parenthood are uniquely personal.* In the
final analysis, they are nobody's business but your own. We do not
need—nor should we permit—pressure from proparenthood *or*
antiparenthood partisans.

Our demographic situation is currently *not* such that we should all
have zero, one, or two children. Especially if some members of
society do choose to remain child-free, that mathematically leaves a
margin for some three- or four-child families. If 20 percent of
couples elected to have no children, another 20 percent one child,
and a third 20 percent two children, then half the remaining 40
percent could have three and the other half four children, and we
would still end up with a two-child average. It may be fun to go
through magazines and song lyrics and vote for the pronatalist
villain of the month. But it doesn't really mean that much.

Although most liberal thinkers would defend an individual's right
not to reproduce, there's no need to *glorify* nonparenthood. But
some groups do seem to be trying to sell the child-free option,
particularly to educated, socially aware couples, by promoting the
view that parenthood occupies the low rung on the life's activity
hierarchy, and that nonparenthood is an "upper-class treat."
Members of the women's movement are protesting.

Ellen Willis writes in *Ms.* that "there is an obvious arrogance in the
assumption of some of the militantly childless . . . that their way of
life is more desirable than other people's. But their position is also
arrogant in a more insidious and ultimately more harmful way: they
seem to regard the worst aspects of motherhood not as oppressive
conditions that should be alleviated but as intrinsic disadvantages
that should be avoided by people with smarts."

Ellen Willis and others also object to the term *child-free.* Pointing
out that if the word *childless* unfairly implies a lack, *child-free* has an

equally unwarranted connotation of superiority. She continues, "I can't help getting the creepy feeling that many apostles of nonparenthood mean to foist what they see as just another disagreeable task—like cleaning toilets—on lower orders who are presumably too dumb ('brainwashed') to object." That does seem a little harsh, however. Even a couple with an intense dislike for children would hardly be inclined to equate them with dirty toilets.

Social pressure—whether it is to have children or to choose to be child-free or to stop at one or two—is very much a part of our lives. One peculiarity of the parenthood issue is that everyone has an opinion on a subject that is really none of his business!

So keep your detection apparatus tuned in for all forms of social pressure, and don't succumb to them. Repeat: *having or not having a child is a uniquely private matter.* There are numerous tactful means of conveying the general message "it's none of your business" when either pro or antiparenthood theorists get on their soapboxes.

⇜ 3 ⇝

Programmed for Parenthood? A Look at the "Reproductive Instinct" Theory

"Well, I would say the primary reason we had the kids was so we didn't frustrate my old lady's maternal instinct," a television repairman explained to me as he removed the back of the set. I had just learned that he was the father of four.

I decided to lead him on. "What do you mean by instinct? Do you mean like the same kind of urge that animals have?"

"Yeah. Right. That's it. You know, women have this need. It's part of them. They can't help it. Y'see, I look at it from the biological point of view. She's got the ovaries and the whole setup. If it isn't supposed to be used, what's it there for?"

I didn't lose my composure. I didn't argue with him. I wanted to see how far he would go. "You mean it's like having an expensive sports car and never driving it?"

"Yeah. Yeah. You got it. Otherwise it would be wasteful. It would frustrate nature. It was meant to be. If you're a woman and don't have a kid, it's like being a gun and never shooting even one bullet."

"Oh. What about you? Do you have a reproductive instinct, too?"

"No. I don't think so. I'm kind of an accessory to the whole process."

He was convinced. If it wasn't Sigmund Freud's theory that explained why he was a father—then it was the omnipotent force of his wife's hormone levels. A reproductive instinct in human beings? We're supposed to be the rational members of the phylogenetic scale. But the old questions are still raised: is there something in either our skull, abdomen, or bloodstream that has us all preprogrammed for parenthood?

If you have nothing to do some year, try reading everything that was ever written about the idea of a natural push toward pregnancy. After doing so for a while, I got the distinct impression that you really weren't anyone unless you also had put in your two cents on this subject. Basically, there seem to be two opposing viewpoints. In one camp you have those who, despite the observations that not all women do choose to have intercourse, a pregnancy, and childbirth, tell you that a woman is basically a reproductive machine, a uterus surrounded by a supporting organism and a directing personality. In the other camp are those who maintain that there is no such intangible force and that it is rational thinking or social pressure that leads to childbearing. I decided to give all sides and the middle ground a fair trial before reaching a verdict.

Psychoanalysis and Parenthood: The Push from Within

In this corner we have Sigmund Freud, Joseph Rheingold, Erik Erikson, Helene Deutsch, Therese Benedek, and others. Let's start with Dr. Freud.

Yes, we're going to have to blame it all on penis envy. Freud felt that the drive toward pregnancy was essentially a wish to incorporate and retain the penis, the final resolution of a woman's phallic phase of development. She finally got something she'd never had. The penis-envy hypothesis is still very much alive. Hyman Spotnitz, a contemporary psychoanalyst and psychiatrist, writes, "In order to explain the devastating gap in themselves, little girls have to invent a story. One of their fantasies is that they once had a penis. The clitoris is left as a remnant to prove it, but someone, usually the wicked mother, took the penis away as a punishment for the bad things they did (e.g., masturbation). It is less humiliating for a girl to imagine that she once possessed a penis than to face the fact that she never had something that boys have." I wonder what psychoanalysis would be like if Freud had been a woman.

Dr. Joseph Rheingold, in his classic and controversial book *The Fear of Being a Woman*, goes along with Freud's feeling that motherhood is basic to a healthy feminine psyche. According to Rheingold, a woman doesn't have any other option in her quest for self-satisfaction.

Let her be dedicated to creative or professional endeavor, let her be rabidly feminist, let her arm herself with defenses—she is female, and from childhood she has striven toward motherhood. Repudiation of this goal is forced upon her by fear and hate, but she cannot and does not renounce the emotional urge.

New York psychiatrist Jay DiMaggio asserts unequivocally that an instinct to procreate exists in all humans—male as well as female. He is quoted in a *Woman's Day* article by Marcia Kamien as saying: "I believe there's an instinctual urge in all human beings to be a parent. Couples who deny that urge and refuse to be parents must either do their nurturing another way—by parenting each other, for instance—or they suffer." At least he leaves the door open for mothering (or fathering) something and/or someone other than a human baby.

There's more along the same lines. Erik Erikson, in his essay "Woman and the Inner Space," clearly concurs with Freud on the idea that reproduction is the woman's primary role in life. The woman who does not satisfy her innate need to fill her inner space, or uterus, with embryotic tissue is likely to be frustrated or neurotic. Each month the efforts of her uterus are expended in vain and her menstrual flow appears, the flow being, as my graduate school physiology professor (male) described it, "the weeping of a very disappointed womb."

Erikson believes that well-adjusted "normal" individuals go through various life stages. In order to develop properly, you have to resolve the issues on one plateau successfully before moving to the next. The seventh stage in this psychological hierarchy is *generativity*, the opposite of which is stagnation. Erikson writes in *Childhood and Society:*

> Generativity . . . is primarily the concern in establishing and guiding the next generation, although there are individuals who, through misfortune or because of special and genuine gifts in other directions, do not apply this drive to their own offspring. And indeed the concept of generativity is meant to include such more popular synonyms as productivity and creativity, which, however, cannot replace it.

According to the Erikson theory, you can forgo parenthood in favor of a career as an artist, but you'll never be able to quite reach generativity and be as enriched as you would have been if you produced babies instead of paintings, because "women especially, but not exclusively, are apt to feel that they are frustrated in something essential if they do not produce children." In this view, a childless individual might be considered like someone who had just one kidney—managing to cope, but not quite all there.

What happens if you don't reach generativity? What if you want to stay home all day and take care of turtles? Erikson says:

> Where such enrichment [generativity] fails altogether, regression to an obsessive need for pseudo-intimacy takes place, often with a pervading sense of stagnation and personal impoverishment. Individuals, then, often begin to indulge themselves as if they were their own—or one another's—one and only child; and where conditions favor it, early invalidism, physical or psychological, becomes the vehicle of self-concern.

In other words, you get "funny." Or you might even get sick. You stagnate. Who wants to stagnate? Stagnation is terrible.

I can't help thinking of my graduate school friend with her Phi Beta Kappa key and three small children and no career. She tells me *she's* stagnating. Maybe it's all a matter of having a choice about which way you would prefer to stagnate!

So you won't think that all psychoanalysts commenting on the reproductive drive are male, I'll review what psychoanalysts Helene Deutsch and Therese Benedek have had to say. In *The Psychology of Women,* Dr. Deutsch emphasizes that pregnancy is the "direct fulfillment of the deepest and most powerful wish of a woman." She feels that the whole maternal urge is visible in childhood. Little girls build houses in order to put something inside them, to "close the gates" and carefully preserve what was built. Their games, Deutsch says, have the character of nest building. (Erikson concurs with this, noting that from infancy on, girls show tendencies toward filling spaces, and boys center their interests on the penetration of spaces.)

Dr. Benedek brings an elaborate biological framework to the reproduction-is-natural hypothesis. It is her view that the natural hormone fluctuation during a woman's menstrual cycle actually orients her toward having sex at the exact time when she is most likely to conceive; that is, at the time her egg is released. During the first part of the cycle the hormone estrogen is produced in increasing amounts by the ovarian follicle. According to this psychobiological theory, this estrogen makes a woman feel alert, aggressive, and very sexy. If women don't have sex at this time, they allegedly get restless and irritable. Their natural drive is being thwarted. Right around the time of ovulation, Benedek emphasizes, this drive and pregnancy orientation is greatest. You might say the woman is in heat. After ovulation, the hormone progesterone is produced in significant quantities, and, Benedek explains, this makes the woman passive and relaxed and not particularly oriented toward sex. And all of these observations (which, it must be added, were based on studies of neurotic women, who, according to some researchers, manifest exaggerated versions of symptoms and orientations of normal women) led Benedek to the conclusion that in the adult woman it is "possible to relate instinctual drives to specific hormone functions of the ovaries."

There is a problem here. No study of female libido has shown that sex interest is greatest in the middle of the menstrual cycle. A number of researchers have attempted to evaluate objectively the idea of a cyclic sexual interest by measuring the quantity of mucus present in the vagina during a cycle. Assuming that the secretions were related to sex interest, the researchers confirmed that sexual height in women occurred just before or after their periods—that is, the observed heightened sex drive was occurring at the most infertile time of the cycle. That doesn't do much for your instinctual "heat" theories.

Benedek had thought of an answer for this challenge. She felt that the premenstrual sex interest is more of a manifestation of depression—and the need to express passive, dependent feelings, the need to be cared for. She maintains that you cannot judge the psychobiological hypothesis of reproduction by what people say. Their dreams, and materials gathered through projective techniques, consistently point to a surge of interest in sex at ovulation.

Dr. Benedek didn't leave the man out, either. "There need be no doubt," she concluded, "that the male biological drive has psychic representations of instinctual, biological origin. The biologic root of fatherhood is in the instinctual drive for survival." Indeed, she claimed, there is a strong urge on the part of a man to be a provider and to re-create himself—to add a meaning to life. She described a father who was going off to combat in World War II. "He was deeply happy in being able to go away with the feeling that his life would be continued, that he had created a tie which gave him a sense of obligation, and, by this, an aspiration to life. Many men were aware of using the fact of survival in their child as a means of increasing the chances of surviving the war."

Is there any real evidence that there is a basic male drive toward fatherhood? Una Stannard, author of The New Pamela, thinks there is. She writes that "women have the babies, but men have the maternal instinct." And she presents historical and anthropological evidence to back up this conclusion.

After all, who was the first real mother? According to the Bible, it was Adam. Remember? God put him to sleep and delivered a female from his rib cage—a variation on natural childbirth. And look to mythology. Zeus snatches up a child (a premature baby), puts him into his thigh, and carries him to term.

Psychoanalysts like to talk about penis envy. But what about womb envy (a theory set forth by psychoanalyst Karen Horney)? When Leeuwenhoek put semen under his microscope in 1677 he saw *animalcules* and thought he had discovered complete, miniature human beings in semen—beings that just needed to be put in the woman's uterus so they could mature somewhat. (Shortly after that, scientists confirmed this theory by noting that the semen of elephants, horses, and animals also had miniature versions of their own species.) Many of the descriptions of early reproductive theory give the male the primary role in reproduction. He provides the life; she provides the soil for the baby to grow. (You still hear "and daddy planted a seed in mummy. . . . ") It was a very controversial day when it became apparent that there was a female egg cell—and that it had an important role to play. Confused and threatened male scientists for a while claimed that the egg was no more functional than male nipples.

The subject becomes more fascinating the more you get into it. (This discussion is, of course, off the main topic of the book, but it is worthwhile deviating for a moment.) Consider the double standard—the girls will be virgins but boys will be boys myth. Why did it originate? At least one suggestion has been offered. Women know that the child they are carrying is theirs. A man can never know that for sure. So how does he increase the odds on assuring that his fertility drive has indeed been satisfied? By demanding undying faithfulness on the part of his woman.

Literature is full of tragic accounts of the aftermath of a man's suspicion that the child his wife is carrying is not his. For instance, in August Strindberg's play *The Father*, Laura, the strong-willed wife, does not want to send her daughter into town to go to school; she wants her at home where she can control her. As revenge on her husband, Laura hints that perhaps he is not the father of the child. She keeps up the insinuations until he gets sick and eventually dies of a stroke. And in *Rebecca*, Daphne du Maurier describes the second Mrs. Maxim de Winter, who lives in a house haunted by the memory of Maxim's first wife, Rebecca. Eventually Maxim confesses to having murdered Rebecca. Why? Because she told him that the coming child was not his. Of course it was all a lie, since Rebecca wanted to be murdered rather than face the pain of dying of cancer. But she sure knew how to get a man angry.

Do you want more evidence about how men may be more

motherly than women? How about Una Stannard's explanation about why, traditionally, when a woman gets married she changes her name to his? He and she are incorporating. Now he has that womb he always wanted. And in spite of the Equal Rights Amendment, that is the closest he will ever get to becoming a mother.

The Drive against the Drive Theory

At the basis of the theories that human beings are driven to procreation is the belief that some nonrational, possibly biologically based force pushes us toward parenthood. Furthermore, the proponents of this view suggest or state that if we dare to frustrate this powerful drive or instinct, we'll have to suffer the psychological consequences. The commentary on this subject has primarily focused on women—but as you see from the above, men have not escaped instinctual scrutiny either.

Today it isn't very popular to talk about instincts and drives, and the commentaries in this area by Freud, Benedek, and others are not taken seriously. We're above all that, right? We're civilized; we can think. Drives are definitely out this year. This faddism is natural, of course. The history of intellectual thought is patterned by swings in attitude about the nature of man and his control over his environment. During the Enlightenment, I think, therefore I am, was the slogan. Then followed the writings of people like Darwin and Freud, and a more pessimistic view of mankind predominated. People believed that forces other than reason and intellect determined behavior, forces of which man himself was not always aware. Now we're back to intellectual control of everything.

"Motherhood . . . a biological destiny? Forget biology!" says sociologist/author Dr. Jessie Bernard. "If it were biology, people would die from not doing it."

"Women don't need to be mothers, any more than they need spaghetti," claims Dr. Richard Rabkin, a New York psychiatrist. "But if you're in a world where everyone is eating spaghetti, thinking they need it and want it, you will think so too."

And Simone de Beauvoir, author of *The Second Sex*, generally goes along with that, noting that there is no such thing as a maternal instinct and that "there is nothing natural in such an obligation; nature can never dictate a moral choice." "That the child is the supreme aim of women," she continues, "is a statement having precisely the value of an advertising slogan. Some women should not have children."

"When a woman says with feeling that she craved her baby from within, she is putting into biological language what is psychological," explains University of Michigan psychoanalyst and motherhood researcher Frederick Wyatt.

"There are no instincts," says sociologist Dr. William Goode. "There are reflexes, like eye blinking, and drives like sex. There is no innate drive for children. Otherwise, the enormous cultural pressures that there are to reproduce would not exist. There are no cultural pressures to sell you on getting your hand out of the fire."

So, there is another side of the reproductive instinct question which claims that there is no internal drive or push toward procreation. Then there are theories that fall in the middle.

Maybe There Is "Something"

The late Margaret Mead and others have noted that if human reproduction were instinctual, a biological or social human necessity, you would expect that all human beings in all cultures would follow the same general pattern—that is, that the desire for reproduction would be universal. As one example of the lack of universality in this area, Dr. Mead has described the Mundugumor, a preliterate cannibalistic people in New Guinea, where women detest childbearing and child rearing and men detest their wives for being pregnant. Beyond this example are a number of observations that suggest that a purely biological explanation of why people have children is too limited.

Think of the five components of the reproductive process: sexual intercourse, conception and pregnancy, childbirth, and child rearing. Right away, the "universally desired" criterion is missing. Not all people demonstrate the "innate psychophysical disposition" for any or all of these reproductive components. Some men and women choose the celibate life and forgo sexual intercourse. They seem to cope. Furthermore, for human beings, the desire for intercourse and the desire for pregnancy are two different matters. The most obvious example of this is the fact that women, unlike most animals, are interested in sex at other than the most fertile times of their menstrual cycle. Less obvious is the observation that some women want the pregnancy and childbirth experience, but not the sex. A New York gynecologist told me that he has over thirty requests each year from single women who desperately want a child—but don't want to carry the psychological burden of knowing who the father is. Stranger than this are the studies of men and women in unconsummated marriages. Unbelievable as it is in this era of sexual revolution, this does happen. One such report of a thousand virgin wives—the median duration of marriage in this sample was over eight years—indicated that a significant number of them did want to have children. Their problem was that they didn't want to have sex. Now *there* you have a problem! Either these couples appeared in their doctor's office for lessons—or suggestions about how to overcome their psychological barriers to intercourse—or only the wife would show up and request artificial insemination with either her husband's or a donor's semen.

There are those who want the intercourse, the conception, the pregnancy—but not the child. I met more than one woman who said, "I like the idea of being pregnant, conceiving, carrying, and delivering a baby. But what horrifies me is that after it is born, you are responsible for it for at least eighteen years! It's really sad. I love every part of it but taking the baby home."

Others want a baby, but not a toddler or an adolescent. And still others claim, "Babies leave me cold. But I do like young adults."

No, the word *instinct* does not fit into this discussion very well. Nor does the word *drive*.

But, as Dr. Mead suggested, there is a middle ground between "it's instinctual and you've got to do it or you will pay some psychological consequences," and "it's all rational and you have to be socially brainwashed to want children." In *Male and Female*, she explained her feelings:

> Men have to learn as children to want to beget and cherish children . . . women, on the other hand, have to learn to want children only under socially prescribed conditions. . . . Girls can certainly learn not to want children, but such learning seems always to be socially imposed.

In other words, Dr. Mead felt that a woman may be somewhat naturally inclined toward having children—maybe there's some biology, psychology, and sociology behind this inclination—but if her life circumstances are such that she revises this orientation, she can certainly have the option to lead a fulfilling life following another route. "There seems to be no reliable evidence," Dr. Mead wrote, "to suggest that learning not to want children necessarily introduces such a deep conflict into a woman's nature that the conflict is insolvable and she must inevitably pay a price, in frustration and hatred of her fate, that will in turn reverberate in the lives around her."

But, unless she "unlearns" the desire for children, there is probably "something" there. Dr. Helen Kaplan, Clinical Associate Professor of Psychiatry at New York Hospital–Cornell Medical College, reinforces this belief, indicating that there is a type of maternal urge in many women from early childhood on, and she feels "it's not just culturally determined either." And we can't leave out the other half of the parenthood team. Maybe that unknown factor is part of the male too, a complex set of experiences, expectations, memories and needs, biological or otherwise. We don't really understand them fully, but it seems they probably do orient us toward childbearing. They may not *require* us to reproduce our own biological children, but they may focus us in the direction of human preservation, or what Erikson referred to as generativity, a concern with the next generation.

Psychoanalyst Abby Adams concurs that there is an impelling "something" that tends to direct women toward childbearing. She suggests that since the equipment is there, there's *probably* a biologically determined impulse to use it. Marcia Kamien quotes her in a *Woman's Day* article: "But it would be a blind impulse, designed to keep humanity going, and that would mean even a mother of ten could keep getting signals to conceive. It doesn't mean a woman *has* to." And Dr. Adams continues, "There have always been women who *couldn't* have babies who have led fruitful and satisfying lives."

Classic dream studies indicate that most women have sexual dreams during ovulation, a time when hormonal changes are taking place. An unnamed doctor in the same article speculates: "What if women have a special hormone, triggered to go off when conception possibilities are at their peak? Wouldn't it then be possible . . . that some women are born with less or none of this hormone so that the urge never really strikes them?" A fascinating theory, if of little practical value at this time.

As long as we're into unproved theories, this seems to be as good a place as any to propose still another. In a recent speech delivered to the La Leche League International in Toronto, author Samuel L. Blumenfeld asserts: "I see motherhood quite differently. I see it as a manifestation of God's will for both mother and child. I see motherhood as the result of God's technology, not man's. The miracle of birth exceeds anything man has ever done or will ever do." Well, okay, at least we have someone to blame if things don't turn out right.

The idea, however, that this generativity can only be reached through parenthood and children is too limited. As New York psychoanalyst Donald Kaplan told me, "There is a need, say after the fourth decade of life, to stand in some leader-type relationship to the younger generation. Now whether that's fulfilled by having children or by pursuing a career as a leader of the next generation—a teacher, writer, or someone who offers apprentice opportunities—is another matter. There are alternate routes to generativity."

We can't overlook the obvious. If the human race is to survive, people have to have children. That doesn't mean everyone has to have children, but one way or the other it's got to work out so that living human beings are replaced. From that point of view you could question Simone de Beauvoir's statement that there is no obligation for reproduction. There's no obligation for specific individuals, but for a community as a whole, there is. And think about Dr. Goode's notion that there is no pressure to tell us to get our hands out of the fire. There are many such pressures around us. Seat belt requirements. Antismoking campaigns. Drug laws. Any health-education measure is an attempt to keep our hands, lungs, or some other part of us out of the fire. Society does have an interest in self-preservation, and very likely each of us carries some elements of this preservation orientation, elements that lead us to protect existing lives and create new ones.

Let's return to the possibility that there is "something"—nothing that merits the term *instinct* or *drive*—but something that is not fully rational, but also not fully socially engendered, which orients us toward reproduction, sometimes so much so that the efforts of modern contraception are thwarted.

Consider the subject of accidental pregnancies. Each year in the United States there are thousands of nontherapeutic abortions and thousands of out-of-wedlock births and legitimate unplanned and unwanted children—all in an era of highly sophisticated and widely available forms of contraception. Of course there are some real accidents, but there is no denying that something less than rational is also going on. What is behind these "accidents"? Probably an intricate complex of human needs, many of which cannot be recognized, and maybe even some biology (shifts in hormone levels exerting their effect) too. We really don't know.

Dr. Hans Lehfeldt of the New York University School of Medicine has coined an expression for what he believes to be an unconscious pregnancy drive: the WEUP phenomenon (willful exposure to unwanted pregnancy). By forgetting to swallow a pill for a couple of consecutive mornings, by neglecting to insert her diaphragm, or by complaining about abdominal pains she attributes to the intrauterine device (though they may be nonexistent or psychologically induced), a woman may be WEUPing, creating a situation where a perfectly acceptable form of birth control is thwarted. Consciously, the woman may tell you she doesn't want a baby. She may even have an abortion after confirming the pregnancy. But deep in her psyche she wants to conceive. Why this type of conflicting behavior? Maybe our WEUPing lady views pregnancy as a form of accomplishment, about the only thing she can do really well. Her husband may not want another child—and she may agree that their already strained budget couldn't take an additional hungry individual. But that's her conscious mind. She still has that inner need for self-fulfillment, and that may be enough to counteract even the most effective pill. Perhaps, on the other hand, she feels pretty guilty about the fact that she is having sexual intercourse. Even if she is married, a rigid upbringing may have convinced her that sex is evil—especially if one enjoys it. For her (and possibly for her husband, too), pregnancy might be a way of justifying a sexual relationship, or of punishing herself for being sexy. (That's what psychologists call *masochistic motherhood*).

Some men and women just cannot use contraceptive devices effectively. Drs. Cornelius Bakker and Cameron Dightman of the Department of Psychiatry of the University of Washington School of Medicine report that immature women tend to "act out" and avoid responsibility; one manifestation of this behavior is inconsistent contraceptive use. Helene Deutsch wrote about some of her patients who had a problem diametrically opposed to sterility. They just kept having babies. The main character in Penelope Mortimer's *The Pumpkin Eater* was like this. She had an irresistible urge to give birth to more and more children. When her husband insisted that they have no more, she became dangerously depressed and sought professional help.

In these cases there *is* something nonrational going on. That's not a judgment: it's an observation. Some men and women desperately want children—maybe lots of them. There is no certainty that the famous little old lady who lived in the shoe wouldn't have had as many children if she'd known what to do. Asking her to use contraceptives effectively might have been like asking a cat to guard a bowl of tuna fish. (On the other hand, a cartoon by Jerry Zimmerman that was carried in *Science Digest* a couple of years ago suggests that even that prolific lady could have too much of a good thing. It shows her marching off with her suitcases, a scowl on her face and a large I Quit sign nailed to the door of the shoe.)

And just as these not fully rational forces may cause some couples to have many children, less intense versions of the same forces may be behind other couples' decisions—or nondecisions—to have one or two. Who is to say? Probably no one.

And there are a great many other questions as well. Adrienne Rich in *Of Women Born* poses some of them:

> Is a woman who bore a baby she could not keep a "childless" woman? What makes us mothers? The care of small children? The physical changes of pregnancy and birth? The years of nurture? What of the woman who, never having been pregnant, begins lactating when she adopts an infant? What of the woman who stuffs her newborn into a bus station locker and goes numbly back to her "child-free" life? What of the woman who, as the eldest girl in a large family, has practically raised her younger sisters and brothers, and then entered a convent?

Presumably, instinct and rationality interact in complex ways.

Why *do* people have children? Quite simply, the desire or lack of desire for a pregnancy is not always rational. Reason has its limits. There may be a constellation of consciously unidentifiable factors at work in eliciting the response "I want to have a baby," or "I don't want any children." External factors such as social pressure—however strong—logistics of timing, and costs of pregnancy may not be enough to explain why we decide to have or not to have children. The answer may be buried deep in the cerebral memory bank.

⚜ 4 ⚜

Why Do People Have Children?

"Because they didn't think about it until afterwards," explained a nine-year-old boy I ran into one morning in the elevator, "or maybe because they just wanted to have someone they could boss around. Why else would someone have a child?"

It's a thought. And he raised a legitimate question. After all, at first consideration it does seem a bit strange, does it not, that a perfectly happy couple would actually choose to change their life-style radically by taking on all the responsibilities and unknown risks that go with being a parent. Erica Jong, in *Fear of Flying*, gives the thoughts of a young woman who herself had considered pregnancy:

> How did people decide to get pregnant, I wondered. It was such an awesome decision. In a way it was such an arrogant decision. To undertake responsibility for a new life when you had no way of knowing what it would be like. I assumed that most women got pregnant without thinking about it, because if they ever once considered what it really meant, they would surely be overwhelmed with doubt.

Whatever the motivation or process of consideration involved, the great majority of couples (the lastest surveys from the U.S. Census Bureau show twenty-four out of twenty-five couples) choose to make this move. Perhaps it is more accurately phrased another way: They don't choose not to have children. But what type of decision-making process, if any, is involved here?

Three points are immediately relevant. First, some people do

53

have real accidental pregnancies. But the birth-control-methods failures—particularly among mature adults—have been grossly overstated. Yes, there are the thousands of unwed parents each year and countless others whose marriage proposal is a succinct "You're what?!" But again, what they might term *accidental* may well have been a full-fledged WEUP. Second, after talking with several hundred individuals, I realized that there are two obvious types of childbearers inhabiting our country: the relatively rational and the not so rational. What distinguishes them? Not much, actually. But there is something. Rational childbearers may be defined as those who, at least to some extent, think through their decisions before acting on them. As candidates for parenthood, they probably have evaluated the effect a child might have on their lives; maybe they even did some financial calculations to see if they could afford a baby at that point; and very possibly they gave some consideration to the option of being child-free. If the potential child were to represent a third or fourth addition to the family, the rational childbearers might possibly include a "population growth factor" in their considerations. However their reasoning process might be characterized, couples who take a rational approach to childbearing are distinguished from their counterparts by their ability to explain, before as well as after the conception, *why* they are having a child. When you ask, you will be spared the "it's natural" or "it's a woman's duty" explanations. The motivations may be presented in somewhat vague terms, but at least you get the feeling that some thought went into their decision. These are the rational childbearers—well, relatively rational.

Then there are the not-so-rational childbearers: those who, prior to the conception, did not consider why they were planning to have a child; those whose babies just happened; those who might tell you that they had a baby because it was expected of them, or because it was a natural part of marriage; those who assumed the parenthood role because they thought it was the logical thing to do; those who didn't know why but felt an overwhelming urge to create a child. These couples may be able to define in retrospect some of the motivations that were behind their desire to conceive or impregnate. But what distinguishes them from their relatively rational counterparts is that they did not consider the whys and alternatives *before* the pregnancy occurred.

Probably you would concur that a rational, well-thought-through approach to any important life decision is preferable to an offhand let's-see-what-happens attitude; it's common sense. Decisions relating to parenthood are no exception. The severe consequences of a wrong move in this area make rational behavior even more imperative. But unplanned pregnancies still do occur, and the results are not necessarily disastrous. The resulting children may be as accepted and loved as they would have been had the conceptions been carefully planned and timed. As you have gathered from the first three chapters, the constellation of motivations that may precipitate a pregnancy is extraordinarily complex, characterized by an intricate network of rational and nonrational components. Thus, stressing the desirability of advance planning and consideration, we should keep in mind that for some couples this does not require a bankbook, calendar of events, thermometer, pencil and balance sheet. The communication about the desirability of parenthood is usually more subtle, more delicate.

When I began to spell out the reasons for having children, I realized that I couldn't avoid another sticky dichotomy: the "right" and the "wrong" reasons. I found three independent, although similar, lists of the wrong reasons for having a child. I didn't find any lists of right reasons.

Where *are* the right reasons? I figured there had to be some. I asked Ellen Peck, founder of NON.

"Good reasons? I personally cannot think of a single one. Having a child is both a personal and a societal decision," Ellen explained, "and right now, in the late 1970s, I can't think of any good reasons to have a child. In earlier times there were several justifiable reasons, chief among them human survival, as well as a desire to share one's own values and delights of life with those of another generation. But not today."

TABLE I
Suggested Wrong Reasons to Have a Child

Planned Parenthood	National Organization for Non-Parents	Dr. Robert Gould* New York Medical College
"You've been married a year now. When are you going to give us grandchildren?"	*"To give your parents grandchildren.*	*"Our parents want grandchildren."*
"You want to have a kid, Evelyn? All right, we'll have a kid. Maybe that'll patch things up."	*"To save a shaky marriage (or to get a guy to the altar)."*	*"We thought it would help our marriage." "A baby will keep my husband attached to me and*

*Dr. Gould's "Reasons" originally appeared in the *New York Times Magazine*, 3 May 1970.

TABLE I
(Continued)

Planned Parenthood	National Organization for Non-Parents	Dr. Robert Gould New York Medical College
		is less likely to stray from home."
"Why knock myself out working when I can have a baby?"		*"A baby will give me something to do."*
"I bet my parents would send us money if we had a baby . . . "		
"Heh-heh, hey Frankie, what are you and Margie waiting for? Something wrong with you?"	*"To be 'fulfilled' as a woman." "To 'prove you are a man."*	*"It's the only way to prove you're a man [woman]."*
"We only want two kids. But if we don't have a boy we'll keep trying."	*"We are trying for a girl [boy] this time."*	
"Sure I want babies. What else is a woman for?"		
	"To carry on the family name."	*"A child is my only claim to immortality."*
	"Johnnie wants a baby brother."	
	"To have someone to love or possess."	*"I need to be needed—if I'm somebody's mother [father] then I'm Somebody."*
	"Because everyone else is doing it."	*"We don't want to be different."*
		"We can afford to have a baby."
		"I want my child to get the things I never had."
		"A baby will keep a woman in her place."
	"To have someone to care for you when you are old."	

"Hypothetically," she continued, "it might be useful for us to call a moratorium on births for some period of time. I don't mean to seem naïve as to the effect such a moratorium would have on our economic and social institutions, but again, speaking hypothetically, it might give our battered and exhausted planet a breathing spell and allow us to base our lives and identities on ourselves and not on our children. From my point of view, giving birth to a biological child today is depriving others already born of care that might be given to them. If one loves children, should one not be able to love children of other races and from other countries? Now, there *are* certainly good reasons for adoption."

No good reasons for having your own? Only bad reasons? I am the first to agree that there are some less than ideal reasons why many babies are brought into the world. But this seems to go more than a bit too far.

I can accept the desirability of a rational—or relatively rational— approach to parenthood and the recognition of nonparenthood as a perfectly acceptable option for some people. But to recommend nonparenthood as the norm for everyone? There is, after all, the problem of survival for the human race. Moreover, people are going to continue to have children, so why paint them as villains?

But let's hold out for good reasons, really positive ones.

In his book *Woman's Doctor,* Dr. William Sweeney says that when he asks a woman why she is having a child, he waits for the response "Because I like babies!" And that Planned Parenthood advertisement referred to in Table I ends with "There are a lot of wrong reasons to have a child—but only one right reason: because you really want one." How do you know what "really" means? There's "really," and there's *really.* Where is the why or the right or wrong of parenthood? A statement about wanting merely stimulates a logical follow-up question: "Why does he or she really want one?"

The Want Factor and Its Triggers

In today's world, the statement "I want a child," is not enough of a reason to explain why someone is having a child, because there *are* a lot of wrong reasons and because the planet *is* overcrowded. On the other hand, the desire certainly has to be there in some form if the child is to be welcome and if the reason is to have even a remote chance of getting into the "good" reasons column. As a matter of fact, that *Want Factor* is so critical to a good decision in favor of parenthood that it merits a definition. And I just happen to have one. The Want Factor can be considered to be *the sincere desire to welcome a child into your life for its own sake and a readiness to share your time, love, and attention with this new human being.*

But even with an official definition, the Want Factor is not enough. *Something has to trigger the desire for pregnancy and parenthood.* And these triggers may be of two different types. One type may be on the conscious-rational level. You may be able to pinpoint and talk about these triggers. Others may be of the unconscious or nonrational variety, possibly located in the depths of your cerebral cavity.

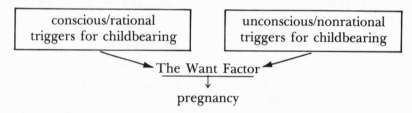

The parenthood decision-making equation isn't so simple as this suggested formula makes it sound. Sorry. First, there is no clear-cut division between the unconscious and conscious categories of childbearing triggers. The real reasons that lead a man and woman to parenthood may be found in either, or more likely in *both*, of these areas. And they all may be interacting with one another. As Dr. Mark Flapan writes in the *American Journal of Orthopsychiatry*, the motivations for parenthood must be understood in the context of a couple's life: "Childbearing motivations," he notes, "involve a [variety] of socially defined and idiosyncratic meanings, some of which may be recognized by the individual." It is probably not possible to identify everything that goes into the triggering of a desire to become a parent: as psychoanalyst Donald Kaplan told me, "It's not a fully rational act. It's not irrational and it's not rational. Basically, you're dealing with the outcome of a long process of inner reasoning."

In other words, as we have already established, the decision to have a child or not is unique, a special combination of feeling out and thinking out your own answer. Although babies probably shouldn't just happen, neither should you feel that you must have *all* the answers before committing yourself either way. You can't have all the answers. For one thing, you're usually dealing with not just one complex constellation, but two. A man and a woman may have two completely different viewpoints on the subject. Somehow, in our culture, where there is an unwritten guideline to the effect that men are not to express feelings, it becomes easy to pass the whole subject of babies and children into the female column. But of course it does not and must not work this way. He is as involved as she is in this process, although he may make his feelings and attitudes known in a more subtle manner.

The parenthood *trigger model* is really just an attempt to simplify a very complicated subject. At the least, it provides a logical foundation. I'd like to build on this structure by first describing four couples who told me about their conscious-rational reasons, or triggers, for childbearing. Then I'll try to identify some of the less-than-conscious, nonrational forces that may be behind a desire to have a child. Keep in mind that these categories, which look so far apart on paper, are really about as mixed up as homogenized milk.

We're Having a Child Because . . .

I drove up from the city to meet with John and Susan in the suburban house where they'd lived for about a year. I knew that they were both in their twenties and didn't have children. As I started up the crumbling brick steps in front of their house, I saw John in the backyard mowing the lawn. He was a tall, heavyset man with short black hair; he was wearing blue jeans and a sweat shirt. When he saw me he turned off the mower and came out front.

"Hi! I hear you want to talk about the children we don't have yet." We both laughed, and he invited me to see the yard before we went inside to join Susan. The house was obviously in need of paint and some repairs. But the yard was beautifully kept. John took me over to a small vegetable garden where he plucked a ripe tomato and handed it to me.

"We're of course planning to have children one of these years," he told me as we walked toward the house. "But we have lots of time. After all, Sue's only twenty-one and I'm twenty-seven. But when we do have the kids, we'll need some extra room. You know, a nursery and playroom. I think there's enough space here for an addition, don't you?"

We met Susan in the kitchen. She was a short, slightly plump woman with dark hair and eyes and an infectious smile. She greeted me enthusiastically.

"I've been looking forward to this all week. I've been doing a lot of thinking too, you know, about children and all. Have a seat." She motioned us to the kitchen table while she put the last dishes from lunch into the dishwasher.

"Could you tell me when you plan to start your family?"

"Oh yes! We can hardly wait to be parents." Susan looked at John and smiled and then addressed me again. "We both love kids—babies, toddlers, and teenagers. But we want to make sure we're ready. That's why we're holding off for a while. Every cent of our money is in this house, and we have so much to do to it. First a new roof, then a couple coats of paint." She sat down next to John and continued, "We think we should have some of these things done and some cash squirreled away before we have the baby, right, honey?"

John was staring off into space. "Oh, right, right. I was just thinking about what Sue said about loving kids. We really do, you know. I used to teach at a boys' camp. I loved it. I still coach basketball at the YMCA each week to keep in touch. Kids are so much fun. But anyway, yeah, we're trying to save some money before we have ours. I'm a policeman here in town. We're not what you'd call millionaires, but we're doing okay. We're saving slowly. I know we could do better if Sue took a job, but that's where I put my foot down. In my family, wives don't work." John's authoritative tone left no doubt about who was the boss. Susan seemed to hang on his every word.

I decided to ask him more about his parenthood plans. "Have you thought about how many children you might have?"

He smiled confidently. He seemed to have all the answers.

"Oh, yes, that's decided too. We're going to make two our limit. We want to do everything right, and I'm not sure we could do it if we had more than two." Susan looked a bit concerned about this but didn't say anything.

"Well, have you thought about why you want children? Did you ever try to put your feelings into words?" I looked directly at Susan, because I already knew that John would eventually have something to say about that.

She smiled and this time spoke more softly. "Well, yes. I'm the oldest of seven, four girls and three boys, and I'm used to being with lots of people." She stopped for a moment and sighed. "I always remembered how my parents loved us. I think I inherited it from them. My younger sister just had her first, and I don't mind telling you I'm green with envy. My goodness, just the experience of having a family makes it worthwhile. The idea of having the responsibility of raising a human being—it's nothing less than thrilling, miraculous." I thought she was going to lift up off her chair. John was watching her intently, thoroughly enjoying her enthusiasm. She took a deep breath. "Children are so refreshing—stimulating. They'll bring such a challenge. I can hardly wait to diaper and feed my own baby. Oh, and cuddle it, too. John always tells me he thinks I'll be a great mother."

I looked at John. "I'm not as bubbly as Sue is about it—I'm just not like that anyway. But I do enjoy being with kids—and I think when they are *my* children I'll love it even more. It's an experience I don't think anyone should miss. At least we're not going to!"

"So, it's the joys, the thrill and stimulation of children—the urge to experience parenthood—that explains why you're going to have a family. Is that it?" I directed the question at both of them.

John answered first. "That's it. That's why we want to be parents."

"Well, wait a second." Susan leaned forward, put her elbows on the table, and held her face in her hands. "You know, there is something else. Let's see if I can explain it. Okay. John, you go out every day to work. But I'm here. I do the dishes, read the paper and whatever magazines are around, and I look at some of those morning TV shows. But, you know, that's that. Do you know what I mean?" She was addressing me.

I nodded and asked her to go on.

"When we first moved here I was busy—you know, buying drapes and furniture and just getting things together. But when that was done, it occurred to me that I really didn't have that much to do. I'd go to bridge parties and people would ask me, 'What do you do?' When they heard I didn't have a job or children, they'd give me a look like, Boy, is she weird—she doesn't do anything." She turned and looked at John and raised her voice somewhat. "Well, let's admit it; I really don't do anything."

John started to talk. "Oh, come on, Sue—"

She interrupted. "No, really, it's true. And I don't want to get a job even if you wanted me to." She looked over at me as if for approval. "Having a career never turned me on. I want to be a full-time mother. So what's wrong with that?" She sat back in her chair and frowned a bit. "You know, this conversation reminds me of an ad I saw the other day. I think it was by Planned Parenthood. It describes all the wrong reasons to have a baby. Probably they would think that mine is wrong, too. But I think it's right. And I don't really care what they think."

I visited with Ann and Richard in their twenty-third-floor apartment overlooking the lights and traffic jams of the city. The doorman had announced me, so they were looking out into the hall when I got off the elevator. Although it was after 8:30 in the evening, both were still in their business clothes. Richard wore a three-piece suit, and Ann was striking in a sweater dress that complemented her well-proportioned figure.

"Come in," Richard said graciously as he took my coat. Ann smiled, but she seemed slightly reserved. We walked into the living room. It was impeccably furnished, the ashtrays and candy dishes symmetrically aligned and dust free. Richard moved a large rubber tree and found an outlet for my tape recorder. I sat down and asked if they could tell me a little about themselves. Ann looked nervously at Richard, visually requesting him to talk first.

"Okay. We're both twenty-eight and have been married for three years this month. I'm a lawyer with one of the Wall Street firms. Ann is an investment analyst at a midtown bank. One of the reasons we couldn't see you until this hour is that we both work late most every night." Richard looked over at Ann and smiled. She still looked a bit uncomfortable. He lit his pipe and went on. "Oh, it's not all hard work. We've squeezed in vacations. We're even planning a Caribbean cruise next month—sort of an anniversary gift. We go away on weekends, to see our parents in Vermont and Massachusetts. We work hard, but we play hard, too." He paused, giving Ann a chance to speak. She didn't. So he continued. "We're doing pretty well; we've saved a bit. And that's why we're planning to have a baby in the near future. I guess that's what you wanted to know, right?"

"Yes. Right," I said. "But could you be more specific?" I turned and looked directly at Ann. "Could you tell me what you think you might be gaining—or giving up—by having a baby? What rewards do you anticipate?"

Ann moved around in her chair and crossed her legs. "Well, listen, I should tell you that I don't exactly feel comfortable talking about this subject. It's so personal. We've never talked with anyone about it before." She glanced over at Richard. "As a matter of fact, we don't talk about it with each other much, either. I mean directly. It's very emotional. I don't find it easy to talk about." I told Ann I knew exactly what she meant. She looked relieved but was still obviously self-conscious.

She uncrossed her legs and leaned back in her chair. "Okay. I'll give it a try. Why do we want children? Well, I would say that by having a child, my husband and I would be merging ourselves in a unique way." She looked at me to see if I knew what she meant. I nodded.

"It's not," Richard interrupted, "that we now notice anything missing in our marriage. But as Ann said, we have this feeling that a child will add even more depth to our already strong relationship. It would be kind of nice to have a living symbol of our love—a symbol of our dedication to each other." He had a very intense look on his face, and he was staring out the window. He tapped down the tobacco in the bowl of his pipe as he talked. "A child would be another person we could both love and give our attention to."

"Right. Right." Ann seemed to be loosening up. "Those are just my feelings too. But there's something else. My God, is this a difficult topic! Let's see. Both of Dick's grandparents died many years ago. I never knew them. But my grandmother lived till she was eighty-five. She was the life of our family parties at Thanksgiving, Christmas, and Easter. Whatever. Believe it or not, despite our ages, we enjoyed playing the role of children at those gatherings. Having all that attention directed at us." Ann smiled as she remembered those pleasant occasions. Then she spoke softly. "My grandmother died three months ago, quite suddenly. At our first family dinner after her death, it was obvious that we had moved up the generational ladder. We weren't kids anymore. There weren't any kids. We began to think about that."

Richard nodded in agreement. "Frankly, we began to wonder whom we would be having dinner with twenty years from now. We really like that feeling of family togetherness, that sense of warmth you don't get always with friends. I don't want to get morbid, but what if one of us died much before the other? Being alone is no fun. A child gives you a family base. For now and for the future."

I asked Ann about her job and how she thought she would handle motherhood and a career.

"Oh, I'm not naïve. I know it won't be easy to swing. And I'll tell you the truth, I'm not enthusiastic about leaving the bank for a few years. Who knows if I'm the nursery type? And from the practical point of view, we'll be losing my income at the same time we'll need a bigger place to live." Ann had a look of real concern as she began to itemize the possible problems she saw in the future. Then she smiled. "But we'll do it. We'll work them out, right, Dick?"

"Of course we will." Richard looked and sounded confident. "I think planning for children is great. But you can't have everything worked out. What's important is deciding if you want them or not. And we've decided yes. Everything else will fall into place. In both the long run and the short run, it will be worth it."

"Do you like children?" I looked at both of them.

"I can't really say that I know that many babies or young children, or even teenagers for that matter," Richard admitted, "but I know I will love my own child. I'm not worried about that."

Ann agreed. "No, I'm not concerned either. I'd be lying if I told you I was mad about little children. I don't know that I am. But I'm willing to give my time and attention to my own son or daughter—and I feel I could enjoy doing it."

I wanted to tell you about these two couples because I think they have offered four of the most common, relatively rational reasons for having a first or second child.

Susan and John are planning to have children as a means of exposing themselves to the *stimulating experiences of pregnancy, childbirth, and parenthood.* It's a part of life they just don't want to miss. Additionally, motherhood provides Susan with *a clear-cut role, the only role she has really ever wanted.*

Ann and Richard see children as a way of *deepening their already well-grounded marriage relationship* and as an *investment in future emotional security—a means of providing a family base.*

If you had to rank these four reasons in terms of which was the "best," you'd probably put John's and Susan's first explanation on the top of the list: the love for children and the desire to be involved in the stimulating experiences of parenthood. You might even go so far as to say that none of the other three reasons alone, rational or not, would be enough to form the basis of an intelligent and informed decision to have a baby. But these other three reasons are very often present among some couples: the general feeling of not wanting to miss a major facet of human life; a strong desire to further enhance a good marriage; the desire to provide for the years to come and/or to create a role for the wife. They may at least initially serve to compensate for a lack of ardent sentiment for children. After all, what does love for children really mean? A woman named Frances Bless, at the birth of her eighteenth child on June 15, 1959 said, "We just happen to like children." What is classified as love or like may to some extent reflect myriad other reasons.

In *Blackberry Winter,* Margaret Mead, who had her only child at age thirty-eight, explains that her own decision to have a child was triggered by her observation of people who actively disliked children. As I have mentioned, she had studied the Mundugumor, the New Guinea preliterate group of cannibals who hated children. "It was the Mundugumor attitude toward children that was decisive," she wrote in discussing her approach to parenthood. "I felt strongly that a culture that rejected children was a bad culture. And so I began to hope—not very logically, but with a kind of emotional congruence—that perhaps after all I could have a child; perhaps I could manage it."

Probably the most encompassing of all the reasons expressed by Susan, John, Ann, and Richard falls in the category "the experience," the desire not to miss a major life event, the eagerness to broaden horizons by having a child. But their specific goals are worth looking at individually.

First, *the desire to provide a family base and make a type of investment in the future.* If that sounds familiar, maybe it's because it is something of a variation on a few of those reasons on the "bad and dumb" list: "I need to be needed," "to have someone to love and possess," and "to have someone to care for you when you are old." You might want to criticize Ann and Richard's reasoning or come back with the rejoinder that "kids don't comfort you in your old age; they just help you get there faster," but they were expressing a basic human need. We *do* need others, at every stage of our lives.

To many persons frustrated by too little love or closeness to others, a baby may seem an ideal object for their affections. Fully aware that even "perfect" marriages often go awry, a prospective parent may think of a baby as someone who will belong to her (or him) forever, who will always be considerate and loving. Beverly Crumley, a social worker at Planned Parenthood in New York, has noticed that even among young unwed mothers, many of them want to have a baby simply because they need *someone* to love. But, too, there is frequently the expectation that in later years the child will even up the output-input balance by repaying his parents for the years of goodness shown to him.

Of course it doesn't necessarily work that way. To begin with, as Holly Golightly so succinctly put it in *Breakfast at Tiffany's,* people (even babies) don't *belong* to people. At best, you might consider a child a temporary investment, one on which there is no guarantee of any returns, either emotional or financial. He or she may take off to Mars if transportation is available by then. On the other hand, as New York University School of Medicine psychiatrist Henry Greenbaum discussed with me, "Future security, however poorly defined that may be for an individual, can play an important role in the expression of a desire to have a child. Man is the only species who knows about his death. He is aware of being mortal. We all have a fear of loneliness in old age, and we all worry about the possibility of being incapacitated. This is not an abnormal or neurotic feeling. It's not like being afraid of going outside your house because you might be hit by a car. It is a realistic fear. As life-spans became even more prolonged, this aspect of family life may become even more important."

But, you say, there are always friends. Not everyone looks at it that way. There are those like Richard and Ann who strongly believe that the bond that generally exists between a parent and a child is on another level than that which exists between friends. They feel that their best friend today may pack up and move to the other side of the world, never to be heard from for twenty-five years. This could happen with a child, but the odds on it are very much lower. Possibly in a subtle way a child can provide a parent a link with the future, a means of making the unknown a little less frightening. This may be especially true for a woman. Demographically speaking, a woman lives on the average seven years longer than a man. And on the average, she is likely to be three years younger than he. There can be those ten lonely years to think about.

An immortality wish exists in almost all of us. Not everyone labels it as such, but the urge to introduce one's genes into the next generation, and hopefully into an infinite number of generations yet to come, indicates a strong push toward the pursuit of life-after-death. In many cultures parents tenderly apply the terms "little father" and "little mother" to their offspring, an affectionate tribute to their assumed future roles. Among Orthodox Jews a prayer know as the *Kaddish* is recited by Jewish sons on each anniversary of their fathers' deaths. Accordingly, a son may be fondly referred as "my *Kaddish'l*" in recognition of the fact that the son will one day assume his father's place, and presumably will beget his own son to honor and perpetuate the tradition.

The desire for immortality is not strictly limited to physical aspects. Adults frequently feel a need to remake their own lives through a child. They want to compensate for mistakes, real or perceived, their own parents may have made. They want to provide all the advantages that they may have felt they themselves lacked. And, perhaps most important of all, they want to correct the self-imposed errors they have fallen prey to—the wasted learning opportunities at school because C grades seemed sufficient at the time; the exciting job not taken because a lack of self-confidence made the dull one seem safer; personal difficulties that might have been avoided with greater fortitude or a better knowledge of one's own self. There persists the secret (or not-so-secret) hope that a child will achieve where his parent or parents have failed.

How often have you heard, or uttered yourself, "If I had known then what I know now, I would have . . ." (or "would not have")? The power of 20/20 hindsight promotes a subtle wish to magically create a new me, fresh, uninhibited, and right from scratch.

Does this aspect of future investment come off as a good reason or a bad one? As with some of the other reasons, it depends a great deal on the handling. If the basic idea is to contribute the knowledge of experience to a young new life, it is probably a good reason. But if you disregard individuality and make too strict an attempt to mold and manipulate a child into precisely what *you* wish him or her to become, the reason becomes a wrong one—and the results could be disastrous. Beginning in infancy, every person is unique. Some characteristics need to be channeled, or even discouraged; others merit an extra effort toward development; but in no case can a complete do-over job be justified.

Second, *the desire to deepen an already well-grounded marriage relationship.* This *is* very different from the save-a-shaky-marriage reasons that all wrong-reason experts come up with. Here we are not dealing with a chain of wedlock that is so heavy it needs three to carry. "I love my child because he is the we of me," one woman told me. "I just wanted to have my husband's baby. I can't really explain it."

"My wife and I care very deeply for each other," a new father explained. "After four years of marriage, we found our love had only grown stronger. We wanted to add a 'forever' factor to our relationship by starting a family. I guess you could say our baby represents a statement of our love."

"This sound a bit morbid, I guess," one prospective mother told me, "but when my husband was traveling recently, I admitted to myself that I was happy his baby—our baby—was developing inside me. If anything ever happened to him, I would have our child."

Psychoanalyst Donald Kaplan feels that it is perfectly understandable that a happily married couple would turn to a child as a focus of their love. "Two people in love are not always going to be looking into each other's eyes; that becomes an impossible expectation," he told me. "They eventually come to stand shoulder to shoulder. They begin looking in the same direction. A child at this point is very appropriate, an opportunity for them to share something which is very much part of their narcissism." Having a child is seen by many couples as a means of extending, of increasing, their love. A folk song says that if you give love away, you end up having more.

Third, *to provide a role for the woman.* Again, that looks like it's directly off the no-no list. ("Why knock myself out working when I can have a baby?" "A baby will give me something to do.") But the fact remains that, even in the age of women's liberation, many women do not want to follow careers outside their homes. They want to have children, and they want to spend all or most of their time raising them. Just as a woman should have the option to choose to work full time and decline her option for motherhood, shouldn't she have the freedom to reverse the options? (Or if she feels up to it, why shouldn't she try to coordinate a career and motherhood?) The wording of the Gould and Planned Parenthood "wrong" reasons is hardly positive, but the same concept could be expressed another way: "I have no intention of assuming a business career. My chosen career is motherhood. And that *will* give me something to do."

In Susan's case, it appears that the choice of motherhood over a career outside the home was made on a positive basis. But it can work another way: a woman may turn to pregnancy out of fear of striking out on her own, or if she is unemployed she may use the baby as an alibi to account for her time. If she is already employed, she may turn to pregnancy as a backup mechanism, just in case the career she has in mind doesn't work out or if she begins to feel unfulfilled, as though she were merely treading water.

A short time ago *The New York Times Magazine* carried a story by Nancy and Chip McGrath entitled "Why a Baby?" After hashing over, *ad infinitum,* all the reasons for *not* having children, they found themselves dissatisfied, even though the not reasons appeared totally logical. Later, when the McGraths had decided positively on the prospect of a new addition to the family, they discovered the reasons for their decision were difficult to talk about and not terribly coherent. Although expressed somewhat differently, the Want Factor had been at work again.

"Maybe . . . a large part of why parents want children [is] to own those moments when an unselfconscious child gives away his undiluted self," Nancy suggested. But there were other reasons, too. "Suddenly, having a baby seemed like the most selfish thing I could do. . . . Whenever I tried to imagine myself in the role of a housewife-mother, I thought of free time [even though] I know that a wish for free time is a poor reason to have children." (As she quickly discovered after the birth of their daughter, neither is it a very logical reason, since free time is soon reduced to precious little.) Nancy's point here was that after years of following the patterns set by parents, schools, and jobs, finally she would be able to establish her own patterns, and she found that idea very appealing.

"Mostly I wanted a child because children are fun, and this still seems to me the best of all reasons," added Chip. "Children are fun to watch and to be with and they give you an excuse to occasionally act like a child yourself. When there's a kid around, you can play with electric trains, and make funny noises at the dinner table."

I have listed several common triggers that precipitate the relatively rational pregnancies—particularly first and second ones. Perhaps you can think of others (we'll discuss possible unconscious triggers later in the chapter), but these four are of immediate interest. Did you notice that they all have at least one salient point in common? Their intentions are directed toward the prospective parent. If you want to be moralistic or dramatic about it, you can even use the word *selfish*, as Nancy McGrath did. Why not admit it? Contrary to the accusations often hurled at childless couples, in the 1980s there is no really altruistic reason to bring a child into the world. Instead, the child is seen by the prospective parents as having the potential to serve some present or future need. That doesn't mean the parents won't be selfless and giving, once the child arrives. But here we're focusing on the motivation of the parents before conception. And no matter how you analyze it, it boils down to the fact that the individual man and woman involved have the interests of themselves or each other—or possibly someone else—at stake, and not the interests of the unborn child. There is not necessarily anything wrong with this. But would-be parents should come to terms with these thoughts. There are, after all, different forms of selfishness, and it helps to know which form is exerting an influence.

What precedes the decision to bring a third or fourth child into the family? Are there any rational triggers here, any good reasons to have more than two children? Steve and Cynthia and Janet and Paul seem to think so.

We're Having More Than Two Because . . .

"We've been married for ten years," Cynthia told me as we drove from her sprawling country house to the neighborhood school to pick up her two sons. She was a petite woman with a glow of health in her cheeks and from the morning activities she described to me it was apparent that she had almost limitless energy. She went on. "I'm thirty-four, Steve's . . . let's see . . . thirty-seven. The kids are seven and five."

"Do you know why you wanted your first two children?" I was hoping she'd give me her answer before Jody and Michael got into the car. I'd found that parents were not so candid about the whys of parenthood when the subjects in question were present. I was lucky this time. When we parked in the schoolyard there was no evidence that school had been let out yet.

"Actually, I just knew I wanted children," she said as she turned to face me. "When we were first married, Steve was in the service in Germany. We were stationed there for two years, and I worked half time as a secretary at the military base." She leaned forward and looked out the front window to see if the kids were coming. They weren't.

She continued: "We talked about children, and we both agreed we'd wait a year or two. Then he said it was up to me." She stopped and laughed. "Two months later I conceived. I was happy it turned out to be a boy because I felt that was what Steve really wanted. Then when Jody was a year old, I learned that Michaél was on the way. I must tell you, though, I was hoping it would be Michele. Oh, but of course we were thrilled with him, too." Cynthia was staring out the front window again, but this time she was not looking for the boys. She was lost in thought.

After a moment, she spoke again. "You asked about why I had the first two, and I gave you vague answers. But one thing I can tell you. I do know why I want to try again. I want a daughter." As she talked, Cynthia closed her eyes and nodded her head to emphasize what she was saying. "I can't tell you how strong that feeling is! Girls are softer. Well, they're just different. I don't want to be deprived of the experience of having one of my own."

"But that's a game of roulette at this point, don't you think? Is that enough of a reason to have a third child?"

"Right. I know. But I *really* want a daughter, so I think it's worth the gamble. I've read about some techniques to increase your chances of a girl, but I'm also not fooling myself. If it's another boy, so be it. Children are my life. I give them all my attention. I know I will love him. I will enjoy having a third child, although I will admit that we wouldn't have it if we already had a daughter and a son."

"But what if your next child is—"

She threw her hands up. "Oh, no, don't ask me if I'd try for a fourth if I had another boy. I can't answer that now. The thought of possibly ending up with *four* boys is a bit overwhelming."

Later that evening I talked with Cynthia's husband, Steve, a short blond man with a full moustache. He was an assistant professor of German at one of the local community colleges. After he had put his two sons to bed and we were walking back downstairs, I asked him his feelings about having a third child. "I understand how she feels, you know, about having a daughter. I let her make the decisions about parenthood, but if we had two daughters, I might have felt the same way about wanting a son. She's a great mother, really selfless. I can't see anything wrong about having a third. I know we can't be guaranteed a girl, but I can tell you one thing—" He stopped and looked directly at me. "If we *don't* try again, we are guaranteed of *not* having a girl." He looked away and proceeded down the stairs. "We've looked into adoption, but we were told that because we already had children, we were not eligible to apply for an infant. And we would want any child we raise to be with us from the start."

Janet and Paul stopped by our apartment one Sunday afternoon. They weren't inside for two minutes before the latest pictures of Marie and Paul, Jr. were brought out for inspection. I agreed they both looked like Paul and promised to meet them in person someday soon to verify this observation. Then we sat down to talk. Janet and Paul were expecting their third child and had agreed to discuss their thoughts about parenthood.

Paul was of medium height and distinctly overweight. His face looked young, but his thinning brown hair made him appear older than he probably was. He shook his head and chuckled. "I've seen all this stuff in the papers about how it's un-American to have more than two kids. What's that all about, anyway? I'm thirty-one and Jan's twenty-nine, and we plan to have at least the third and maybe a fourth. Now what are you going to do about that? I bet that gets you all upset." He grinned and looked prepared to meet any argument.

I shook my head. "No, right now I'm most interested in finding out why you wanted to have your third child—and possibly more." He seemed disappointed. I think he was expecting more of a challenge.

"Well, I'd say we want more kids because we're good parents. Especially the little woman here. She's great with them." He put his arm around Janet for a moment and then turned to me. "But you wouldn't understand that. You couldn't unless you had kids of your own."

Janet sat forward on the couch. In contrast to Paul, she was tall and thin, with long, heavy reddish hair. "You know, it isn't easy for us. Paul teaches school all week and works at a restaurant on weekends, and when the kids are sleeping I type term papers at home to bring in extra cash. But I think my life is great. I wouldn't have it any other way. This sounds corny, I know, but my children are my jewels. I love being with them." Her eyes sparkled as she talked. "I think there are mother types and nonmother types. I'm willing to give them my full attention and time, and why not?"

I tried to turn her last comment around. "Let's turn from the why not to the why. Can you tell me why you want to have a third and maybe a fourth child?"

She didn't say anything for a moment. Then she smiled. "Yes, actually I can. You may not like my answer, but I can." Paul and she exchanged a quick glance. "I really think Paul and I have something to offer in the way of intelligent, well-adjusted children. I'm not saying that our genes are any better. It's just that we've made parenthood our specialty." She paused again and, when she resumed talking, sounded more distant. "And there's something more—I'm not sure how to put it. Even this early in their lives, I can tell that both my son and my daughter are very much more like Paul than they are like me. They are more interested in books and problem solving than they are in people, for instance, or sports or outdoor activities. Don't get me wrong. I mean, I love them the way they are. But I'd also like to have one child like me." She laughed and looked at Paul. "Maybe I'd also like to have one who looks more like me!"

Paul laughed, too. "I understand that. I do. Each kid is different—do you know what I mean? That's part of the fun. We both enjoy it. Someone's got to have the children, and I feel we can do a better job than most. You know we're not asking anyone to pay for our kids. We carry our own weight. It's a struggle, but we can afford 'em. So there you are."

Do you think we should call out the ZPG enforcement squad and send them after Steve and Paul and their fertile wives? If you take some of those "wrong" reasons literally, these couples are definitely guilty. Steve and Cynthia are trying again for sex balance, and Janet and Paul could at the very least be indicted on the grounds that they think they can afford to have a baby.

It's easy to sit down with a typewriter or pencil and paper and, in a totally removed manner, come up with wrong reasons for parenthood, such as the ones listed in Table I. In fairness to the authors of those reasons, I should say that their main purpose was not to set strict codes, but simply to get couples to think about what they were doing. A judgment on such a personal issue of having a baby does not lend itself well to subway posters. You can't, for instance, condemn a couple for wanting a child, even the third, of the "other" sex. There can be very different feelings toward a son and a daughter (as feminists well know!). D. H. Lawrence, in *Sons and Lovers,* presents an interesting example. "A son's my son 'til he takes him a wife. But my daughter's my daughter the whole of her life." Different but equally intense feelings might be expressed about a son.

If the would-be jury sensed the intensity of that desire, the verdict might be very different. "My feelings about having a daughter were so strong," one mother of three told me—I detected she was holding back tears as she spoke—"I thought about almost nothing else during my third pregnancy. Of course I loved my sons, but I thought I could be closer to a girl. I had the wardrobe all picked out, although I never actually bought it. And I used to think about how much fun it would be to dress up a little girl in frills and comb her hair. Well, my third was a son, and of course I love him very much. But it's funny, when the doctor said 'It's a boy!' I felt that I had lost a child as well as gained one."

Another mother told me she had endured a miserable childhood as a "lonely only." As soon as her year-old daughter became a few months older she and her husband were planning to "get to work" on her second pregnancy. "Frankly," she explained, "I always envied my friends who had big families; in fact, I still envy them. Gale and I plan to have at least three, probably four children. I guess it's my way of compensating." Pure enjoyment of an oversized family—is that a wrong reason?

And with regard to Janet, Supermom, are we going to tell her not to have her third or fourth? Are we going to explain that she has no right to try to create another child because she wants one who is different from her first two? And that it is wrong to feel that you have a unique capacity to raise the type of children who will contribute to society? No, we're not there yet, and hopefully we never will be. In our culture at this time in history, the childbearing decision-making process remains a personal one. ZPGers and others would argue that point. But the basic human question is, can you condemn someone else's motivations and needs? However important population issues are, it is at least as important *not* to legislate feelings. In the past, such a course has led to fascism and persecution, which are hardly appropriate remedies for population growth rates. We *can* develop less drastic alternatives. For instance, it is worth remembering that not everyone has to follow the same demographic formula to ensure a slowdown in population growth rates. There is room for differences—differences that will balance each other out. For instance, national surveys taken during the 1970-75 period indicate that only 30 percent of young married wives are planning to have three or more children. The other 70 percent report they want two or fewer children (57 percent want two, 9 percent one, and 4 percent intend to remain child-free). Considered in this perspective, and taking into account that the option of nonparenthood may become even more attractive, a range in family size is indeed acceptable.

To return to the question of motivation, all the examples I've given you so far are unique in that they have a factor whose presence you can't always depend on: the husband and the wife generally agree on the decision to have children. Steve appears not to have taken a very direct role in the thinking about pregnancies or about the third child, but he still saw Cynthia's point of view and understood her desire for a daughter. Often, it doesn't work that way.

"I know I'm really hurting my wife's feelings," one thirty-five-year-old child-free husband told me in a very serious tone. He frowned with concern. "I know she wants to have a child. We've been married for six years, so I hardly have time as an excuse. I just don't know if I want that responsibility."

A twenty-two-year-old newlywed reflected the same situation from another vantage point as she explained how she was trying to stall on the parenthood issue. She shook her head and smiled sadly. "He just loves children. And he wants to start right away. It is a source of contention between us, and I get by by saying 'just a few months more and then I'll be ready.' But I have no reason to believe I will be ready in just a few months."

"Our problem is a little different," declared Vivian, a neighbor of mine. "I have two teenagers from a previous marriage who live with us, as you know. When Gary and I were married two years ago we didn't really talk about the idea of adding to our family. But now Gary desperately wants to have a child of his own.

"I'll be forty years old in a few months and I'm aware of the various risks that go with having a baby at that age. I'm afraid. I know there are ways of testing now before the baby is even born. But I can't help asking myself, 'What if the test were positive—for mongolism or whatever? Then what would I do? How would I handle that?' If we were then to start all over and try one more time, I would be just that much older and the risk that much greater."

She seemed lost in thought for a few minutes and I assured her I understood her dilemma very well. Finally she continued, "And all the time I'm worrying about the physical risks, I'm not even sure if

I'm being honest with myself. Gary even once suggested the possibility of adoption. I think that's when it all really hit me—I'm not sure I can go through all that again—the bottles and the diapers and the smelly laundry. I've *done* that already. I'm into other things now; my children are into other things. I have a good job that I really like—a medical research project that will continue for another two years. If I go through the baby bit again I may never have the same career opportunity that I have right now.

"That must sound selfish. I love Gary very much and we have a wonderful relationship. I hate to see him disappointed. He doesn't really bug me about it, but I feel guilty sometimes just the same. And then I resent the fact that I should feel guilty. Wouldn't it be nice if men could have some of the babies? Maybe then they would understand how it feels to be looked on as a baby-machine."

All of these situations are common—and they cause real problems. In Vivian's case, she related a number of issues that often cause friction between husband and wife, ones that cannot be readily smoothed away. Ideally, parenthood is a question that if raised, discussed and, hopefully, decided before marriage. But a decision is subject to change and in practice, it may seem like an option appropriate to the distant future (or, for Vivian, only the near future). When that future comes, the couple may realize to their discomfort that they disagree. Or their attitudes may fall short of unanimity. Timing may be all that is keeping them from agreeing; in that case, a compromise may be the answer. But when one person registers a loud aye, and the other a loud nay, there's trouble. There is still no easily available source of help to which most couples can turn to resolve this question. The few preparenthood counseling services are confined to a few large cities. A man and woman who see the parenthood question from different angles should attempt to identify each of the factors in their own pro and con columns and see if there is any room for give-and-take. Otherwise, a gifted and sympathetic marriage counselor might help to thrash it out.

The Psychic Lower Level

Amoebas are simple. Human beings are complex. There is no uniform way of explaining most human behavior, and childbearing behavior is no different. Even if you think Sigmund Freud contributed about as much as Peter Rabbit to our knowledge of what makes people run, you'd probably concede that our behavior *is* often guided by unconscious motivations that we are not always fully able to grapple with. Probably the most significant group of reasons that come from the nonrational level are reflected in the argument, "I don't know why I want a child, but I want one." Or "I'm not absolutely sure I want to get pregnant, but I know that if I *don't* have children I may be sorry. If I *do,* I won't be sorry." And this is nothing to pass off lightly or label as irrational. *Non*rational maybe, but, again, we're not dealing with a fully rational deck to begin with. You can probably think of a number of examples, both in literature and in real life, of nonrational forces at work in bringing about a pregnancy.

For instance, when Rabbit in John Updike's *Rabbit, Run* learns that his inebriated wife has accidentally drowned their child, he pleads with another woman to bear his child as soon as possible. And in *Life Signs* Johanna Davis tells the story of a woman who agrees to terminate her unplanned pregnancy until she comes to terms with her desperate desire to have that child.

In line with this desperate—almost panicked—urge to have a child, two real-life people told me similar stories. "When I married my second husband, we were both over thirty-five, and we each had children of our own," an attractive woman of about fifty told me. "But I had this overwhelming desire to have his baby. I didn't have that with my first husband."

And a college professor who was close to retirement age and had earned a reputation as one of the leaders in his field spoke candidly about his sudden surge of interest in becoming a father: "My wife found out shortly after we were married that she wasn't able to have children of her own, and somehow we never got around to adopting. We had full lives; actually we still do. We are both very active in university matters, too. I never really missed children, never really thought about it until recently. And then it hit me." He leaned forward and lowered his voice. "I don't want to die without having at least one son or daughter. I've accumulated so much knowledge myself, I want to pass it on. I want my name or some form of me to be carried on in some way. I've already asked two women if they would be willing to have my child and, frankly, I have been turned down."

This expression of urgency or intense desire isn't always there. Sometimes the nonrational explanation is just that it appeared natural. "No, I can't say I actually thought about why I was having a child," one sixtyish mother explained to me. "I just knew that we wanted one. Things were different back then. Life was simpler. We were married just after the war, and it seemed like the logical thing to do. We weren't concerned with all the material possessions and so-called personal freedom young people seem to want today. Our family came first. If having a baby meant using up all the cash we got for wedding gifts, which in our case it did, then so be it."

Today, particularly because of the Pill, more couples are postponing their first child—and owing to this factor alone, they have to think. They have to decide to go off the Pill, and that can lead them into the rational arena. It *can* lead them in a rational direction, but not necessarily. There is a long list of propregnancy factors that may be lurking in the depths of their minds—and these factors may gain dominance before reason even comes into play.

Table II gives a list of subconscious factors that may trigger a pregnancy. They don't look too good, do they? They even appear to be tailor-designed for the forbidden-reason list, and you'll find that some of them have already been put there. There is no way to defend any of these irrational triggers, any more than there is a way of defending the more rational ones that occur without the all-important Want Factor. To use an unborn child to manipulate someone? For instance, to please (or hurt) your parents, or to drag a prospective mate to the altar? Definitely not the intelligent path to parenthood. To prove or establish your masculinity or femininity? There must be other ways. To be like most couples? That's hardly the most positive invitation to an unborn child. To draw attention to yourself? You could do that by taking off all your clothes and running down the street. To establish your claim to immortality? If that's all you want, it would probably be more constructive—and more humane—if you built a bridge. To be creative? You could try sculpture. And on a much more subtle layer, to punish yourself for enjoying sex? (As I have mentioned, this is the so-called masochistic motherhood motivation.) Instead, you could deny yourself Boston cream pie, or, better yet, you could see a professional counselor and try to work out your conflicts.

Obviously, in any combination, these nonrational triggers—even if they reach the rational level—do not constitute a good reason to have a child. But before you label them as 100 percent evil, look at them again. Even though they are not legitimate reasons within themselves or in combination, *a couple having a child may indeed derive fulfillment—and psychological benefit—from every one of them.* By having a baby, for instance, you may please your parents—or get them angry. You will in some respects be further establishing your sexual identity. (If you're a man, you might even hand out some phallic representations—in the form of cigars.) You'll be drawing attention to yourself and establishing your maturity by moving up the ladder from child to parent. You also may be perpetuating yourself—or at least your gene pool.

And if you are the type who can't shake hang-ups about sex, maybe the birth will cure you. But don't count on it. Something as deep-seated as the masochistic-motherhood (or fatherhood) wish may prove complicated.

TABLE II

Why Do People Have Children?

(Just a few childbearing triggers* to think about)

Conscious/Rational Triggers	Subconscious/Nonrational Triggers
The individual and/or the couple desires to:	*The individual and/or the couple desires to:*
—deepen an already well grounded relationship.	*—reward or manipulate someone (parents or a prospective or current spouse).*
—provide for a family base and potential relationship for the future—an attempt to ensure that they will always be needed by someone.	*—prove and/or establish masculinity or femininity.*
—undergo the experiences that accompany pregnancy, childbirth, and parenthood.	*—be like most couples.*
—provide a clear-cut role for the husband and/or wife.	*—draw attention to themselves.*
—have a child of the other sex.	*—demonstrate their maturity or creativity.*
—have a child who is different from the ones they already have or who will give them another chance at having an "ideal" child.	*—establish a claim to immortality and validate their existence.*

These two categories are not really distinguishable! These triggers can shift back and forth between the conscious and the subconscious levels.

There's obviously no set recipe for the right reason to have a child. The ingredients are too personal. Only one basic ingredient *must* be there: The Want Factor. The stronger the better. And it requires real thought, real introspection, to know if it is there. Prospective parents and nonparents alike will benefit from the time-honored sage advice, Know thyself. That accomplishment is a major one, and it is a crucial prelude to making an intelligent decision. By introducing some degree of forethought, planning, and evaluation, and by at least considering the option of not having children, you can't help but understand your own needs, assets, and limitations and thereby increase your odds on making the "right" decision.

The problem with getting a meter reading on your Want Factor and measuring your potential for parenthood is that before you have a child, you're not exactly sure what you're going to be getting and how much it is going to cost. It's like going into a store and handing over a blank check for a mystery box.

In the next two chapters, I'll try to describe what is in the parenthood mystery box—and what the emotional numbers on that price tag are.

⤳ 5 ⤺

"Tell Me about the Good Parts . . ."

"I know more than I really want to know about jolly jumpers, breast pumps, and singing potties," complained one thirty-year-old child-free husband I was chatting with at a cocktail party before the first edition of this book was written. "I hope your book will include something about the positive aspects of parenthood. There *are* some positive aspects, aren't there?"

"If there are, *she* certainly wouldn't know about them," his wife broke in. "How can a nonparent even begin to discuss that subject?" I took a big gulp of my rye and ginger and resolved then to look closely at the generally unpublicized "good points" of parenthood.

Actually, I thought I was in a pretty good position to discuss both the positive and the negative aspects of parenthood. If I had had children at the time, I could have been accused of being myopically concerned with justifying my own decision. Or if I had made up my mind not to have children, it would have been easy to stack the deck in a way that would understate the "good parts" of having a child.

The question was where to begin. That there were positive aspects of parenthood—indeed, very positive aspects—had been confirmed by every parent I had ever spoken with. The problem was and is putting those confirmations into words. It's really much easier to write about potties and pumps than to identify and describe the joys of parenthood. As *Ms.* editor Letty Cottin Pogrebin puts it, it's like describing the sea to landlocked people. One puts sand in their palms and conches to their ears and leaves the rest to the human imagination. Here, I felt, we had a case of the landlocked leading the landlocked!

I started my quest at the local stationery store. I bought fifty newborn congratulations cards (thus convincing the owner that I was the high priestess of a neighborhood fertility cult), and studied them to see if I could get some feeling of what the thrills of parenthood were all about. The greetings I found in a few typical cards are as follows:

Babies . . . they come in assorted
sizes, shades and shapes, and
they're all adorable.

With a special magic of their own,
they add a sparkle to your eyes
and a glow to your lives!

They manage to wrap you around
their tiny finger, and their
trust in you is endless.

You watch them grow from infancy
to childhood, and even when
they're all grown up, your love
for them never changes.

Ask any Mother and Dad.

A baby is
the Smile of God,
A bundle
of pure mirth.
A sacred little source of joy
From the moment of its birth,

A warm and cuddly comic
With a secret sense of fun,
The pleasure of whose company
is felt by everyone . . .
And, if God's love seems distant
From our worldly point of view,
We find it in a baby
Where the Smile of God shows through!

What else can bring
  more happiness
Or joy beyond compare
Than having life's
  most precious gift
Entrusted to your care!

WHAT ARE BABIES MADE OF?

Powder and pull toys
  and tiny white socks,
Lullabies, laughter,
  and alphabet blocks,
Wonder and Pride
  and contentment and love . . .
That's what babies
  are made of.

God created everything—
  The golden daffodils,
The serenade of birds
  that sing,
The green and rolling hills . . .

He made the summer breeze
  so mild,
The moon and stars above,
  But when He made
  a little child—
Then God created love.

To wonder at birds
and bright butterflies,

Delight at bubbles
that float through the sky,

Marvel at water
that splashes and flows,

Thrill at the feel
of sand on bare toes . . .

The small things in life
are discoveries of joy,

When discovered again
through the eyes of your boy.

A bundle of pure energy,
a free-for-all of fun,

Here, there, everywhere—
always on the run!

Jump-rope-jumper,
hop-scotch hopper,
climber-in-the-trees,

Kitten-hugger,
puppy-chaser,
crawler-on-her-knees!

A gift of love and happiness
that sets your world a-whirl,

An angel (when she's fast asleep)—
that's a little girl!

Love. Preciousness. God. Miracle. Sparkle. Mirth. Warmth. Closeness. Company. Trust. Not only are these concepts difficult to write about, they are also almost impossible to understand or predict out of context.

"If I had written a piece a few years ago declaring that my children were my greatest pleasure," the English author Margaret Drabble has commented, "people would have assumed that I was simply being polite, dutiful, womanly and deceitful. Before I had children," she continues, "I never really liked them. I thought they would be boring, irritating, expensive and a drag on my yet undecided career. Now they are my greatest pleasure."

What are the components of this pleasure? Can we cut the *Mona*

Lisa into pieces and examine it under a microscope? Can I verbalize some of the ingredients in the joy of parenthood? Before I try, I want to issue a disclaimer. I am not trying to sell parenthood. I am not trying to negate the value and appropriateness of the decision to remain child-free. I just think it is vital that people considering nonparenthood and parenthood have at least a glimpse of the good parts—if you can get such a glimpse from another's commentary. During the year and a half of my initial research into the parenthood question, I was always disturbed because my note file entitled "joys" was slender compared to its "trials and tribulations" counterpart. My initial research involved books, magazines, and medical journals, and people *haven't* written so much about the joys of parenthood as they have about the other side, perhaps because it's such a slippery subject and it's difficult to get a grip on it. Keep in mind that the joys of parenthood, like any other emotional subject, are very fragile, easy to destroy with one-line rejoinders.

You Change. You Grow Up.

"You become more of a person when you have a child," Marion, a forty-year-old mother of two, explained to me. "When you become a parent, you grow yourself. When I look back, I realize I discovered traits, capacities, resources I never even knew or had forgotten I had." She smiled and went on. "I think that's a real joy of parenthood—seeing yourself mature. Children bring out the best of you."

"Can you pinpoint exactly how your personal horizon was broadened? Can you give me some examples?" I asked.

"Well, yes." I could tell that Marion was talking about one of her favorite subjects. "When you have a child, you have more in common with the rest of mankind. You can relate to your neighbors better." For a moment, she seemed at a loss for words, but then something occurred to her. "I remember shortly after my first child was born. I called my father's office, and his secretary answered. I had talked to this woman a hundred times before, but we had never really shared ideas. Now, all of a sudden, we had common ground. She wanted to give me advice—and I wanted to tell her my experience. Parenthood brings you more into the real world. My husband noticed it too. People at work who had never spoken two words to him before started asking about our son and seemed eager to exchange comments."

People do not stop growing at adolescence. Human personalities are dynamic, continuing to change with each stage of life. Parenthood is such a stage, a time that Dr. Benjamin Spock refers to as the shift from care-receiver to care-giver. Inevitably parenthood brings new depth and adds a special type of experience. In their report *The Joys and Sorrows of Parenthood,* the Group for the Advancement of Psychiatry stresses this point and goes so far as to label this growth process as "the most enduring joy of parenthood." And Wenda Wardell Morrone, writing in *Glamour* on motherhood and its capacities for personal growth, points out, "We have a tendency not to make ourselves grow until we must."

"You grow at every stage," Marion continued. "In talking about parenthood, it's easy to overemphasize the baby stage. You know, children are babies for a very brief period. They grow every day. And you grow with them because you find yourself seeing life from a whole new vantage point—from the point of view of an infant, toddler, school-age child, teenager, young adult, and beyond. It's broadening. And I'd like to emphasize the effect that being a parent has on your relationship—your capacity for empathy—with the people around you. Before I was a mother, I didn't know what tenderness and intimacy really were. There's an Italian proverb which says, 'He who does not have children does not understand love.' I think there's something to that. I became more interested in my neighbors and their concerns. I understood my own mother and sister better after I had my own children."

Other mothers voiced similar comments. Many spoke of rediscovering the joys of bicycling or ice-skating while accompanying their children in these new learning ventures. "I finally had an excuse to go swinging in the park again," one told me. "How long has it been since you really looked at an ant crawling up a blade of grass?" another asked. "And have you ever thought of what a challenge it is to describe the word blue? There must be several hundred different shades." What did all of these mothers have in common? A new awareness of the world around them, a world not only to be shared with their children but with each other; a feeling of extended youthfulness; the satisfaction of knowing they were able to teach, that part of themselves would go into the creation of a new being.

Dr. Helene Deutsch tells a story about the time she was traveling on a train from Vienna to Switzerland. It was 1933 and racial hatred was rampant. Her compartment was filled with women, including a number of Orthodox Jews who were fleeing Germany. There were German women too, complete with their swastikas. Let's say they were not the most compatible of traveling companions. One morning the train pulled into a station and one of the women went out to get a newspaper. The headlines carried a story of a well-known young Nazi leader who had been skiing in the mountains before he was buried in an avalanche. The description of the tragedy was read aloud as the train began moving again. It seems that the young man's mother had struggled over snow and ice, finally collapsing in exhaustion when she could not find her son. Dr. Deutsch reports that the hatred in the train's compartment subsided for a moment. Everyone wept. The common maternal feelings, and knowledge that their behavior would have been similar, was a bond—even between enemies.

Carol Milford, the protagonist in Sinclair Lewis's *Main Street,* offers another example of the common bondage parenthood can offer. Carol, a politically active idealist, marries a physician and moves to a small town where she begins to feel her own form of stagnation. She tries to awaken an interest in social reform, and she manages, in the process, to disturb and actually alienate her neighbors, so much so that she is practically ostracized. After three years of marriage, she discovers that she is pregnant. And when her son is born, she realizes that she has a whole new position in life. She becomes part of the town. She has more in common with her former enemies. She understands more and she is accepted more.

Sinclair Lewis obviously understood that by having a child you *do* have something in common with other parents, even those you do not know. You have added another facet to your life. That doesn't mean that your life is *better* than that of men or women who choose to pursue careers and enrich their lives through business accomplishments. It's just different.

It's Stimulating. It's Exciting. It's Simply Thrilling!

I met with Pam and Brian in the yard beyond our apartment house one warm Sunday morning. Both in their late thirties, they have two young children—a son and a daughter. They had been reading *The New York Times* and pouring coffee from a thermos as they watched the children batting tennis balls off the side of a building. They agreed to take some time to tell me about their personal joys of parenthood.

"It started the moment I found out I was pregnant," Pam began.

She was looking in the direction of the children, smiling as she talked. "I was bubbling with excitement. The first person I told was the taxi driver who took me home. He was very enthusiastic. Then I told Brian. He kept saying, 'Are you sure? Are you sure?' I think he was sort of in a state of shock." We both looked at Brian. He was nodding in agreement. Pam went on. "I remember I was dying to call my mother. But I didn't. She would have been so happy. But I was afraid if I ever lost the baby she couldn't take it. So I held off for a couple of weeks."

"Were you just as enthusiastic after the baby was born?" I asked Pam.

"Let me talk about that," Brian said as he leaned forward on the bench. "I have to say I wasn't all there for a while after I got the news that Pam was expecting. I was really very hesitant about having kids. I just didn't know if I could do it. I thought, why invite disaster? But Pam was really up for it, so I agreed to try—halfheartedly, I must admit." Then Brian turned around and looked over at the children. "The afternoon she came home with the news, well, I'll never forget it. It was sobering. I didn't react right away. It took a while to sink in. But in spite of myself, I began to get excited. And by the time she was about to deliver, I could hardly wait to see my child. *My* child. It became very important." He was nodding emphatically.

He paused for a moment, sat back, and continued. "Okay, you want specific joys. Well, the first one I experienced was the thrill of seeing this tiny person, someone who was part of me. When Joanie, and then later Fred, first came home, I was almost afraid to pick them up. You know, they were so delicate and all. When Joanie first smiled at me I was ecstatic—even though Pam tried to convince me it was just gas. My children became interesting to me right away. And now, they are two of the most interesting people I know."

"There are the *firsts*, Brian; you can't forget them," Pam added. I began to feel that this interview was going on without me. "Remember the day you and Joan and I were eating breakfast and Freddie was staring at his cereal bowl, waiting for me to feed him?" They looked at each other and laughed. Pam turned to me and continued, "Well, all of a sudden, Freddie picked up the spoon—he had never done that before—and he filled it with cereal and put it in his ear! We knew he was trying. A moment later, he put the full spoon in his mouth and we all cheered. It's just thrilling to see a child grow, to be part of the first time he walks or talks or says 'Look, mom, I can button my sweater!' or 'I did it! I tied my own shoes.' Did you ever stop to think how complex a task it is to tie shoelaces?"

Pam poured us more coffee and spoke again wistfully. "How can I forget the occasions when I saw their individual senses of humor developing? The time two-year-old Joan hid Brian's glasses and sat there so innocently waiting for him to figure it out. There are so many firsts. And children are so enthusiastic about them. It's refreshing."

Brian was not to be outdone. "Yeah, it's fascinating to watch them develop their own judgments and insights, and you realize that your child—*your* baby!—is figuring out things on his own. Looking at things in a way you never would, sometimes identifying the obvious factor that totally eludes you. I took Freddie to an amusement park one year. I wanted him to see the circular movie theater that was advertised. When we got there, the sign said 'Welcome to the 360-Degree Theater!' and he was concerned that it would be too hot for us to go in!" We all laughed. Brian sipped his coffee and went on. "Or the time after his first day in nursery school when he wanted to know why the place where we kissed him was called a *fourhead*. And then there was the day Pam's father was helping us to redecorate the kids' room. He asked Joanie to get him a screwdriver and she arrived first with the orange juice. Or the evening she was struggling over her math problems and I looked in on her. It was an exercise where you had to fill in the next logical word in a series. It began, 'The fox ate three little rabbits; the fox ate four little rabbits; the fox ate ____ little rabbits'; Joan had written in 'the poor' as her response, and she added, 'But, Daddy, I felt so sorry for those rabbits!' I didn't know whether to laugh or cry."

For Brian and Pam there were some specific joys. The new sense of awareness children can bring to your life. The thrill of a child developing. The reward of knowing that child is part of you.

When I talked with Sally and Peter, both of whom were in their mid to late forties, I got an even greater sense of the excitement that can be part of being a parent.

"I'm in psychology," Sally began. "I'm a high school counselor and I really get a charge out of seeing kids develop. Especially my own. At the beginning at least, I could literally see the change from day to day. On Monday my son was staring at his hands, wondering what they were. On Tuesday he was beginning to use them—grasping everything in sight. One day you are routinely feeding a child. And the next he wants to feed you." She got up from the couch, opened a drawer, and pulled out two photo albums. "They're older now. Linda's twenty-two; Joe's nineteen, and the twins are sixteen. Oh, here's one of Linda when she was a baby. Peter and I used to refer to her as an affection sink. We just kept pouring it in, and it appeared to go down the drain. But then it began to come back." She looked back at the picture and grinned. "The first smile, the first hug. There's something incredibly rewarding about being part of the development of a human being. I hear many people complaining about the chores and nuisances of parenthood, but I never looked at it that way. Kids keep you young. You've heard the expression, Children make a rich man poor? Well, don't believe it for a moment. Children make a poor man rich and a rich man richer. Will you put that in your book?"

Peter came into the living room and stood next to the door. He had overheard some of what Sally had been saying while he was working at his desk in the den. "I'm not too big on schmaltz. Sally can tell you more about that. But what I really liked was learning that my children had some innate talents, ones that I thought I could help develop. Can I tell you about my older son?" We nodded enthusiastically, and he came in and sat down.

"When Joe was ten months old—I remember exactly—we gave him a bunch of blocks of all different colors and shapes. They were meant primarily to amuse him." He paused and glanced over at Sally. "Do you remember that?" She seemed puzzled, but she nodded. Peter looked back at me. "We left him alone for ten minutes and came back to check and found he had put all the triangles together, all the squares—then all the circles. We complimented him lavishly. Then to our amazement he mixed them all up again and recategorized them by color! At ten months!" Now Sally was laughing. She obviously remembered the incident. "We thought we had something there," Peter went on, "and we set to work on it. When he wasn't even four he explained to me, as someone would a mathematical proof, why nine must be an odd number." Peter mimicked a youngster's tone. " 'Well, the number sets go one, two, three, four, five; and the system goes odd even, odd even; and four and four make eight, five and five make ten. So nine must be odd, right?' I had to think that one through myself."

Helen Keller in *The Story of My Life* speaks of the joys and stimulation children brought to her. "If there are children around, nothing pleases me so much as to frolic with them. I find even the smallest child excellent company. I often tell them stories or teach them a game, and winged hours depart and leave us good and happy."

Nancy and Chip McGrath, mentioned in the last chapter, described their excitement with their daughter, Sarah. Wrote Chip: "In some ways . . . she is the embodiment of something perhaps otherwise unsayable about Nancy and me and the way we feel about each other." And from Nancy: "Sarah has made such a present of her eagerness, her quick sense of humor, her cockeyed, pell-mell walk, her crooked grin and . . . her almost boundless affection, that I'm sure I haven't lost out on the deal. . . . In a way that a grown-up simply cannot be, Sarah is always pure Sarah."

Children can be amusing. They can be exhilarating. They keep you on your toes. It can be rewarding to hear their first opinions ("Yes, Daddy, it was a very nice house. They had old antique rugs on the floor") or to see that these developing individuals are following your instruction to the letter ("Mommy, an older boy—I think he was five—I met at school today told me I was cute. But I ignored him, Mommy. We don't talk to strangers, do we?"). It can even be thrilling for some parents to get up in the middle of the night for a feeding—or just to check to see if he or she is all right. As one new mother put it, "I actually remember feeling delight at two o'clock in the morning because I so longed to have another look at him."

Life Is Fuller

Does having a child make your life fuller? Before I even asked anyone, I knew the answer had to be yes. Dealing on a day-to-day basis with an additional human being would have to have that effect. But "fuller" to one person could be hectic and harassing to another. So I pursued the point with a few parents and asked them to be specific about what it was that children contributed to their lives.

Gerry, Ed, and I sat in beach chairs and talked while their son was riding his raft in on the waves, and their two daughters were taking turns burying each other in the sand.

"We didn't think we were going to be able to have any children—it took a long time," Gerry began. She had told me earlier that she had just turned forty that week, but her figure suggested she was more like twenty-five. "I was doing pretty well as a model. I was making an awful lot of money. But when I got to be in my late twenties I was ready for something new. I wanted a baby. And then when it didn't happen," she sighed and bit her lip nervously, "well, anyway we did have them. But the fact that there was some doubt—maybe that's why the joys of parenthood seem so vivid to us."

"Can you think of some of the specific things about children that really give you pleasure?" I looked again at Gerry.

"Well, first of all I want to mention the effect that our first child had on our marriage." She picked up a handful of sand and absentmindedly let it sprinkle through her fingers. "We couldn't help but look at this little boy as an extension of our joint selves, a product of our love."

Ed reached over and squeezed her hand and then picked up the conversation. "We can see qualities and likenesses of both of us in him—and in our two daughters. It rounded us out to have children." He hesitated for a moment as if he wondered whether he should say what was on his mind. "And I tell you quite honestly that sex got better, too. Both of us felt differently about each other. There is something about stopping off in the baby's room before you both go to bed and seeing those soft little bundles peacefully sleeping. You kind of look at them and think, Gee, we did something right."

Gerry nodded slowly. "And what Ed just said reminds me of something else—the sheer physical joy of being close to your child. I found that brought a whole new dimension. The reward of hugging something terribly soft. There is nothing like holding an infant in your arms—the responsiveness of a living, breathing human. I really enjoy cuddling my children. Their little bodies are so wonderful."

She stood up for a moment and squinted as she checked on her son in the water. "I think it's the physical closeness," Gerry said as she sat down, "that lays the groundwork for what follows—the intense emotional attachment. It's like nothing else you've ever experienced. It's different from the type of feeling you have for your husband. The child is so helpless, so dependent on you, it makes you feel good to be so totally needed by someone."

Ed concurred. "As the children grow older, I can see this emotional closeness leading to other rewards. I love watching the three of them interact together. Sometimes after I lecture my son on a point and I'm sure it has gone over his head, I hear him in a very authoritative way reciting my words verbatim to one of his sisters. Of course they have the fierce fights that siblings always do, but they are very close, too. They trust each other." He dug at the sand with his feet. "We have so many shared experiences, even at this point when they're only seven, nine, and ten. We have the sense of communication you find only among family members. I was always aware of this with my own parents. There was something very special about an intellectual conversation among my brothers, my father, and me. Even when it turned into a heated argument, we knew and respected each other so much, the conversation was on an entirely different level than it would be with friends. Now, I'm beginning to see this develop in my own home. I think the joys of fatherhood grow as the children do."

Gerry came back into the conversation. "I'm not sure this fits into your question about children adding a new dimension to life—making it fuller—but there is another point, one I kind of touched on before. Well, in my case at least, what I'm about to tell you did make my life fuller." She took a deep breath. "Children look up to you. They make you feel very important. You can't help but feel special and needed. And that did something in terms of rounding out my own self-image."

The two girls ran up and asked if they could go in the water. They were given explicit instructions about watching each other and not going out too far. Then they ran toward the surf.

Gerry resumed her discussion. "They are three more people who are concerned about me. When I was sick last month they brought me illustrated get-well notes. And they are sometimes so grateful for my efforts that I have to laugh. Once when I made one of my daughters an apron she lit up and exclaimed, 'Mommy, you do the most beautifulest things in the world!' It makes you feel good. Oh, there are so many examples. My son once came home from school and told me that his teacher had gone around the room asking what mothers do for you. He said some children said, 'My mommy drives me to school,' and others responded, 'My mommy takes me for piano lessons,' but when it came to his turn he said, 'My mother does everything in the world for me.' You want to melt when you hear that. Or when they would run into the house and throw their arms around me and say, 'Mommy, Mommy, Mommy, I love you, love you, love you.' It's hard to react adversely to that."

A woman who had been sitting nearby walked over to us. "Excuse me, but I couldn't help overhearing some of your conversation. Would you mind if I added a little story of my own?" I assured her we would like to hear it.

"It happened last fall," she began. "My daughter came home from school the day before Halloween to inform me that her second-grade teacher had asked if anyone thought their mothers would be willing to bake cookies for the Halloween party. Tracy said, 'I told her my mother made the best cookies in the whole world and I knew she would just *love* to make cookies for the party.' Zing!" We chuckled in anticipation of what was to come. "I didn't really have time to bake cookies on such short notice but there were those trusting eyes glowing at me from a face full of love—and, well, after all, I now had a *reputation* to uphold. So, of course, I not only made the cookies but decorated all of them with little jack-o'-lantern faces. I knew I had been manipulated, just a little, but how could I ignore that kind of flattery? And, incidentally, I don't really make the best cookies in the world; I distinctly remember that honor belonging to my own mother."

The type of emotional depth children can bring to family life is worth considering. Psychologically speaking, the bond between parents and their children is generally the strongest of all those that hold human beings together, in some cases perhaps closer than that between husband and wife. Literature is full of references to this strength, particularly the mother-child relationship. For instance, in Edith Wharton's *The Old Maid,* Charlotte, forced to give up her illegitimate child for adoption, assumes the role of aunt and stays with her daughter just to be close to her and to participate, if only peripherally, in her upbringing.

In W. Somerset Maugham's *Of Human Bondage,* Louisa becomes deeply emotionally committed to Philip Carey, the physically deformed orphan, and she is only a stepmother. And, although the emphasis in much writing about parents and children has concentrated almost exclusively on the mother (Aristotle pointed out that "mothers are fonder of their children, for they have a more painful share in their production, and they are more certain that they are their own"), the deep attachment of fathers is beginning to get the attention it has long deserved and been denied.

In *How to Father,* Dr. Fitzhugh Dodson emphasizes that "we are living in a time when, more than ever before in recent generations, the father's vital role in the child-rearing process is beginning to be valued. Not only have women been denied opportunities in the traditionally male realms, but men as well have been taught to believe that too much involvement in the upbringing of their children is somehow unmanly and likely to compromise their masculinity." We are beginning to accept the importance of the two-parent commitment to raising children. Thus, now particularly, the deep attachment of fathers must be equally stressed.

And the reciprocal commitment? The feelings of children toward their parents? Everyone has heard of ungrateful children, those who denounce their parents and sever ties. You may *hear* more about the exceptional cases of the child who totally abandons his parents, but they are in the distinct minority. As James M. Barrie wrote, "The God to whom little boys say their prayers, has a face very much like their mother's."

In later years, despite the nature of whatever hostility may exist, the child's tie to his parents is generally greater than that which characterizes even the best of friendships. Studies of adults under stress—for instance, men in battle—report frequent references to family life. American soldiers talked of their mothers' homemade apple pies. Germans talked of their mothers' dumplings. Even old people over eighty or ninety have been known to call for their mothers when they are very ill and near death.

And it's worthwhile to pause here to elaborate on the physical rewards of pregnancy and parenthood, some of which Gerry mentioned above. For instance, some women perceive the pregnancy state as a thoroughly enjoyable, physically rewarding experience. "I loved every minute of my pregnancy. I don't think I ever felt better!" a twenty-five-year-old high school teacher told me. "I felt particularly maternal and am not embarrassed to say that I was proud to have a protruding abdomen. My husband enjoyed the pregnancy, too. We both read every expectant parent book there was, and he kept asking me to describe how I felt and what it was like to feel the movements of a growing child. When the baby would start kicking, he loved to put his head on my stomach and listen to it. Our only fear was that I might give birth prematurely—we'd have to give up some of those precious pregnancy days."

Pregnancy can be viewed and experienced in exactly the opposite way, too. "You're not serious, are you?" the woman's friend and fellow teacher broke in. "I felt just awful during my pregnancy and hardly enjoyed it one bit. I consider those nine months as something you have to go through to have a child, and I really don't look forward to my next turn. The whole time I just felt like I was carrying a load. I was grumpy, ugly, and uncomfortable, and my husband was less than thrilled over the new profile I temporarily acquired. Let me tell you, that's one phase of motherhood I would gladly have delegated."

The physical component of parenthood continues after birth. "A lot of women don't like to admit it, but there is something very physical and just plain sexy about breast-feeding, complete with all the tingles," one new mother confided to me. "I was never really oriented toward my breasts and expected that, when I first put these two rather curious structures into operation, I would have some new feelings and sensations. But I wasn't prepared for the intensity of the pleasurable effect." Since, from the physiological point of view, breast-feeding and sexual intercourse are very much allied, this woman's reaction is understandable. During both coitus and lactation, there are nipple erections and very possibly uterine contractions, stimulation of the clitoris, and various vascular changes, and there is no denying the physical aspects of these events. But this new mother was right about the fact that many women don't like to mention this aspect of breast-feeding because they have trouble accepting the idea of deriving sexual pleasure from an infant.

And there are physical aspects of parenthood that go beyond breast-feeding—the fondling and cuddling of a soft, responsive infant or a squirming affectionate child. "I'm really not the physical type," a three-piece-suited tax attorney told me. "I don't routinely express affection toward my wife or anyone else—especially in public. But I must say there is something irresistible about my daughter. When I get home from the office, I can hardly wait to pick her up and hug her. I never thought I would ever get that thrill out of contact with a child."

They Begin to Grow Up

What about the teen years, that period after the cuteness and innocence of childhood have begun to wane? Do children really acquire a totally new and automatically unpleasant personality as they enter the world of adolescence? Newspapers, television, and the gossip hot line are fraught with stories about teenagers who are rude and unmanageable, given to fits of cruelty and violence, and who have become victims of every conceivable kind of outrageous bad habit.

Fully aware of the media's inclination to promote sensationalism, and the public's apparent enjoyment of it, I couldn't help wondering whether such horror stories were really the exception or the rule in our present society. Speculating on the probability factor that there might exist an entire generation of juvenile delinquents, I set up an appointment with Marilynn, a friend who lived in a nearby suburb. She had a son and a daughter, both in their teens, and had invited two neighbors, Marie and Connie, also mothers of teenagers, to join us.

The attractive warmth of the living room was mirrored in all three faces. They seemed eager to talk, even after spotting my tape recorder. Marilynn giggled when I voiced my fears about today's teenagers. "I guess it's like anything else," she answered. "People always find it more interesting to talk about what's wrong. After all, you can't write a book or make a movie about ordinary average people doing ordinary things. And who would write a news story that went: 'Lisa and Kirk were polite to all their teachers in school today. And they didn't terrorize their classmates, vandalize the halls, or smoke in the bathroom.' " She laughed again. "I realize that sounds silly—but think about it! You hear about all the ugliness and occasionally you hear of a teenager who has made some outstanding achievement, but you hear very little about most of the others, those who live and behave and do most of the same things in the same way that most of us did when we were their age." (Thinking back, I decided that probably meant they were something of a pain in the neck.)

"Of course, many things are different nowadays," put in Connie. "Norms have changed, attitudes have changed, and obviously, the fads are always changing. You have to swing with it; you have to remember, to constantly remind yourself, that this is *now*, not twenty-five years ago. For instance, I find it hard to approve of girls wearing eye shadow to high school. It simply wasn't done in my day, but today in most places it's part of the teen culture."

"I agree with you," added Marie, who at forty-five was the oldest of the mothers. "But you have to weigh the issues. You can't say no to everything. When I was in high school there was a constant hassle about whether or not I should wear lipstick—and I remember it was *so* important, because almost all the other girls did. So I allow Vicky to wear eye shadow, and I save my no's for the more important issues."

The conversation continued along those lines for a while longer, reassuring me that the teens were not necessarily impossible years, or at least not much worse than I remembered. "But," I asked, "what about the positive aspects of adolescence? Is this a stage simply to be waded through as best you can, or are there definite pluses as well?"

The three mothers nodded and Connie was the first to speak. "I have to admit I had some reservations about ever having a baby in the first place. I knew I like babies and very young children, but I kept wondering what it would be like at the age of five and ten and then, heaven forbid, *fifteen*. I had to ask myself some long, hard questions about whether I was prepared to handle all that. Well, surprise. There really isn't all that much 'handling' to do anymore. Rhonda contributes so much. She does a lot of the cooking, which means we eat some rather strange dishes from time to time because she likes to experiment." She paused for a moment as her face took on a still warmer glow. "But one of the biggest pluses is our mutual interest in theater and dance, something my husband was never very big on. Now Rhonda and I spend frequent evenings together at a play or a movie or the ballet while my husband goes bowling with the boys. We all have a good time, and Rhonda and I spend many hours discussing what we have seen. She comes up with some good points, her own ideas, and I find that thrilling. I really *enjoy* her company, and I think I can safely say she also enjoys mine."

Marilynn, who was director of nursing at a retired persons home, spoke next. "Something that tickles me is how much I learn from my daughter. I've never exactly thought of myself as dowdy, but wearing white uniforms five days a week, and little makeup on the job, fashion tends to take a backseat on my list of primary interests. I just got out of the habit of keeping up with the latest thing the way I used to. But lately Lisa has taken it upon herself to get me 'with it,' as she says. A couple of weeks ago she insisted I borrow her little gold belt for an outfit I was wearing. She was right—I liked the combination enough that I went out and bought a belt of my own. And just yesterday she showed me how much better her own type of eyeliner was, compared to the same old thing I had been using for the past ten years. It makes me laugh. You spend all those years trying to teach them; then all of a sudden they turn around and start teaching *you!*"

Now it was Marie's turn: "It probably isn't so true in the big cities, but I'll bet if you took a survey in any smaller community you'd find that just about all of the over-forty disco dancers have at least one teenage child. And how else does a parent become acquainted with the BeeGees or the Electric Light Orchestra? My younger sisters and brothers think I'm quite mad to go disco dancing at my age—but my husband and I really enjoy it, and it's good exercise. Besides, Vicky and Lennie really get a kick out of showing us off to their friends. Whenever they have a few people over to dance at the house, they always invite Mom and Pop. Of course, we don't really hang around in full view for very long, which is probably one of the reasons they keep reinviting us. But it's fun and we get to know their friends in a very comfortable way."

Marilynn's husband, Lee, had arrived home a few minutes earlier and sat listening. "Seems to me it's time to add a word about the boys," he interrupted. Lee then told me that as an engineer he had always been interested in math, and was especially intrigued when his older child, Kirk, started school and became involved in the so-called new math. "I studied it right along with him," he said. "And today we still get a bang out of hunting out some good mathematical brainteasers to work on. And all four of us enjoy an occasional rousing discussion on some current-event topic or other. You know, things you read about in the papers are often inclined to pass right on out of your head in a day or two but they're often topics that are studied in some detail by the kids in school. We learn from them, and they from us, as we discuss the various sides of the issue in question. We always try to compliment them for their own contributions, and for developing original viewpoints."

"Speaking of sons," added Marie, "my husband has always delighted in Lennie's baseball knowledge. Since he was about seven years old he knew every player on every team, what position they played, and usually what their batting average was. Whenever Bill or one of his friends has had a question about who was traded where in what year, they've called in Lennie—and Lennie always knows. That sure is one sport my two 'men' have enjoyed together."

Lee spoke again: "That's great. It happens to be my opinion that when you give kids credit for the positive things they have to offer, they are less inclined to adopt the know-it-all attitude that's often so typical of teenagers. They have things to say, too. If you don't listen, or you scoff at their sometimes ludicrous ideas, it then becomes the parent who is guilty of a know-it-all attitude. And, let's face it, we *don't* know it all and never have."

"I started working full-time when Rhonda was two," said Connie, "but I made sure I took some time every evening to chat with her, no matter how tired or busy I was. Oh, it wasn't anything formal. I never said, 'Okay, it's 7:15 and time for our 15-minute talking time.' It's just that I always took the time to *listen*, even though it frequently interrupted a conversation Rick and I were having. But he was good about listening too. That pattern has continued all these years and Rhonda knows she can always come to talk with either of us—and that we are there to listen, to explain, perhaps to offer advice, but never to judge. It's really a matter of keeping the lines of communication open. There are never any guarantees, of course, but I do feel that if she were ever in trouble she would come and discuss the problem with one or the other of us, and ask our help before little trouble turned into big trouble. At least I hope I'm right about that."

I was beginning to wonder if these youngsters weren't too good to be real. "Don't you ever have any problems?" I asked. "And how about other families you know that include teenagers—are most of them as compatible as yours seem to be?"

Their response was that of four comedians reacting to a straight man's innocent question. But they quickly grew more serious and agreed unanimously that problems did indeed exist. "My sister-in-law insists that nothing ever changes; the fingerprints just get higher up the wall," Marilynn began. "I don't see it quite that way. The problems change but we try to deal with them in the same kinds of ways we always have; that is, we try to be reasonable, to be firm but gentle."

"You have to understand that both of our children were planned and very much wanted," added Lee. "A great deal of time and energy—and caring and thinking and loving—have gone into their upbringing. This isn't necessarily true with some of our friends and acquaintances, and they tend to have many more problems with their kids than we've had. I don't mean to imply that we have all the answers, but I do believe that that little extra some of us put into the raising of our children does *help* to minimize the chances of trouble later on."

"Definitely!" agreed Marie. "Our kids have always known that privileges are granted according to the amount of responsibility they are willing to assume. Now if you think about that for a minute, you've got to know that hasn't been a very smooth road to follow. But it has worked pretty well for us. Maybe we've just been lucky."

No, not merely lucky. All of these parents had been willing to share their love and knowledge, and whatever else they had, with children they had planned and genuinely cared about. Evidently, these parents had enjoyed each new stage of the passing years. With little difficulty they had discovered that raising a teenager isn't all that much different from raising a child of any age; that it's a matter of caring and knowing when to teach, when to guide, and when to let go.

It's the Second Time Around

We all live vicariously in some ways: through books, movies, and television. We identify with other individuals and share in their successes and failures—once removed. It's a normal part of human experience to project yourself occasionally onto some other individual, and, so psychiatrists tell us, it is a useful way of working out certain conflicts within ourselves.

There is no doubt that parents relive their own childhood experiences through their daughters and sons. This may be particularly true if the child is of your own sex. I asked Pam and Brian, who were so articulate about other aspects of parenthood, to tell me about participating in past life experiences once again, through their children.

"The most immediate example that comes to mind is Christmas," Brian started off. "Totally unconsciously I went through the stocking-hanging and gift-opening routines with my kids in exactly the way my parents did for me. Like I followed it to the letter. It took a Christmas or two before I realized what was going on, but finally it surfaced. I was reliving the whole joyous childhood experience that goes with the tinsel, bells, and Santa Claus bit. Only this time I think I was enjoying it more!" Both Pam and I understood and laughed with him.

Pam added her experience to this. "I find that in the playground, the kids shy away from the seesaw and concentrate on the swings and the jungle gym. I was always afraid of the seesaw, and I must have subtly communicated this to them. When I'm out there on a bench watching them, I can't help thinking back to when I was the child and my mother was doing the sitting. And—I guess it's natural—I start to restructure my life, think about other routes it might have taken." She frowned slightly. "I never had dancing lessons or was encouraged to develop a number of hobbies. I'm leading my kids in these directions, and I'm almost waiting for one of them to put a limit on my vicarious living and say, 'Gee, Mom, I wish you hadn't been deprived of so many things as a child.' "

Dr. Frederick Wyatt from the University of Michigan has discussed the principle of *inner duality*, that human capacity for splitting ourselves into two prototypical roles—one of which we project on a child, or possibly on some other person with whom we have an intimate relationship. Particularly with a child, this type of identification gives the parent the opportunity to relive important life phases, possibly directly reenacting them, and even revising moves and resolving elementary frustrations and tensions. It's part of the personality developmental process. With one self-image we live our day-to-day lives; with the other projected one we attempt to resolve past psychological conflicts.

Along a similar line, Dr. Esther Greenbaum points out the concept of *unfolding*, the repeating of events that occurred during the parents' own early years. As she puts it in an article that appeared in *The Journal of the American Academy of Psychoanalysis*, "At each developmental phase, the children trigger in their parents memories of the corresponding time when they were children, their feelings as well as their attitudes toward them." This gives the parents the opportunity to have a new focus on human relationships, to relive events, but this time from a new, more enlightened perspective.

A continual remembrance of things past would be regarded by many as being unconstructive or even morbid. But, in fact, much of our lives involves reliving earlier events. Novels, for instance, can evoke powerful memories of childhood experiences. Charles Dickens's "child," David Copperfield (Dickens's reversed initials here are a thin disguise for himself), especially during the first half of the book, is a classic example of the desire to relive one's childhood.

So there is a variety of joys. There are thrills and rewards. But there are costs, too. And your only hope of getting an accurate reading on your Want Factor is to consider them alongside the possible joys.

≼ 6 ≽

The Psychological Costs
of Children—or,
You Didn't Expect Something
for Nothing, Did You?

Unlike the joys of parenthood, the emotional or psychological costs are fairly easy to document. We're always more voluble when we're negative. Part of the plumpness of this chapter is due to my attempt to be specific about the problems that may occur and to be equally specific about how individual couples have adjusted to them.

I started my search for the joys of parenthood with greeting cards. Given that a form of sympathy card that might counterbalance the thrills is not in print yet, I decided to look at some daffy definitions—of a baby or a child, and of a mother and a father.

First, what is a baby? According to Webster's *Unafraid Dictionary*, a baby is a "sample of humanity entirely surrounded by a yell." Other sources yielded different definitions:

Henry Ward Butler: "A mother's anchor. She cannot swing far from her moorings."

Ralph Waldo Emerson: "A curly, dimpled lunatic."

Elizabeth I. Adamson: "An alimentary canal with a loud voice on one end and no responsibility on the other."

Mark Twain: "An inestimable blessing and bother."

Carl Sandburg: "God's opinion that the world should go on."

Arthur Gordon: "A little rivet in the bonds of matrimony."

Other anonymous definers suggest that a child is "an individual out of whose mouth come things you wouldn't want neighbors to hear," "a home accident," "a disturber of the peace," "an individual who screams, throws up in a bus, and rides for free," "the most desirable pest," "an island of curiosity surrounded by a sea of question marks," "something that gets you down in the day and up at night," "a bald head and a pair of lungs," "a tight little bundle of wailing and flannel," "a perfect example of minority rule," "someone you first teach to talk and then beg to shut up."

According to a Yiddish proverb, a child is "a person who when he is young disturbs your sleep and when he's old disturbs your life."

And the definitions of a mother and father? A father, Margaret Mead has said, is "the children's mother's husband."

He's been defined as "a banker provided by nature," "the other half for whom the tenth month of pregnancy is the most difficult," and "the one who replaces the currency in his wallet with snapshots of the kids."

And mother? She's "someone who is disorganized around her children," or "a person who, seeing there are only four pieces of pie for five people, promptly announces she never did care for pie," or "someone who can't quite leave the children at home even when she doesn't take them along."

Shakespeare called motherhood "the pleasing punishment that women bear."

Marital trials. An anchor for the mother. A source of anxiety. A cause of disorganization. The definitions pretty much cover the gamut of costs, or rather, possible costs.

Babies and Marriage

Comedienne Joan Rivers, in her book *Having a Baby Can Be a Scream,* humorously describes the experiences of herself, her husband, Edgar, and their new baby, Melissa, during the early weeks: "I think I can truthfully say I had no idea that motherhood involved so much work. If it wasn't changing the diapers, it was sterilizing the bottles or mixing the formula—and all that screaming, grabbing, crying, and upchucking—so finally I told Edgar, 'If you don't stop acting like this soon, I won't have any time for Melissa.' "

The first child brings to marriage what psychologists refer to as a crisis. Not necessarily a crisis in terms of shock, tears, and hysteria, but a crisis in the sense that your lives will never again be quite the same as they were before. As Drs. Barry and Patricia Bricklin point out in their book *Strong Family, Strong Child,* "When the first child arrives . . . a great many . . . psychological changes occur. The child will produce the most negative impact within the people who are highly immature, secretly dependent and who themselves still wish to be children."

In D.H. Lawrence's *The Rainbow,* Anna Lensky and Will Brangwen fell in love, got married, and went away for a long honeymoon, ensuring their complete separation from the outside world. But after two weeks Anna got restless and decided to bring a little variety into their new life by scheduling a series of parties. Will was furious. For him, marriage meant just being with her. It was a rude shock for him when the outside world entered their life. But this was nothing compared to the shock he experienced when he heard that Anna was expecting a baby. He was not prepared for any type of intrusion on their privacy and did not at first adapt well to parenthood.

For all couples, the birth of a first child means changes and some surprises. Probably the most encompassing and jolting ones come from having to learn to be on somebody else's timetable. "You just can't set your daily routine ahead of time," one new mother told me as she scurried around looking for a stuffed animal to distract Junior during our interview, "and that does sometimes interfere with your schedule with your husband."

And the second most likely jolt, her neighbor, a veteran mother of four, added, "comes with the realization that you've changed status. All of a sudden *you're* the parent. And it doesn't take you long to start sounding like a mother. After a full day of disciplining children, you're apt to say sternly to your husband, 'No, you *cannot* have another martini!' "

So a first child brings great changes to a marriage. Given that a baby is a voracious consumer of time and energy, there is, by definition, a decline in the number of hours a man and woman have with each other. Often, in the interests of efficiency, the parents choose to do their chores separately—they may even eat separately. A 1962 study noted that the arrival of the first child cut the couple's time together in half. This change can be a strain on a marriage, but whether it is devastating and whether it is preventable is another question.

Ellen Peck, in *The Baby Trap,* calls attention to this aspect of the parenthood crisis and casts the child as villain, the surest way a woman can lose her husband's love. Typical of this line of reasoning is the statement that "Dad may simply have gotten fed up with all those Dresdenite-finished shoes, minivaporizers, cradlettes, musical floatees, Busy Boxes, and little doodits and decided he wanted a dark-beamed oak den, black leather sofa, fake zebra throw and a bar, and a woman."

Does it have to reach this extreme? That's too individual a question to answer generally. But you might get some clues about the potential pitfalls by looking at the specifics of the first-birth impact.

The sexual aspect of the marriage relationship may change soon after a pregnancy is diagnosed. Depending on the opinion of the doctor you are seeing, sex may be proscribed during the first and last months of the gestation (some people think that nature has built in a reduced libido during the early weeks as a precaution against miscarriage), or a woman and her husband may be given no ground rules at all. One outspoken obstetrician I spoke with identified only one contraindication to sex during pregnancy—labor. Even then, he said, the deciding factor might be a private versus a semiprivate room. Even with a sex proscription at some point during the pregnancy, most couples I talked to spoke of the time as an intensely emotional, bonding experience. "My husband and I never felt closer than we did through the months of my—I mean our—pregnancy," a young mother wistfully told me. "It was so much a part of us, I can't imagine feeling any other way. He was so solicitous, he enjoyed taking care of me, and I enjoyed his attention."

The fact that there is an intense mutual feeling during the gestation may be the reason that the next phase is more difficult. "During my wife's labor," one new father explained to me, "I was still very much with her. We had studied her exercises together, and I really felt like I was helping out. But whammo. Everything changed when they wheeled her into the delivery room. I have never felt so helpless and out of place before in my life! All those gadgets! I couldn't help but wonder if my wife was having a baby or if we were going to the moon. It was downhill from there. They decided to give her a spinal, and the doctor came up with this needle. It was big enough to take care of an oversized horse. When I saw it, it was all too much. I fainted."

I learned, from his wife, that this understandably squeamish father-to-be was picked up off the floor and rushed downstairs for some emergency revival measures; fortunately, he got back upstairs to see his daughter born. What he was not prepared for, however, was the birth of a second daughter about two minutes thereafter, and he was again in need of the hospital's services.

The birth may be the first in a series of events that make the father feel helpless and unnecessary. Where do I fit in? might be the question of the hour. The cartoon of the pacing father in the waiting room asking "Is it a boy?" and being told "The middle one is," gets that point across very well.

Sociologists who have studied fathers' feelings about birth find that a husband's general life orientation is a good predictor of his reaction to his wife's pregnancy and the eventual birth. Those with a romantic orientation demonstrate a feeling of wonder and awe about the whole series of events and are a bit overwhelmed with the idea of having to be the source of support for a child as well as a wife. Career-oriented types more often regard fatherhood as a burden that has the potential to interfere with other life priorities. ("This is our last chance to be human beings, dear. After this we are going to be parents.") And the real family-oriented type sincerely looks forward to the responsibilities, more likely seeing the child as a gift, a means of becoming even closer to his wife, and eagerly anticipates his new image as a family man.

Whatever his paternity orientation, it is not at all unusual for a new father to feel left out and downright jealous. Anthropologists have identified a series of customs that serve in some societies to reduce this natural anxiety, this feeling of helplessness. The custom of *couvade,* from the French word meaning "to brood or hatch," is used to designate the regulations a prospective and new father may follow during the period around the childbirth. For instance, he may be required to avoid certain foods; go into seclusion; or, through projection or in reality, help his wife to expel the child. It's not unusual for men to want to be involved in what physiologically and emotionally is half theirs.

After Brian and Pam had spoken in such glowing terms about the joys of parenthood, I asked if they could describe any of the ways their lives changed for the worse during the year after their first child was born. Brian thought for a moment and then began. "As I told you before, I had some mixed feelings about the fact that we were expecting a child. But I became gradually more enthusiastic as I adjusted to the news. I bought Teddy bears and fancy mobiles to hang over the crib, and, as I said, I loved Joanie instantly. It was all great. But it you want it straight, things did change pretty abruptly. One night it was the two of us sitting in the living room watching television after dinner. Then a week later Pam was home, giving her complete attention to the baby. I guess the first thing I noticed—a little thing—was that she used to always greet me with kisses at the door when I came home from work. That turned into more of an exception than the rule during the first year. Before the baby was born, I had her undivided attention at meals, but once we had the baby, she would pop up and down. It would really disrupt things."

"We cured that problem real fast." Pam laughed. "For some reason I thought I would be less of a mother if I asked his help. Of course that was ridiculous. Here he was jealous of my time, and if I had only gotten him involved from the start, we both would have been better off!"

Joint participation in the baby-care process may indeed reduce jealousy: either the husband's feelings about losing his wife to an intruder, or the woman's feeling that he is having all the fun out in the real world. But there are other strains of jealousy that may be more subtle. "It's hard to believe," Pam mentioned to me as we were parting, "but I had the distinct feeling that Brian was at least a little bit jealous of my breast-feeding. 'Aren't you *finished?*' he would say once in a while. It was really interesting to see his reaction."

Want to recall some real jealousy? Shakespeare in *The Winter's Tale* presents a portrait of King Leontes, who falsely accuses his devoted wife Hermione of adultery with his best friend; this was his projection of the jealousy he felt upon the arrival of a new baby. He was reacting in a rather extreme fashion to the very natural feelings that accompany what is presumably temporary displacement.

While we're on the subject of jealousy, consider something even more subtle than the friction that may come between a man and woman at the arrival of the "intruder"—something that may come up some years later.

According to Freudian theory, a child in the pregenital phallic stage typically develops romantic feelings toward the parent of the opposite sex—the much-discussed Oedipal complex.

In normal development, a child goes through this stage and moves on to other levels without any problems. But a fascination with one parent—whether specifically sexual in nature or what-ever—may crop up again, even in young adulthood. "My daughter, very frankly, got in the way sometimes," a fiftyish mother of two teenagers told me. "She occasionally became really obsessed with her father and would only relate to him. I would be ignored from the moment he came in the door. A year ago he died, and my daughter, even more than my son and myself, went to pieces. She insisted on spending the first two nights after his death in her father's bed. I'm just now beginning to realize how much her father meant to her. I guess you could say I was a bit jealous when it was going on, but I understand now."

A child can be a divisive force, whether it is his or her seeming fascination or preference for one parent, or whether the child's problems prove to be a source of conflict between mother and father. ("But Daddy said I didn't have to take a bath tonight.")

Children can also be sexually divisive. I've mentioned that there may be some limits on the prospective parents' sex life in the last weeks of pregnancy, but what about sex after the baby is born? Does libido just fizzle until nine months before the child's first sibling is due? No, not quite. But there can be some changes. Again, the reaction and adaptation to those changes have a great deal to do with the couple's ability to meet a new set of circumstances.

Avery Corman, writing in *Cosmopolitan,* refers to the arrival of the first child as "The Beginning of the End of Sex," and notes that leaking milk is hardly a come-on. "It is," he writes, "as one of the characters on Sesame Street says, 'yucky.' " As a preventive measure, his wife took to wearing a bra during their lovemaking, and they both began to feel like backdrops in a sadomasochistic play.

"Is it really like that?" I asked Gerry and Ed on the beach after we chuckled over the descriptions of the lactation drip and its consequences.

"Well, sex does change, especially at the beginning," Gerry admitted. She turned and spoke to me in a confidential tone. "You're supposed to wait six weeks, and if you've had an episiotomy, it can hurt for a while. I didn't find the milk bit a problem, but there were other things. Compared with before the birth, there were many more occasions when either or both of us were simply too tired. Chasing after a child all day can be pretty exhausting. And also, even on the occasions when you're both in the mood for love, you can get pretty turned off if beforehand you have to remove what the baby has just vomited onto your sexiest nightgown. And, maybe this is just me, I really can't relax when they are up and crawling or running around. In that way, sex becomes much less spontaneous. Having said all that, I know I sound like I'm contradicting what I told you earlier. But I meant that, too. Sex does get better. It does have more meaning for us—when we have a chance to get around to it!" Gerry looked over at Ed. "Well, what do you think?"

"That's about it. We just learned to adjust," he said. "We've learned to take full advantage of any opportunity that presents itself. Like times when the kids are napping. Or when they put on one of their favorite albums, we know we have half an hour. You work it out. No, I'm not going to say it is the same as it was before. It is different—but it has its points."

I guess it's a matter of human ingenuity in time of need, but people do come up with some clever ideas on how to keep their sex life in one piece and still raise children. Major League baseball player, author, and ex-sportscaster Jim Bouton offers this suggestion: take a big bag of jelly beans and scatter them all over the backyard. That'll give you about half an hour.

And then there's always the possibility of just closing a door—or getting one of those minigates with locks. One couple I spoke with told me that they have a baby-sitter who comes in every Sunday afternoon from two to six. They retire to the bedroom, and if the spirit doesn't move them, they read, knit, or play cards—$2.25 an hour.

Adding a third, and fully dependent individual to what was previously an independent two-person pad will cause an impact, an upheaval in the status quo, some type of shift in the marital relationship. And that's a psychological cost of parenthood. How much of a cost—and how that cost is counterbalanced by positive effects—is a completely individual matter.

Mother's Anchor?

Babies are not only lovable, they are also messy, demanding, impatient, and totally exhausting.

A 1950s study of new mothers found that the birth of the first child raised the number of housework hours from thirty-two to sixty-eight a week. Presumably some of the work-savers that have entered our lives since that time would bring the number of hours down somewhat, but it is still pretty safe to say that motherhood can double the amount of time spent cooking, cleaning, clothing, and comforting. A trip to the grocery store seems to take twice as long as before, especially in wintertime with the struggle to insert two unyielding baby legs into a snowsuit, and later on meeting the challenge of boots and mittens. (They do come in pairs, after all, and where a young child is about, pairs have an uncanny habit of separating themselves in even the most organized of households.)

A significant amount of this time is borrowed from the husband-wife relationship, but other parts, if not taken from the wife's career schedule, are transplanted from what would be sleeping hours and her previous commitments out of the house. Perhaps before the baby was born she took some university courses a few days a week—or maybe she enjoyed playing tennis with friends. A large group of mothers was once asked what was the most significant change in their lives since they returned from the maternity ward; the overwhelming cries were, "less freedom" and "I'm tied to the house!"

In *Up the Sandbox,* Anne Richardson Roiphe interweaves descriptions of the realities of domesticity with wild fantasies of a liberated woman and conveys that same sense of entrapment. "I could starve him—or leave him behind me, dropping him on the cement, crying in the park till the police come and assign him some nameless future. But he has nothing to worry about because despite an angry thought or two, we are connected deeply and permanently."

And Carol in *Main Street* was tortured during her pregnancy about the prospect of losing control of her life and freedom. As Sinclair Lewis put it, "She was encircled by greasy eyes. Every matron hinted 'now that you're going to be a mother, dearie, you'll get over all these ideas of yours and settle down.' She felt that willy-nilly she was being initiated into the assembly of housekeepers; with the baby for hostage, she would never escape; presently she would be drinking coffee and rocking and talking about diapers."

A few years ago *Redbook* conducted a study of seven middle-class couples from pregnancy throughout the first year of parenthood. Conversations with these couples were then resumed about three years later when most of the children were of nursery school age. "Becoming a parent is one of life's major crises, a crucial psychological adjustment for a woman," writes Alice Lake in her summary of the study. All of the couples admitted that "although waiting for the baby brought them closer together, living with the baby was another story indeed."

In the beginning, interviews with the seven couples were very much alike. There was general agreement among the wives that baby-sitting experiences in earlier years, together with a built-in "mothering instinct," would conquer all difficulties with minimum fuss. Their husbands had agreed to be "partners." Confidence reigned. Four years later Ms. Lake wrote:

> Today each of the seven households has changed drastically, and in different ways. Confident predictions have been shattered. There have been bitter quarrels, anger of surprising intensity, irrational panic. The

mothers have experienced exhaustion, boredom, loss of self-esteem. Some of the fathers have felt themselves demoted from kings to vassals. One couple have separated, probably permanently. One woman, fearing emotional collapse, has sought psychiatric therapy.

It sounds bleak. Yet on the positive side, despite the surprises, the inconvenience, the lost freedom, three of the mothers had given birth to a second child, and a fourth was about to do so. One mother was quoted as saying, "At this moment I'm happier than ever. My marriage is richer through sharing the acute joys and sorrows of having a child."

Presumably a sampling of mothers everywhere would agree with that mother, but not all of them do. The transition from the pampered days of pregnancy to the realities of dirty diapers, middle-of-the-night feedings, and general panic ("What do I do now?"; "Why is he crying?") is not an easy one. Many mothers simply never do make a comfortable adjustment. Exhaustion and frustration bring on feelings of resentment, guilt, and irrational anger (at baby or spouse or both). And logical or not, a mother often directs the blame at her husband, their financial state, her parents, his parents, her husband's employer, or the neighborhood in which they live. In a sense, there often exists an unwillingness to recognize the fact that a family of three is simply not the same thing as a family of two.

The *Redbook* study quoted a mother of a three-year-old as saying:

> Now it's starting to be fun. But if you don't have yourself squared away, if you haven't worked out your own identity and values, it's practically impossible to be a mother. It brings you down to earth to have a child. Without [our baby] I think I'd still be buried under all my problems.

After they became parents, most of the seven couples discovered gradual changes in their attitudes about many issues such as religion, war, and general life-styles. One father mentioned that he sold his motorcycle because riding it seemed too dangerous now that he had additional responsibilities.

At the end of the four-year study period, *Redbook* attempted to discern whether there were regrets among any of the couples for having chosen parenthood. For these seven couples regrets existed primarily in the sense that parenthood was perceived as the loss of their own childhood. And in spite of many episodes of disharmony, almost all of these parents expressed satisfaction at having been able to tackle a whole set of new problems with a certain amount of success.

"Things do change. Be sure to tell them that," a mother of two young children told me. "I was tied to the house for the first five years. I should have known better and gotten more help, but I was stubborn. Now that I'm not chained to the house, I'm chained to the car. In our neighborhood, there's just no other way to get to school, piano lessons, dancing class, and Girl Scouts. We try to pool the driving, but there's no getting around the fact that I've been promoted from bottle washer to chauffeur."

I talked some more with Sally, the high school counselor, and Peter; they live in the city and didn't have the chauffeuring or some of the other problems, but they did have their own concerns. "Did you feel you were chained to the crib and the bottle warmer after your first child was born?"

"Did I ever!" Sally exclaimed. "I was used to my daily routine of getting up, having a quick breakfast, and rushing off to school for a pretty full day with the teachers and kids. Wanting to be a dutiful mother, I resigned my job a few months before the delivery and wrote 'motherhood' over the front of my five-year calendar. I thought I could have my two or three quickly and then go back to work. Boy, was I ever naïve! It was fun, a novelty for the first few months, but let me tell you, as a full-time activity, motherhood can begin to wear on you very quickly. Yes, I know, happy parenthood is joint parenthood, and Peter did help out. But the reality of our lives is that he had to go to work every day—we just couldn't see the president of his bank going for a half-time arrangement. He brings in the money—and I assumed the care of the children. I guess if we each had the types of jobs that allowed part-time work, we would have considered splitting it up so we would both have our turn at home. But for us, that wasn't a possibility.

"My neighbor had a baby just about the same time I did," Sally continued. "We had never really talked before, but when we were both wheeling carriages, we found we had more in common. She complained about the full-time drag of motherhood and felt the same way I did about not being prepared for the round-the-clock nature of the job—but I had additional pressure. You see, she had never had a career orientation. I kept trying to deny it, but I couldn't help thinking about that five-year schedule. *Five years!* One afternoon, an associate of mine stopped over to discuss a paper she was preparing for publication. It occurred to me that her visit elicited from me the first polysyllabic word of the day. Maybe I would be writing papers, too, I thought. And then out of nowhere it hit me. I wanted to be paroled. I wanted to go back to work."

Peter was becoming increasingly uncomfortable during this conversation. Finally he interrupted. "All right, I know what the next part is going to be all about, and I'd like to present my view of it. When Sally told me about her decision to return to school, I was not very happy about it—particularly because I knew she didn't have the option for part-time work. It was all or nothing. I was concerned." He sounded more than a little defensive. "Who would take care of the child? Would the baby develop problems because his mother wasn't around? And it wasn't just me. Our mothers still haven't stopped talking about it. 'How *could* she leave that baby in the care of someone else?' They believed—and I did for a while too—that motherhood was a full-time job—with no exceptions. They would say, 'Have someone inferior take care of your baby? Terrible and very selfish!' But I went along with Sally's decision, and after a while I came to agree with it. I know now that all of us are better off."

For a great many women there exists an imperative need to maintain, or achieve, some semblance of self-identity. "Sometimes you forget who you are," a mother of a two-year-old told me recently. Before Craig was born I had been an executive secretary for a news wire service. It was an important job and I didn't mind too much that I was often referred to as 'Mr. K's secretary' instead of 'Audrey.' Then the same kind of thing happened after I got married—I became 'Larry's wife.' Still I could put up with it. But now, out in the playground, I'm 'Becky's mother' and sometimes I want to scream. I want to tell the world, 'No, no, I'm *not* just somebody's mother or wife or secretary—I'm *me*! I'm Audrey. I'm a special person with special things I enjoy and think and do and talk about. I am me!' "

Audrey stared wistfully out the window a few minutes, then suddenly grinned. "Well, at least I'm not totally paranoid about it yet—not as far as the playground goes anyway. I remember when I was in kindergarten and had a best friend down the block with what to me was an unpronounceable last name. So when speaking to her I simply addressed her as 'Donna's mother,' which seemed to amuse her intensely. But she and I are very different kinds of people. All of the 'regulars' at the playground know the names of all the kids—and which mothers' faces belong to them. But with only a few exceptions most of the mothers don't know each other's names. You happen to see one of them at the grocery store or someplace and you think, there's Stuart's mother or Carla's mother or whoever. It's as though we're all extensions of our kids rather than the other way around, as it seems it should be. It's frightening in a way."

Some mothers, probably with a strong sense of self to begin with, are able to handle identity crises more easily. In *The Balancing Act* five mothers relate their stories of juggling motherhood and career. One of them, Jane Stevens, discusses how she successfully coped with her added role:

> I continue to identify myself as I always have: I am an intellectual, an artist, a lawyer, and sometimes a writer. Now I also spend some of my time playing with and taking care of babies. The concept of "motherhood" is meaningless to me. Perhaps it is to everyone, except as a superficial description of a female who has a child. "Mommy" to me still means my mother. When I think that for Vanessa and Rachel I will be the image of "mother," it seems absurd. . . . In fact I rarely identify myself to myself as a "woman." I take it for granted that I am a woman, and go on to other things which seem more uniquely me.

Just as each baby is unique, so is each mother. While some express delight simply in being recognized as a *mother* as they push their baby carriage down the street, others are dissatisfied with the image they're projecting. They may find themselves wanting to shout: "But I'm not *just* a mother. Please, world, don't think I'm only a mother and nothing else."

For the last few decades there has been heated debate over the question of whether it is psychologically necessary for the child to have the mother in full-time attendance. I don't think there is any professional child specialist today who would insist that a baby or young child needs his mother every waking moment. In fact, all of the psychiatrists and psychologists I spoke with about this question emphatically said, "Tell mothers to get some help. A teenager on Tuesday afternoons, a baby-sitter at least one weeknight if possible." All agreed about the desirability of getting away from the child and giving the child the opportunity to relate to someone else occasionally. Almost invariably such relationships promote easier social adjustments later on and tend to make a baby less subject to what is known as "stranger distress."

But with regard to full-time work for mothers, there is no agreement. Indeed there is heated controversy.

Dr. Benjamin Spock has written: "I myself would say it is much more creative to rear and shape the personality of a fine, live child than it is to work in an office or even to carve a statue."

"Day help? I think it's a pity," Dr. Henry Greenbaum, Associate

Professor of Clinical Psychiatry at New York University School of Medicine, told me. "The woman deprives herself of the period of mothering. The mother can become alienated from her child. I've visited the Scandinavian countries. As you know, they have day-care centers to which children are sent at a very early age, sometimes at six months. There's also a high rate of social problems such as suicide and alcoholism in those countries. I wonder if there isn't a connection." Pointing out that his wife, also a psychiatrist, gave up her practice for some three years and didn't return to work full time until the child was seven, Dr. Greenbaum emphasizes that the development of the mother-child relationship can suffer if the mother goes outside the home to work every day.

That's one point of view, and it is consistent with what is known as the Bowlby theory—a school of thought that dominated the 1950s and 1960s. Bowlby's theory was that, for a young child, prolonged maternal deprivation may have a grave and far-reaching effect on the character and future of his life. That is, that "prolonged breaks" during the first three years of life leave a characteristic impression on the child's personality. Clinically, such children appear emotionally withdrawn and isolated. In defending this point of view, people pointed to animal studies. In certain animals—for instance, goats, cows, and sheep—when infants are separated from their mothers immediately after their birth for a period as short as one to four hours, the mothering behavior becomes distinctly aberrant. The mother doesn't feed her children, or she feeds her own and others indiscriminately.

But not everyone goes along with Bowlby's theory—or the opinions of Greenbaum and Spock. First of all, the prolonged separation studies that provided the basis of these theories have generally involved institutionalized children. Prolonged separation here meant months or years away from their parents, at a very early point in their lives. Second, just as animal studies have indicated aberrant behavior in early separation, later separation has shown no significant effect. If cows and other animals (although not all) are with their offspring for the first four days and separated on the fifth, they resume mothering as usual when they are reunited. There can be some good arguments in favor of a mother's working—at least part time—if she wants to.

Over 40 percent of mothers in the United States with children under the age of eighteen are employed. Thirty percent of mothers with children under age six are employed, leaving behind 6.1 million children to be cared for. (These figures were 20 percent and

13 percent respectively in 1949.) This does tend to undermine the prevailing argument that maternal employment is deviant. There is no statistical evidence to suggest that children of working mothers turn out any differently than do those of mothers who stay home with them all day. Nonemployed women do generally express fewer doubts about their own adequacy as mothers, but their self-confidence does not appear to make their children any more emotionally stable, socialized, intelligent, or mature than children of working mothers.

Dr. Mary C. Howell of Massachusetts General Hospital has looked very closely into this matter. Writing in *Pediatrics,* she concluded, after reviewing and evaluating hundreds of studies in this area, that "no uniformly harmful effects on family life, nor on the growth and development of children, have been demonstrated. It is concluded that conditions of employment and the attitudes of other family members probably influence the employed mother's relationship to her family by affecting her self-esteem and energy sources." In other words, if she doesn't really want to work, or doesn't like her job — or if her husband or some other family member is reacting adversely to her working—then problems may come up.

Madame Curie managed it. As her daughter Eve put it, "The idea of choosing between family life and the scientific career did not even cross Marie's mind. She was resolved to face love, maternity and science . . . and to cheat none of them. By passion and will, she was to succeed." Margaret Mead managed it. "Nor did I worry about what a child might do to my career. I already had a reputation on which I could rest for several years." And other successful women have managed it, too.

Indeed, Margaret Mead, as well as a great number of other child study specialists, feels that it is useful to avoid exclusive upbringing by a mother. In her extensive studies of variations in child-rearing patterns, she concludes that a number of early attachments can promote the child's development and avoid overdependence on one or two individuals. And Dr. Mary Howell has observed that the maximum amount of time the most interested and able of adults can invest in a meaningful interaction with children is approximately six hours per day. Thus the conclusion one might derive here is that the difference in positive interaction hours between a mother who stays home all day and a mother who works half or three-quarter time and spends the remaining hours with the child is not all that significant.

But there are caveats. Even those who are very open-minded on the question of working mothers are not enthusiastic about an immediate return to work. The have-a-baby-and-go-back-to-the-fields approach might indeed interfere with the attachment phases. "Ideally," Dr. Howell writes, "a mother should return to work gradually, and only when she feels that she and the baby are ready to leave their exceptionally intimate postpartum relationship."

And then there's the problem of finding a mother surrogate. It can be argued that a loving, middle-aged maternal type who declares love at first sight when she sets eyes on the crib may enhance the developmental pattern. Baby gets used to being with mother and father, but he also learns to adapt to someone else in his life. He develops a relationship with her and, as a result, may be more socialized than his counterpart who takes longer to expand his vocabulary beyond the *momma* and *dada* level. But here we are talking about the ideal. Too often, working mothers are forced to choose from a group of potential helpers who can offer little more than the promise of keeping the baby from going hungry or from pulling down the one portion of the house that you neglected to babyproof. Often mothers complain that their day helpers are more concerned with keeping the child quiet and orderly than they are in helping him learn and grow. The child's day is more structured. He can use crayons—because they won't be too messy. But should he want to try some finger painting, the answer is no. The chaos that could result from painting would make more work for the mother's helper, and she's not being paid for that.

This undesirable situation is made even worse by the fact that this type of day helper, who has little or no emotional interest in the child, will not stay around very long. A group of young working mothers in New York City indicated that the typical child-care employee feels she is eligible for a gold watch if she manages to stick around for a full year. Six months is about the average.

A really first-rate mother substitute may bring about other problems—simply by being too good at her job. A superbly honest mother of a ten-month-old confessed to me one afternoon: "I often find myself overcome with almost uncontrollable jealousy. I wanted to find the best available care for Geoffrey, someone who would really take my place, someone he could love and depend on and relate to just a well as me—except *not quite.* I still want to be Number One in his life. Just yesterday the sitter and I were both in the room when Geoffrey bumped his knee. He ran to *her* to have it kissed and I almost went to pieces. I suppose that's proof that a baby doesn't really need a full-time natural mother, that an unrelated stranger can do just as well, and I should be pleased that I have one less thing to worry about. But my feelings fight with each other constantly. I want the independence but I want my baby to know that *I* am his *real* mother. When it was the sitter who witnessed his first smile instead of me, I was somehow furious, filled with unreasonable remorse, jealousy, and guilt. I seriously considered quitting my job. Maybe as Geoffrey gets older and our own relationship becomes more firmly established, I won't have those kinds of feelings. I hope not, because right now I'm having trouble keeping them to myself."

Daily contact with a loving mother substitute may enhance the sociability of the child, but a continuous mommy-go-round could present some serious problems. As psychotherapist Joanna Ehre told me, "If you change mother surrogates every six months, you may run into some serious problems. You will be interfering with your child's developing an object relationship. That is something he really needs during his first two years of life."

And there are other problems. Sally, our working mother, can tell you about them: "Finding a helper was one thing. I went through four agencies before I came up with a woman I really felt secure about. And she let me know right off that housework was not her bag. I'd have to get someone else to help me there. The mathematics of the whole thing"—Sally put her hand on her forehead and groaned—"and the fact that I just about broke even between her salary and mine, was only part of it. What was really fun were the mornings when I was about to miss my bus and Mrs. No Show calls to tell me that she's not feeling well and won't make it. Then there's the anxiety—be sure to tell them about the anxiety, especially at the beginning. I'd be sitting in a conference at school, and all of a sudden I'd break out in a cold sweat. Was she taking care of him? What if she was negligent and let him fall out of the crib? Was she watching him every moment, or was she on the telephone with one of her friends? Was she making him feel loved, or just acting as a custodian? You can't help thinking about it. And you can't help having guilt pangs when you leave in the morning and the child is going through his heartbroken routine. One morning he piled all his blocks up in front of the door. That got to me."

"I always thought I was opposed to mothers working while their children were still very young," Janet, a nurse in her late twenties, told me one Sunday afternoon in the park. "But complications developed when Debbie was born—nothing terribly serious, but it left us with some whopping medical bills. Finally, after a year of trying to get them paid off, along with the house payments and the car payments and what not, we realized we just couldn't hack it on one salary. I went back to work two days a week, which helped some, and it didn't seem to bother Debbie in any way. Then out of the blue I was offered a marvelous supervisory position—full time. My husband and I thought about it very hard and I decided to accept it. I've been there a month now and it all seems to be working out pretty well. But let me tell you, it's tiring!"

Janet paused, shook her head and smiled. "What probably surprises me most, though, is my own change in attitude about 'career mothers.' It's really a matter of priorities and compromises. As long as we were continuing to get farther behind in our bills, I think Debbie would have suffered more in the long run than she is now with me working full time."

During the past few years a growing number of modern couples have elected to share not only the work load jobwise and in the home, but also to share child-care responsibilities. In the late 1970s, according to the Bureau of Labor Statistics, more than 234,000 men stayed home to care for their children on a full-time basis for at least part of that year.

In *The Balancing Act,* all five husbands assumed part of the baby-care duties, with varying degrees of success. Baby-sitters were also used during part of the week, but the couples preferred to avoid full-time mother substitutes as long as possible.

There are caveats here as well. However much a new mother may require and desire her husband's participation, she often finds herself confronted with ambivalence. She may be the most modern and liberated of females but, steeped in tradition, she may be subconsciously convinced that no man could possibly change a diaper or administer a bottle as well as a woman. There is a frequent tendency to criticize and worry. Father may be doing the caretaking but mother usually continues as the "psychological parent," the one more concerned with balanced diets and clean clothing. And, as with a good professional mother substitute, there is the tendency toward jealousy. A number of mothers have admitted attempting to steal smiles from the babies perched on their husbands' laps. And as long as they are successful, they accept this as reassurance that they still occupy first place in baby's heart.

The truth is that a devoted, loving father can be just as fine a mother as a mother can. It must be admitted that they are sadly lacking in breast-feeding equipment, but that is a situation for which the only imminent solution is an alternative feeding method. In *How to Father,* Dr. Fitzhugh Dodson writes: "If a baby is bottle-fed it makes little difference whether he is fed by his mother or his father.

There is no 'male' or 'female' way of bottle-feeding a baby. Either parent may perform this task, depending on which one has the available time."

Of course, no matter how progressive or enlightened a husband is in other areas, he may exhibit a great deal of reluctance to stay at home and play mommy. Sociologists are quick to explain that most of them unavoidably view such a role as a tremendous threat to their masculine image. In a *Redbook* column, pediatrician T. Berry Brazelton writes of a father who shared about 50 percent of the care of raising his young child. During a routine examination when the baby girl was about a year and a half, Dr. Brazelton noticed that her father seemed somewhat upset. After a bit of probing, the father finally blurted out: "Well, she's confused about me. She calls me 'Mommy' when she's in trouble and 'Daddy' when she wants to play!" Dr. Brazelton hastened to explain that the baby wasn't in the least bit confused; she had very cleverly managed to sort out two different roles for the number one man in her life.

In *Good Housekeeping,* writer Edward Susman related his mothering experiences, assumed voluntarily so that his wife could take advantage of a journalism fellowship at Stanford. The role reversal lasted throughout the first six months of his daughter's life. After Susman had again returned to his newspaper job, he wrote: "Although I can't say I miss the daily burden of caring for Perrie—her cranky moments, her upset stomachs—being a mother has its wonderful moments. Watching a baby discover life is an experience no man or woman should miss."

It may be well to note here that however little a baby's father is involved in actual share-the-care, some degree of participation is indispensable. To again quote Dr. Dodson: "A growing child needs a model for feminine behavior and a model for masculine behavior. *One parent cannot possibly play both roles.*" The ultimate Women's Libber may take offense at that statement, but the fact remains that every baby was conceived from the union of a female and a male. In that respect he has two parents—of different genders.

I'll give you some specifics about the economics of private child care in Chapter Nine. The numbers are quite unsettling. Of course there's group day care as an option, but generally the child has to be at least three years old to qualify. And don't think that's always an ideal solution. There's the cost of transportation to and from the center, and, as one enlightened mother put it, "I never knew how many holidays there were in a year until I registered Tommy in the local day-care center." Even a full-time mother substitute in your home will mean occasional use of a back-up sitter. Baby tenders get sick, take vacations, and get called for jury duty just like the rest of us.

On the other hand, many women with rewarding careers do manage to take a few years out of their lives to become full-time mothers and find their new role just as satisfying and challenging as their chosen careers had been. A number of these mothers take this opportunity to enroll in a college course or two—either for their own enjoyment or in preparation for a higher or better-paying position for the time when they are ready to return to the business or professional world.

A few months ago, *Woman's Day* carried the story of twenty-seven-year-old Kitty Costa, a highly successful banking executive who had planned to return to work as soon as her baby was a year old. After daughter Christy was born a little over two years ago, Kitty underwent many of the usual adjustment problems, often feeling exhausted and isolated, and convinced that her life had become totally chaotic—"a nightmare" as she described it. In the early months she could hardly wait to return to her job with its regular hours, clearly defined duties, and the camaraderie of her co-workers.

To her surprise Kitty gradually began to honestly enjoy watching her daughter's physical development and the unfolding of a new little personality. Soon thereafter she decided that for the time being, motherhood will be her career. "It was a difficult decision," said Kitty. "Working was very important to me. I couldn't picture myself without an interesting, demanding job. Which is exactly what I have now, the way I see it, as a mother and housewife . . . . I can always go back to work. But I want to make the most of this time *now*. Because I'll never have the chance again."

Kitty feels that her life is very full right now: college courses twice a week, a daily exercise program with Christy, piano lessons, and a myriad of other activities. While her working (i.e., away from home) friends have difficulty understanding what she does with her time, Kitty insists that, energetic and efficient as she is, she has trouble fitting everything in. Nevertheless, she stresses (just as this book has) that staying home is *her* choice, and certainly not right for everyone: "Whether or not a mother works is a very personal decision. What's right for one may be wrong for another. And I know how many women have to work to support their families."

In a number of ways, Kitty's story typifies many others. Unfortunately, the women's liberation movement has convinced many mothers, or would-be mothers, that to stay at home playing "mommy" means to turn into a bleating sheep or a blowzy fishwife, with nothing to talk about and nothing interesting to do, and that, consequently, life always and necessarily becomes dreary, unstimulating, directionless, and pointless. As countless women *and* men know, even with a career, life can become dreary, unstimulating, directionless, and pointless—with or without a baby. In other words, as that favored cliché goes, life is still what you make it. Staying home with a baby doesn't have to be dull. Most certainly there is no reason to feel there should be any stigma attached to assuming the motherhood role for a while.

Kitty Costa has chosen to resume her own career at whatever time she feels she is no longer so importantly needed as a full-time mother. For some women that time may come when baby is two weeks old; for others it may be a year, five years, ten years, or never. But just as the decision to have or not have a baby is a matter of individual choice, so is the decision to combine baby with career.

Anxiety and the Emotional Gamble

Sally brought up one aspect of this psychological cost of parenthood—the concern about leaving the child with another person—but there's more.

Children are a rich source of anxiety for both the mother and the father. The anxiety is evident even before the birth: will I be able to take the pain of labor and childbirth? Will the baby be normal? Will he develop any of the dreadful congenital anomalies that have been known to occur? Did I eat the right things? Are we going to be good parents?

Anxiety about the pain before and during childbirth is worth commenting on specifically and right away. Studies have shown that over 60 percent of middle-class first-time mothers express this concern. *Are* labor and childbirth painful? According to gynecologist Waldo L. Fielding, the answer is yes. He writes in *Pregnancy: The Best State of the Union:* " 'Labor' is one of the most accurate terms in medicine; it is hard, physical work . . . the process of delivering a baby can never be guaranteed to be free of discomfort and pain."

A woman with first-hand experience (Margaret Mead, writing in *Blackberry Winter*) described labor more optimistically as "far from being 'ten times worse than the worst pain you've ever had' . . . or 'worse than the worst cramps you ever had, but at least you get something out of it' . . . the pains of childbirth were altogether different from the enveloping effects of other kinds of pain. These pains one could follow with one's mind; they were, like a fine electric needle, outlining one's pelvis."

Writer Margaret Drabble has spoken even more positively about childbirth: "The feel of a newborn baby's head on your thighs is like nothing on earth."

Women still compare notes on their labors and deliveries in the same manner that men talk about their war experiences. And pregnant women still get unsolicited advice about the "right" and "wrong" way to deliver and about what type of pain and discomfort they should expect. The fact remains that modern medicine offers a wide variety of safe, effective means of minimizing pain and facilitating birth. There is nothing cowardly about taking advantage of these. Even those who have the fullest possible respect for the schools of natural childbirth techniques do admit that not everyone can successfully go through a drug-free delivery. One gynecologist I spoke with estimated that at least 50 percent of women don't have the psychological makeup to go through unmedicated childbirth, and he pointed out that for them there are all kinds of options for making labor and birth tolerable.

"Yes, I was a bit apprehensive about my hours in the labor room and my moments on the delivery table," Gerry confided to me. "But I consoled myself with the idea that women have been doing this for centuries, even without our fancy new drugs. And the majority, after going through labor and childbirth once, elect to do it at least once again. If they could do it, I could do it. As it turns out, it wasn't bad at all—or at least I don't remember its being bad."

Gerry wanted to discuss one of the anxieties she had before the birth, one not related to the birth itself. "My husband and I really planned the pregnancy—remember, we had to try really hard. We did all the right things. We talked about it, considered our options, and then went ahead. Finally, when it happened, I woke up in the middle of the night thinking, My God! What did I do to my life? I started getting very anxious. What did I want a baby for? I was so used to dropping everything and running whenever I wanted to." She grimaced and shivered noticeably. "One night when I was eight months along I had this terrible dream. I was playing with my baby and the phone rang. My friend asked me to join her in a shopping tour downtown. And I just dropped everything. I somehow decided the baby would be safe in the kitchen sink, and that's where I put him. I came back six hours later and looked in. He was all blue and very dead. I woke up screaming that night, too."

Babies do present you with anxieties before as well as after they are born. Margaret Mead and Ken Heyman, in their book *Family*, write: "As long as a mother is carrying her child, she cannot know its sex or the color of its eyes. She cannot know whether it will be strong and sturdy or weak and ailing, whether it will be a laughing baby or a sad and lonely one. Until it is born, she cannot know how intense its need of her will be or even whether it will live. She accepts on faith the child's coming into being and the child's identity, as yet unknown. . . . Motherhood begins with the willingness to accept the unknown."

The same thing can be said about fatherhood. People seem to overlook the anxiety the father must assume. Ed pointed it out. "When Gerry came home and told me she was pregnant," he began, pausing to pour some lemonade from a cooler, "there was a drop in the pit of my stomach. I knew we had decided to try for a baby—but all of a sudden here it was! My whole life seemed to appear right in front of me at that time." He took a big gulp and went on. "I was free-lancing as a writer, but that next day I began looking for a full-time job. That was just the beginning. We had a one-bedroom apartment in the city; we had talked about moving, but now I was studying the real estate section as if I were preparing for a final exam. Why does everyone focus just on the anxiety and emotional burden of the mother? My whole attitude toward work changed. I was responsible for a dependent being's support. It was ironic, though, that at the same time I thought I should be working harder to bring in the money we needed, I was feeling increased pressures to be home early so I could be with the child before he went to sleep." Ed sipped the lemonade and continued. "Hearing about the pregnancy was sobering. But the night after the birth was something even more incredible. I visited Gerry at the hospital, then drove out to our new home in the suburbs. We'd lived there for four months, and things were beginning to shape up. I walked in and sat in a chair. And I realized, *I have never felt so alone in my life.* What had I done? All of a sudden I was a father, and there was nobody home. My whole former life was gone. I was in a new world. You know the joke about how when baby gets his shots, daddy does too—Dewar's, Smirnoff, Old Crow? I understand that now."

The father has his own type of anxiety—which in some ways may be made even more intense than the mother's because he is once removed from some events. "When I had my Caesarean," Gerry added as we left the beach, walking toward the car, "I really felt sorry for Ed. They gave me medicine for the pain. He had to take it unmedicated, and without a real understanding of what was going on. He had to make a lot of sacrifices that I didn't. He traded his free-lance position for a nine-to-five job, and he traded his fifteen-minute bus ride for an hour's commute to and from the suburbs. He's been through a lot."

Occasionally the parenthood decision is complicated by recollections of some new mother's encounter with the "after-baby blues," or what is known in medical circles as postpartum depression. It's understandable that either a prospective mother or father might easily react with a startled "Oh, no!—I certainly don't want to go through any of *that!*"

The phenomenon of postpartum blues is almost universal in the American culture. It is indeed real, although it occurs in varying degrees, sometimes as only infrequent, mild attacks; sometimes serious enough to require medical assistance. But however serious it may be for a time, it is a temporary state.

The condition may begin as a postdelivery letdown while a mother is still in the hospital or it may not start until several weeks later when she feels that life should have settled down into something more nearly resembling a normal routine.

The cause is usually a combination of disappointment and fatigue. After a few weeks of sleepless nights, life may seem to have taken on a merry-go-round tempo with a seemingly endless cycle of feeding, changing, bathing, rocking, soothing, cleaning, shopping, washing, and cooking. There never seems to be enough time for husband and wife to spend together—alone. Even an invitation to a special social event may arouse little interest: an exhausted mother would rather sleep. There may be feelings of confusion and helplessness. On the other hand, baby may be a quiet one—the kind that sounds like a delight at first, but who presents so little problem that his mother begins to feel unfulfilled, unneeded, as though there were really nothing to do. The result is the same: you can't help asking, "Is this all there is to it?"

There are ways to minimize postpartum depression. (And do note that it is only *almost* universal; it is not inevitable.) If you are going to plan a baby, you will need to plan for some kind of help, at least for awhile. Figure on full-time help for the first week or two (grandparent, baby nurse, maiden aunt—whoever is available and reliable). After that you should try to arrange for some kind of part-time help, either with the baby or with the housework.

Remember that fathers can be excellent caretakers, with a little encouragement. Accept any offers of help from neighbors, friends, and relatives, and pay attention to any shortcuts they might suggest.

A baby should not be allowed to completely dominate family life; in fact, it's neither necessary nor desirable. Parents need to save some time especially for each other. A mother owes it to herself to spend at least half an hour a day doing something just for her (a manicure, perhaps, or a special hobby). Adequate rest is essential; no one can cope with even minor problems through a haze of perpetual fatigue. There's no need to immediately resume your entire prebaby social regime—new activities should be added only as you feel comfortably able.

New parents are still a couple. The lines of communication must be kept open; you need to tell each other how you feel. A wife must understand that her husband may find it difficult to refrain from feeling jealous and neglected at times; a husband must try to be patient when his wife dissolves into tears for no apparent reason or displays an unreasonable fit of temper. Sensitivities come into play on both sides and must be dealt with sensibly. (There is no logic in each blaming the other because the baby is crying, for instance.)

In addition, even after the new mother is given the go-ahead to resume sexual activities, she may feel too distraught or exhausted to show much interest. It almost goes without saying that such reactions may be extremely upsetting to her; most certainly they will be upsetting to her husband. Again, the new parents need to talk it out, look for possible solutions, and keep in mind that a few more weeks will bring the relief of more sleep and a greater sense of competency as parents. Kitty Costa, mentioned earlier in the Chapter, found herself a typical victim of the postpartum blues during her baby's first few months. And just as typically, she managed to pull out of her depression after she had become comfortable with her new role.

It is interesting to note that although postpartum depression commonly occurs most often with the first baby, there are no specific limitations. A woman of my acquaintance, whom I shall call Ellie, had carefully mapped out in advance at least the first two decades of her married life. Her first of two well-planned pregnancies was realized right on schedule, and precisely 40 weeks later a son was born. Ellie sailed through early motherhood without a hitch. Then, still in keeping with her well-regulated schedule, three years later she again became pregnant. And this time, to the amusement of her friends, Ellie was 100 percent convinced that the new arrival would be a girl because, as she said, "I *planned* it that way!" Three weeks before due day, however, her obstetrician advised her that the baby was not a baby, it was babies.

Ellie immediately lapsed into a state of semishock from which she did not emerge for several months. (Fortunately her husband was able to provide an excellent full-time baby nurse.) The obvious lesson here is that when it comes to babies, there is only so much planning ahead that one can do.

As a postscript I must add that Ellie did indeed get her wish for a girl—and at last report, she was enjoying both of them very much.

"The Awesome Responsibility"

Some hospitals still have a series of standard lectures they deliver to new mothers. There are the normal tips about infant care and child management, but there is usually some additional sage advice: as a new parent, you should never again expect to sleep as soundly as you once did. You are now responsible for the welfare of another human being, and that will be with you no matter what the time of day.

"It *is* an awesome responsibility to have a child," Gerry emphasized as we walked. "Everyone is making a fuss over you when you are pregnant and when they visit you in the hospital. But then there you are alone with this tiny, fragile infant. I was an overly cautious mother, you know, the kind who decorated the baby's room in Early Antiseptic. And I got a bit morbid, too. I never read the details on liability on the back of a plane ticket before I had a child. By the way, don't ever do that. I began to be obsessively concerned about fire engines, ambulances, and seat belts and weighed the odds on a plane falling in the playground. Only a mother understands what it means to lose a four-year-old in a crowded subway. You're always thinking of the worst that could happen; that's why you're so guilty about leaving them." We stopped for a moment to wait for Ed and the kids to catch up. Gerry told me more about anxieties. "Last week Ed and I went to an afternoon concert. We had the teenager across the street come in. As we returned, one of my daughters ran up to me screaming hysterically, 'HE HAD A HEART ATTACK!' She was speaking of the cat, but that did not occur to me for a few seconds. Her source of knowledge about feline cardiology now escapes me."

"When I was a teenager," Sally told me when I asked her about parenthood anxieties, "my mother was constantly worrying that I would 'do something foolish.' Her idea of sex education was giving me the bra and girdle section of the Macy's catalog, and her favorite line was that 'a man won't buy a cow if milk is cheap.' At the time, I would just moo and ignore her concerns. But looking back, I can understand what she meant. You are so afraid that your child might be taken advantage of, hurt in some way, and on many occasions you are really helpless. They are on their own so fast."

Children who are normal and healthy are huge responsibilities. Tragic though it is, you must remember that they are not always fully normal, and all children are sometimes sick. There remains the possibility, slight though it may be, that a child will have a serious problem, a birth injury, congenital problems, mental retardation, or orthopedic or some other problems that need correction. And most children develop some illness—any of the many childhood diseases, for instance—that will give you moments of great concern. If you have a child you'll find you're getting up in the middle of the night, if he's a baby, to see if he's breathing or why he's crying (or why he's *not* crying), or if he's a teenager, to see if he's home yet.

Risks of Disappointment and Loss

Some people treat their children like wheelbarrows. They push them, right from the start. I talked with one new father who was so achievement oriented that he listed the Harvard Admissions Office on his important phone call list. You know the type—"My son can be anything he wants, as long as he is a doctor or lawyer first." And the mother who has her daughter's future husband's profile picked out at the christening.

Children can disappoint you. Children can be ungrateful, and, as King Lear put it, "How sharper than a serpent's tooth it is to have a thankless child." You can be the best parent in the world, but the child will turn out *his* way. Sometimes an apple does fall a long way from the tree. You can be a doting parent or a don'ting parent. Or you can follow whatever the voguish parenting manner is. The Group for the Advancement of Science describes a sign that summarizes some of those fads:

1910: spank them
1920: deprive them

1930: ignore them
1940: reason with them
1950: love them
1960: spank them lovingly
1970: the hell with them!

You can try all of them. But the child may well surprise you with his independence.

In *Letter to a Child Never Born,* Oriana Fallaci writes after the discovery of her pregnancy:

> "You existed. It was as if a bullet had struck me. My heart stopped. And when it began to pound again, in gun bursts of wonder, I had the feeling I had been flung into a well so deep that everything was unsure and terrifying. Now I am locked in fear that soaks my face, my hair, my thoughts. I am lost in it. It is not fear of others. I don't care about others. It's not fear of God. I don't believe in God. It's not fear of pain. I have no fear of pain. It is fear of you, of the circumstance that has wrenched you out of nothingness to attach yourself to my body. . . . I have long awaited you. But still I've always asked myself the terrible question: what if you don't want to be born? What if some day you were to cry out to reproach me: "Who asked you to bring me into the world, why did you bring me into it, why?"

It is a question every child inevitably asks at least once in his life. And it is a question every parent fears to hear. Too often the only answer at that moment is an angry "I wish I knew!"

The sense of loss. I'm not talking here about misplacing your toddler in the subway, or about a child or grown adult who flees his parents, never to return. I'm talking about the emotional loss a parent will someday inevitably feel. "Kids leave you emotionally long before they leave you physically," one psychiatrist explained to me. "I wish I could offer a pain-dispelling drug to mothers during this second birth, this delivery of children into the adult world."

Kahlil Gibran, in *The Prophet,* expressed this sense of necessary separation, the need to let go of a child.

> Your children are not your children.
> They are the sons and daughters of Life's
> longing for itself.
> They come through you but not from
> you,
> And though they are with you yet they
> belong not to you.

You may give them your love but not
your thoughts,
For they have their own thoughts.
You may house their bodies but not
their souls,
For their souls dwell in the house of tomorrow, which you cannot visit, not even
in your dreams.

A cover of the *New Yorker* once captured this parental sense of loss. It showed a woman, dressed completely in black, with a grim facial expression, opening the door to let her radiant daughter, in a bright red dress, walk out with her lunch box. And a tranquilizer ad that commonly appears in medical journals shows a bride and groom coming out of the church and the groom's mother sitting in a limousine crying. She is letting go of her son and of a part of herself at the same time.

"We were packing my teenage daughter's things the Saturday we were to drive her to college," a grandmotherly lady recalled to me. "I went up and down the stairs ten times. Then, on the final trip, I saw how empty the room was, and realized I was losing my last child! I sat on the bed and sobbed."

"Parenthood," Therese Benedek has written, "as a psychobiological process ends only with the death of the parent." But children make a break. This may happen for some children in early childhood; for others it may come much later. Parents have to let go. But not all parents do. They want more than their children can offer.

In Robert Anderson's play, *I Never Sang for My Father,* the son, Gene, is considered an "ungrateful bastard" by his parents because at age forty he has struck out on his own and defied them. When Gene's wife is gravely ill and he is at her hospital bedside, his parents still consider themselves his sole responsibility. ("We miss you so. Our day is nothing without you. Couldn't you come up?") When his first wife dies, they are incensed by his interest in remarriage. They can't let go. A lot of people who see that play know what Gene is going through.

Home Sweet Zoo

Judith Viorst, in *Yes, Married; A Saga of Love and Complaint,* says she was never meant to be the mother of three boys. In citing the traumas of parenthood, Mrs. Viorst points to the time she has spent in the poison clinic and hospital emergency rooms and her familiarity with crushed fingers, twisted ankles, and chipped bones. "Mrs. Viorst," her doctor explained, "when you have sons, you've got to figure that several times a month you'll be filled with terror."

Jean Kerr, in *Please Don't Eat the Daisies*, warns that a mother must quickly learn to be very calm and reasonable. ("Just because he ate your crayons is no reason to hit him on the head with a Coke bottle.") And one must learn to cope with usual daily routines. Mrs. Kerr describes a typical school-day morning that begins with the children spelling out their names in butter on place mats, making sandwiches of boiled eggs and puffed wheat, and stirring orange juice with an old pocket comb. She mentions that the calendar has recently been thrown into the toilet, and the youngest son has been using his sister's toothbrush to paint his model cars.

"There's only one way to describe the first years of parenthood," Pam told me candidly. "It's a fog of fatigue. The next time you hear a young mother tell you her son is eating solids now, be aware that she is talking about keys, newspapers, and pencils. The only saving grace is that babies naturally take a deep breath of silence between screams. Our childless neighbor across the street enjoys our kids, and she has said on occasion, 'I would give ten years of my life for two healthy children like yours.' I love them dearly, but sometimes I think that's what we paid."

No honest parent is going to tell you that having children isn't sometimes a hassle. Children have amazing memory banks. ("You told me two years ago that when I was six you would let me stay up later.") And they constantly ask questions that put you in a spin. ("How come a Coke will spoil my appetite and a martini improves yours?") And there are the midnight phone calls from teenagers reporting as a slight accident what turns out to be the conversion of your extra car into scrap material; the possibility of "academic difficulties"; and the terrors of finding a gory mess resulting from your son's confusing a catcher's head (your daughter's) with a softball while trying out a major league swing.

Especially if there is more than one child around, parenthood requires hard work. As the saying goes, two of anything else make a pair. Two children make a mob. Take a close look at some of history's most classic art. Raphael's *Madonna del Granduca*, *The Mother* by Max Klinger, and Pablo Picasso's *Mother and Child* are typical in that each painting shows a plump, glowing baby, full of vitality, sitting with its lifeless, emaciated mother.

Two factors contribute most significantly to the zoo effect. First, the loud noises that can emanate from those tiny bodies. "It's so frustrating," a newly initiated mother said wistfully, "especially early in his life, to watch a baby screaming for apparently no reason at all. And there is nothing you can do about it. I guess they just take some time to get used to their own feelings and sensations. But to sit by and hear it for hours . . . "

History books are full of stories of women being harassed by children. There is more than one reference to restless children being fed alcohol and opiates. Turning to art again, in Hogarth's *March to Finchley,* the infants are sucking on gin bottles. Gin and drugs are out these days, but a significant number of frenzied mothers probably give some consideration to filling the baby's bottle with glue.

The noise and confusion can go beyond infancy. "Once in a while I do get a little bit crazy," a mother of two young sons told me. "Like when we are in a department store and they are shrieking about something and I say, 'Be quiet, boys, and I'll buy you a drum.' Sometimes our two-bedroom apartment does not seem big enough for the four of us. I have on occasion taken the *Times* out in the hall and read it on the steps just to get some peace and quiet. Oh, and if there's anything a mother should save for a rainy day, it's patience, lots of patience!"

The second factor: Lewis Carroll, in *Alice's Adventures in Wonderland,* describes what happens when Alice comes across a duchess nursing a baby. The baby is sneezing and howling "without a moment's pause," presumably, Alice concludes, because of the pepper in the soup. Then, as Alice is holding the baby, it turns into a pig and begins to grunt. Carroll's choice of animals was probably influenced by direct observation: babies make messes. All kinds of messes. One man described for me the first time he fed his daughter strained prunes. "Hey, honey," he asked his wife, "she wants more. Should I give her another coat?"

"The FBI may have eighty thousand fingerprints," another parent complained to me, "but my house has more. I can always tell if someone I visit has a child or not. The first thing I do is see if they have anything breakable closer than nine feet from the ground."

Infants and young children are constantly learning—about what diapers and toilets are for, about which orifice food is put into, and about what red nailpolish looks like when it is mixed with whipped cream. And that makes a mess.

Fran Lebowitz, writing in her monthly *Mademoiselle* column on the pros and cons of children, notes that "Even when freshly washed and relieved of all obvious confections, children tend to be sticky." Obviously, however, Ms. Lebowitz doesn't consider children to be all bad. As another antireason, she mentions that "All too often children are accompanied by adults," and as a pro reason she writes: "Children ask better questions than do adults. 'May I have a cookie?'; 'Why is the sky blue?'; and 'What does a cow say?' are far more likely to elicit a cheerful response than 'Where's your column?'; 'Why haven't you called?'; and 'Who's your lawyer?' "

~~§ 7 §~~

Two's a Family, Three's a Crowd

"I met with husbands who . . . did not wish to have their wives, during the whole period of their good looks, in the nursery. . . . [Childlessness] allows comfort, society, amusements. . . ."

"There seems to be a movement for childlessness among American women. . . . Children make the mother ugly and come between her and her husband."

"There would seem to be an increasing propensity to fight against the maternal instinct. Some wives are bold enough to declare that they do not want any children; and a few even dare to proclaim openly that they will forgo propagation if possible."

"Why have babies if you do not feel *driven* to it? It is a purgatory and *such* an absurd sacrifice. If no compelling force drives you to it, be thankful and get on with your own life. There are always your friends' babies if you must sentimentalize and blather about children."

These are some recent evaluations of the trend toward the child-free existence, right? Wrong. Consider the sources for the above quotations. The first is that of Foster B. Zincke who wrote in 1868. The second is attributed (by social historian Arthur W. Calhoun) to W. H. Dixon's *New America* in 1869. The third is that of Dr. Thomas S. Sozinskey, published in *Potter's American Monthly* in

1881. And the fourth is a passage from *The Retreat from Parenthood*, a book by Jean Ayling, published in London in 1930. The interest in voluntary nonparenthood is nothing new. However, today there is a renewed and intense interest in the option of nonparenthood as an acceptable way of life.

Although there were some examples of interest in this subject during the 1960s (for instance, Gael Greene's 1963 "A Vote against Motherhood" and Nigel Balchin's 1965 "Children Are a Waste of Time," both published in the *Saturday Evening Post*), the most learned sociologists and demographers were concluding that voluntary childlessness was a demographic dodo bird (the 1960 Growth of American Family Study concluded it was "nearly extinct"). In 1967, one in one hundred couples expected to have no children.

Then, quite suddenly, in the early 1970s, the trend reversed.

Ellen Peck published *The Baby Trap*; magazine articles and news stories began to appear with greater frequency; and NON was founded as a nonprofit organization to represent the economic, social, and personal interests of those who elected not to have children. Most important, by 1976 more than five in one hundred couples stated that they did not intend to have children, according to the United States Census Bureau. Individual surveys indicated that intended childlessness was often as high as 18 percent. Also in 1976, statistics revealed that 18.9 percent of all married women in the United States were childless compared to 14.2 percent in 1965. While in part these figures reflect the current trend toward delayed parenthood, they also indicate a definite movement toward nonparenthood.

But that trend isn't so unique as it may look. Earlier statistics from the U.S. Census Bureau suggest that at least one group of women actually went beyond talk: among women born between 1905 and 1909, the childlessness rate was about 20 percent, as compared with an average of about 10 percent for other generations. The difference between the usual 10 percent and the observed 20 percent figure in this cohort of women presumably represents an increase in voluntary childlessness, since a sudden jump in the frequency of sterility doesn't make sense. Remember that women born early in the century were those who reached their childbearing years in the late 1920s, an era of severe economic hardship. Babies were expensive. Social psychologist Dr. Susan Bram told me that probably more than economic factors lay behind this high rate of childlessness. "The 1920s," she explained, "was also a time of great social upheaval, particularly in the area of women's rights. The suffragettes, flappers, and other groups began to point to social inequities, and female participation in the labor force increased. Women began to look outside the home for activities."

It is probably no coincidence that Jean Ayling's *The Retreat from Parenthood*, pointing out the disadvantages of having children and recommending that women seek roles outside the kitchen and nursery, appeared in 1930. Referring to "the darker side of motherhood," Mrs. Ayling describes the potential adverse effect full-time motherhood can have on the husband-wife relationship. ("By day they see as little of each other on Sundays as during the week. And now that amongst her other experiences the wife knows what it is to wash two or three dozen [diapers] every day or two, the relations between them during the night are no longer either pleasant or straightforward.") She stressed the advantage of being free of the burdens of children, or at least of delegating some of those burdens, so that a woman could have some time of her own.

It is no surprise that another book, *Children, Why Do We Have Them?* by Dora Russell, appeared about the same time and looked at some of the more questionable motivations for childbearing, posing the challenge, "Shall we ever succeed in transforming the impulse that makes a child the vehicle of the parental ego?"

The late 1920s and early 1930s were times of worldwide insecurity and a concern that the planet was not fit to receive children. In Virginia Woolf's novel, *Mrs. Dalloway*, Septimus Smith and his wife considered the world "too horrible" and elected to forgo their option to have children. Many circumstances, but particularly the grim economic realities that began with the infamous 1929 stock market crash, made childbearing a relatively resistible alternative.

The similarities between the conditions of that period and those of the mid-1970s are clear. First, there is a renewed interest—indeed positive unrest—in the area of women's rights; as a consequence, more career possibilities have been opening up for women. Second, we are now experiencing a significant period of economic turmoil during which, relative to other "goods and services," babies, however sacred, are very expensive. Third, there is the same concern about the "fitness of the world"; and fourth, more as a consequence than an independent variable, the birthrate in this country is lower than it was even in the days of the early Depression.

But what is distinctive about today's child-free trend? How do men and women go about choosing the nonparenthood option?

I contacted a number of child-free individuals to see if I could learn how they arrived at their decisions. Barbara and Jeff invited me to their recently purchased renovated brownstone. When I arrived, they gave me a tour. They had four small bedrooms and a small private courtyard just off the living room. "People keep asking us why we want all this space when we don't have kids." Jeff laughed. "But we just tell them we want it for us." We sat by the fireplace and Jeff poured some wine.

"Did you decide before you were married that you were not going to have children?" I asked.

"No, as a matter of fact, we didn't," Barbara started, then her voice trailed off. She was staring at my tape recorder with a look of concern. "Are you really going to record this? We've never talked like this before, I mean about not having children. I don't know if I really want this . . ." She glanced over at Jeff and then back at me. "Oh, I guess it's okay." She began again. "Well, when we first got married, we did talk about having two kids. The whole deal. The boy would come first. He'd be Jeffrey Junior, and the daughter would come a few years later. We thought the name Dawn might be nice for her. It all seemed so romantic and very much part of the future—the distant future. We planned to take full advantage of the freedom of the first three or four years of marriage."

Jeff nodded. "I think that's the key, the freedom we had. With two salaries we were doing quite a bit of entertaining and traveling, and Barbara decided to go to law school at night. Just about every moment was full, and we were thoroughly enjoying life."

Barbara seemed more relaxed as she spoke again. "I'll never forget one afternoon about six months ago when I was riding home from work and began to think seriously about what impact a child would have on our lives." She sipped some wine and went on. "I'd probably have to give up my job, at least for a while, and law school would have to be put on a back burner. Our income would take a plunge, and we would hardly be able to afford this rent on one salary, much less think about getting a larger home. All my life I had assumed that I would be a mother—sometime. But that night it sank in that, for me, the sometime might never happen. And I had to face the fact that there was a good chance we wouldn't have children. It hit me like a ton of bricks."

The Path to Nonparenthood

Psychologists have determined that there are two general paths couples take to voluntary childlessness. One is that which Barbara and Jeff appear to be following. They assumed they were going to have children, but one postponement led to another, and, eventually, either for logistic reasons (being tied up in career plans) or for emotional reasons ("we're just used to being alone!"), parenthood no longer seemed a workable, desirable alternative. The other, less-traveled, path to nonparenthood involves a conscious decision in favor of a child-free existence *before* the marriage occurs. In these circumstances, the decision to remain child-free may actually be a condition of the marriage.

Jean E. Veevers, a sociologist at the University of Western Ontario, has done extensive work in the area of voluntary childlessness. In one study of Canadian child-free wives Dr. Veevers found that about one-third had entered into their marriage with childlessness as a firm condition. She reports that "generally the negative decisions regarding the value of children were made during early adolescence before the possibility of marriage had ever been seriously considered." But the other two-thirds of her study population, like Barbara and Jeff, postponed parenthood until some future time—a time that never came.

As described by Dr. Veevers, "These temporary postponements provided time during which parenthood was gradually reassessed. At the time of their marriage, most wives involved in the postponement model had devoted little serious thought to the question of having children, and had no strong feelings either for or against motherhood. Like conventional couples, they simply assumed that they would have one or two children eventually; unlike conventional couples, they practiced birth control conscientiously and continuously during the early years of marriage.

Dr. Veevers has concluded that for a great majority of voluntarily child-free couples, there is a gradual, yet distinctive four-stage pattern. The *first* stage involves the postponement of children for a definite period. In Barbara and Jeff's case, for instance, Barbara had decided to work for three or four years. After that point, they assumed they would leave their downtown apartment and join the young families in the suburbs. In fact, during this first stage, couples like Barbara and Jeff are indistinguishable from those who do eventually have children.

In the *second* phase in the path to nonparenthood, the couple remains consciously committed to the idea of having at least one child; but, unlike the first stage, the "when" of parenthood becomes increasingly vague. There are so many other aspects of life that are distracting them—their careers, travels, involvement in community activities. ("Yes, we still plan on having children, but there is so much to do first! Besides, we want to save a little more money so we can afford a house in the suburbs.")

At some point the couple enters the *third* phase of the path. For the first time, they actually acknowledge to themselves, and perhaps even to each other, that they might not have children. The emphasis is on the *might*. But this represents a definite qualitative change. Before, the possibility of not having children never entered their minds. Now it does. And it may come to them as a jolt, one they may reject before they fully accept it. Finally, in the *fourth* stage, the couple does decide not to have children. Perhaps the wife, reaching age thirty-three or thirty-four, says, "We have to make up our minds one way or the other; I don't want to have a first child when I am over thirty-five." They may discuss the matter and opt to permanently forgo parenthood; they may even decide to turn to sterilization to confirm the decision. More likely than not, however, a couple in this final stage may find sterilization too difficult a step, too final a decision. So the decision remains implicit. They carefully use contraception and avoid parenthood, and both husband and wife gradually accept the implications of their tacit agreement. As the *when* of parenthood surges toward *now or never*, the *how many* begins to point toward zero.

Susan Bram has noted that it is usually the wife who, after about three or four years of marriage, first comes to terms with the realities of how parenthood would change their lives. As Dr. Bram points out, given that the child-free wife is probably better educated and more career oriented than those who do have children, and given that the major changes children would bring generally would require more alteration in her life than in that of her husband, it is she who does the more serious thinking.

Well, Why *Aren't You Having Children?*

"Right, we're definitely entering phase four." Jeff laughed when I told him about the Veevers concept. "But the way you describe it—in phases and all—it sounds like nonparenthood is a disease. I would hardly put it in that category. It's a perfectly logical option. I think the longer you delay parenthood, the more your life-style doesn't include kids. I don't know what other child-free couples do, but we never really talked about it much. It was a sensitive subject for a while, and most of our communication was very subtle." He got up and poked at the fire. "You know, we'd come home from a football game and reunion at our college, commenting on the hassle our friends seem to experience keeping their kids in line, and one of us would say, 'Thank goodness we don't have those problems.' Or when we'd go to the shore in July for a two-week vacation, the car packed up with food, clothes, pots, and pans—you name it—one of us would look in the back and say, 'Gee, guess there is no room for a baby.' " He walked over to stand next to Barbara. "When I think about it there was no positive decision made. We'd keep checking in with each other, 'Well, what do you think now?'—and eventually it was a matter of what we probably weren't going to do. Neither of us even now is ready to sign a paper saying we won't under any conditions have any children. We're both thirty-five, and that's the way it will probably be. But why rule out the option completely? After a while, time will take care of that anyway."

"You really want to know why we aren't having kids?"Barbara leaned forward intently. "I'll level with you. It's strictly a matter of personal freedom. When I sat down and thought about it, I wasn't sure I even liked kids. I'm a lousy housewife, for one thing. I'm not interested in that stuff. I want to *live!* I want to accomplish things in this world. Okay. You can call me selfish, but the way I look at it, my great-grandmother sacrificed everything for my grandmother. My grandmother did the same thing for my mother, and in turn my mother gave up everything for me. The hell with that! I think somewhere along the line, someone ought to live—and I elect me!"

She took a big swallow from her glass. And a deep breath. "There's something else," she said after a minute. "I'm not sure I am motherhood material. Little babies make me nervous. I'm always convinced they are going to throw up all over me. And when I hear a child screaming in the subway, I can't stand it. I change cars."

Jeff broke in, "Me too. I'm like Barbara. I don't think I'm the father type. I sometimes get angry at kids I don't know, especially when I have a terrific headache and I'm trying to line up those arrows on an Excedrin bottle." We all laughed, and then he became serious. "I'm just not a homebody. I'm very happy the way I am. I know what it's like being married to a wife—and I like it. I don't know what it would be like being married to a mother, and I don't know that I want to risk it." All of us stared into the fire; no one said anything for a moment.

Then Jeff spoke again, still apparently fascinated by the leaping flames. "I thought of something else. We both have ambitious plans for the future, and I doubt we could have those and children, too. If we *did* ever have children, I'd want to do it right. I just can't see bringing a child into the world and then handing him or her over to a substitute mother." He shrugged and looked at me. "What would be the point of that? If I were a father, I would feel it was my obligation to spend as much of my free time as possible with the child. I feel that it would be my duty to plan every weekend around it, to go to Boy Scout and PTA meetings. I would do it right—or not at all. So I'm being honest. When people tell me I'm being selfish by avoiding parenthood, I tell them that just the opposite is true. Having children and not giving them your full commitment—now *that's* selfish."

I met a number of couples who, like Barbara and Jeff, wanted the freedom to travel and pursue joint careers and emphasized that they wanted to do parenthood up "right" or not at all. Other couples, however, had different reasons for not having children.

Emily had just turned thirty, and Stuart was in his early forties. When we met at their two-bedroom apartment, I noticed a number of photographs of children.

"I've been married before," Stuart explained. "I was exactly twenty years old when I said 'I do,' and exactly twenty and seven months the day our first child was born. You get the picture." He slowly brushed his hand over his thinning hair and went on, speaking more slowly. "In the first six years of our marriage, three more children arrived. My first wife had something against contraception, and since we were having problems from the start, I think she thought that children were a good way to hold on to me. I stayed with her for fifteen years, and then I left. Emily and I were married two years ago."

He looked over at Emily, who smiled somewhat sadly, and then he picked up his train of thought. "I send a hefty check to the five of them out in Seattle every month, and the kids visit with us each summer for two weeks, but that's about the extent of our contact. I enjoy them during that visit; I enjoy hearing from them when they write or call; but, frankly, I have no desire to do it all over again. I did my time, I've been through it. I want time for myself now. When I come home I want a martini, not a baby. And from the practical point of view, I can't support two families on my income."

Emily shifted somewhat uneasily and looked at Stuart as she talked. "Stuart told me how he felt before we were married. I had always wanted children, myself, but I could certainly understand how he felt, too." Then she turned to me. "I'll be honest, I still do think about how great it would be to have my own son or daughter. But I bring myself back to reality. I chose to marry Stuart, and, for us, it just wouldn't work out. I enjoy having his kids here when they visit, and I make an effort to get involved in their lives. I try not to dwell too much on the fact that I will never have any of my own.

Things are changing. Today when a child reads a fairy tale, the characters are likely to include Father Bear, Mother Bear, and Little Bear by Mother Bear's first marriage. Very often this can mean that one or both partners enter the marriage with preset attitudes about parenthood, and possibly years of personal experience. Of course the decision about parenthood in a second marriage need not be a negative one. But when one partner feels that he is too old to "start all over again," and when realities such as the economic burden of child support are considered, this decision may seem inevitable.

It's not just previously married couples who take into consideration the money factor. As I've indicated, if money is free and economic pressure relatively unimportant, as it was in the United States during the 1950s, men and women may enter parenthood more casually—and may have more children. They can afford them. Now, as during the late 1920s, inflation has made parenthood a very expensive option, and some couples are thinking twice before choosing it. Various estimates on the cost of raising a child today to the age of eighteen average out to about $60,000, and this is likely to increase in the 1980s. "We're always short of money as it is," a neighborhood couple told me. "How can we afford a baby?"

Peggy and Tim, another child-free couple I talked with at an art museum one Saturday afternoon, appeared to be around thirty. I asked them if they could tell me why they chose nonparenthood.

"In terms of background reasons, I guess we were ambivalent about undertaking the responsibilities of parenthood," Peggy said as we headed toward the museum's coffee shop, "but for us there was another important consideration. Tim has diabetes, and while I don't have it, my mother does. We got some medical advice on our situation and were told that if we had a baby of our own, there was a significant chance that the child would have diabetes. I guess if we'd really had the urge, we might have taken the chance. But then maybe we wouldn't have. When you think of it, it's not really you who's taking the chance. It's an unborn child. Do you think that would be a fair move to make?"

I started to say something, but Tim interrupted, somewhat impatiently. "Anyway, the question is academic now. We might have fooled around with the pros and cons and ifs and maybes for years, but Peggy needed a type of uterine surgery—and her doctor put it on the line. 'It's now or never,' he told us. So we talked about it seriously and opted for the never. She had the operation, and now there's nothing to decide anymore." Then he smiled and put his arm around Peggy. "You can never be sure about these things, but at least we can get on with the business of life."

I met Joan and Andy at a Friday-night meeting of the local chapter of the National Organization for Non-Parents. They were child-free, but unlike Barbara and Jeff, Emily and Stuart, or Peggy and Tim, they didn't seem more or less resigned to their status; they were enthusiastic about it.

Joan was an energetic twenty-five-year-old who headed up the publicity committee for the group. She told me she had done a great deal of public speaking about the rights of the nonparent. She and Andy were more than willing to tell me why they weren't having children. We found a corner of the room where we could talk privately.

Joan sounded almost breathless as she began to talk. "We wouldn't *dream* of having children of our own. As a matter of fact we had better *not* dream of it, because Andy had a vasectomy about a year ago. We just can't see bringing children into this world. The population growth rate is staggering, pollution is so bad you can hardly breathe, and it just wouldn't seem right. I mean, I think there is some human instinct or innate awareness which tells us when enough is enough. Rats and some other animals stop producing when conditions become too crowded, so why can't we?" She caught her breath. "The environmental issue was important in our decision, but of course there was the personal issue, also. I don't think I'm cut out to be a mother. I think you have to be more of a giving than a taking person to be a good parent. I've thought about it, and I've concluded that there are a number of occupations I don't have an interest in and in which I probably would not do very well. Architecture, for instance—it leaves me cold. And so does motherhood, so why get an advanced degree in it? And I keep asking myself, who needs kids? I see what my college classmates are going through, and I read about the glories of motherhood in the women's magazines. People tell us that we won't be complete if we don't have kids." She laughed, and I detected a bit of contempt. "I think if we ever did, we'd be *finished*."

Andy had listened quietly as Joan spoke. He didn't exude the same kind of enthusiasm about nonparenthood as did his wife, but after I heard what he had to say, I could tell he was equally committed. "I think every couple should at least give some consideration to the idea of remaining child-free. The world would be better off that way, and so would many unwanted kids." He spoke earnestly and shook his head sadly. "Do you know how many cases of child abuse were reported last year? It's incredible—just the *reported* cases. There's an estimated minimum of one million cases a year, and a lot of them even die from the maltreatment. Maybe if people took some time to think before they procreate, we'd all be better off." He put his arm around Joan's waist. "I'm really proud of the decision Joan and I made. It was our way of showing that we have a commitment to the world and an interest in humanity."

Personal freedom. Lack of interest in children. Lack of confidence about accepting the parenthood role. Economic factors. Environmental issues, and, less frequently, genetic concerns. That's why some people choose not to have children. Being child-free offers some real benefits, some of which are painfully obvious to couples with children. "You can just get up and go," Joan pointed out to me during a later conversation. "You are really free to do as you please. I just couldn't stand the thought of being tied down to a child. Andy and I pack our bags on an hour's notice and take off for the weekend. We don't have to go through all the confusion involved in getting a baby ready and organizing and lugging all his equipment."

Peggy and Tim stressed another aspect of nonparenthood. "We enjoy being with adults," Tim said emphatically. "We are not big on baby talk or Teddy bears. We don't enjoy crawling on the floor to get someone's attention. I learned the alphabet once—and that was enough, thank you. And I'd rather read stock reports than *Winnie the Pooh*."

As I mentioned earlier, Gael Greene, in her landmark article, "A Vote against Motherhood," in the *Saturday Evening Post*, proclaimed: "I don't want to have any children." (As a side point, Gael told me that the *Post* editors made her and her husband promise not to change their minds on this for at least a year after the article was published. They didn't.) "Motherhood," she wrote, "is only a part of marriage, and I am unwilling to sacrifice the other important feminine roles upon the overexalted altar of parenthood." She chose to forgo the so-called joys of parenthood in favor of developing herself as a woman.

"All I want is just an hour a day to be me," she overheard a friend of hers complain to her husband, "not to be a chauffeur or a bandage dispenser or a screaming harpy in a torn muumuu."

The joys of nonparenthood, the freedom to travel and to be yourself, are attractive in themselves. No contest. But equally important in the decision to remain child-free may be the assurance that by doing so you are going to escape what you see as the darker side of parenthood. Thus the interest in nonparenthood life may be twofold, a positive force that attracts and a negative force that repels. But here we're just talking about the relatively rational factors that may precipitate the nonparenthood decision. Other, more elusive, factors may also operate.

Any Other Reasons?

Just as it is important to go beyond the most obvious reasons for having a child, it is a good idea to look at the more subtle reasons that might be lurking behind the decision not to. By doing so, you will get to understand yourself better, and perhaps you will be able to see why you are going in the direction you are; this should make you feel more comfortable with your decision later on.

I spoke with psychologist Donald M. Kaplan about the new interest in the child-free life-style. "What we're talking about," he pointed out, "is the generation of men and women born in the 1940s and 1950s, children raised by parents whose character style had shifted from what sociologist David Riesman called 'inner directed' to 'other directed.' These parents took care of their children's every need. They put their whole selves into the art of parenting and instilled in their offspring a great desire for accomplishment—a sense of ambition. And where there is such an emphasis on the desirability of individual accomplishment, there may be no room for the self-sacrifices which can go with parenthood."

Thinking about the child-free couples I met, I understood exactly what Dr. Kaplan meant. Most of them, contrary to what the word *child-free* implies, work unusually hard—and they are committed to a career interest. The converse of this is that most of them "play hard" too. Vacations and periods of free time become very important. They are well earned. The emphasis is on self-advancement and, after the work is done, self-reward.

The shift from child to parent—that is, the change in status from one who is cared for to one who does the caring—is difficult anyway; but among couples who have for so long been in the focus of activity themselves—in the sense of pursuing development—that shift may be even more difficult.

I pursued Dr. Kaplan's point with Barbara. "Right. Right. I know what he means. I talk with my mother about three times a week and tell her what Jeff and I are doing in our work. She and my father always encouraged me to keep moving ahead, and they're always eager for our progress reports. Jeff's family is like that, too. They get vicarious thrills from our accomplishments." She stopped and slammed her fist down on the arm of the couch. "The maddening thing is that after giving us this sense of ambition, they're upset that we won't slow down for a few years, to leave some time for grandchildren!" She took a deep breath. "But as I see it, you can't have it both ways. I'm not sure that I would be able now to turn the attention from myself and the ladder I have been climbing to someone else."

Jeff had been looking on sympathetically. Now he spoke. "I understand all that, especially the part about the Superparenting. My mother and father gave me everything. They followed Spock to the letter. They lived for me—and they still do, I'm afraid. Now here's the problem I was raising earlier. I do not feel that sense of commitment. And I don't think it would be fair to give a child any less attention than I got, especially with all the problems kids face today! And I wouldn't be satisfied if my kids didn't do at least as well as I did. With Barb's and my records, those are pretty high goals to set. You know, it is ironic. Here we both have Superparents who are begging for grandchildren, and one reason we may not be having children—is because they were Superparents!"

The nonparenthood decision can be very complex. For example, there may be deeper motivating forces that *accompany* the practical ones already identified. But, in some cases at least, buried fears or anxieties may be the *dominant* force in the decision or nondecision.

Some men or women may worry about their capacity to impregnate or conceive. Maybe they have a medical reason to believe that they can't have children, or they may have a vague suspicion that they could be sterile. Similarly, a woman may have an unreasonable fear of labor and childbirth or of the effect that motherhood might have on her physical appearance. Perhaps one or both partners are afraid that by undertaking parenthood they will be fusing their identities with another person and losing themselves. The option not to have children can provide a convenient escape hatch for unconsidered anxieties—for better, or perhaps for worse.

Psychology Today recently carried a nonparenthood study by physicians Nancy B. Kaltreider and Alan G. Margolis that included fifteen women who had had tubal ligations (the most common technique for female sterilization). Of the fifteen, eleven had come from broken homes, two had lost their parents at a young age, and two had parents who were mentally ill. The study did not indicate whether there were additional reasons offered for the decision to remain child-free, but the significance of these women's backgrounds undoubtedly contributed to their reluctance to bear children of their own.

In a *Woman's Day* story ("We'll Never Have Kids!"), Marcia Kamien relates the story of Cher, who had been a battered child. Cher is only too acutely aware that the parent-child relationship can be ugly and destructive. To quote her: "Everything you're told about motherhood glorifies it. All the pictures show smiling mothers, smiling children . . . satisfaction and happiness guaranteed. I wish young people could be taught a more realistic viewpoint. Not grim, just not unreal." But though Cher has chosen not to have her own children her life is filled with those of other people. She now holds a position as deputy director of the juvenile justice unit in a New York State agency, doing as much as she is able to help "the unfortunate ones who are already among us, already suffering. I'm doing everything I can to save them from being destroyed. I believe that's a meaningful contribution—more meaningful than my becoming pregnant."

Along a similar line, another woman falteringly told me her story at a friend's house one afternoon. After twenty years, the memory was still obviously painful, but she seemed to feel it was important that I understood. "I was nine years old and best friends with Darlene, who lived down the block. Darlene had a little brother who often played with my younger sister. They were a nice family and our parents were friendly with each other, too. Well, one day . . ." She stopped and bit her lip for a moment, then blurted, "One day Darlene's mother just went to pieces and drowned her little brother in the bathtub!"

Again she paused, desperately trying to suppress the vividness of her recollections. "I guess I never quite got over it. First little Freddie was gone, then their mother was gone, then Darlene was sent to live with an aunt in another city. And no one could ever explain to me *why*. My husband really wants at least one child. But I'm afraid—just really *afraid*. I've even gone to a therapist, but he could never quite explain to me how mothers can do such things. And, of course, there was no way he could give me absolute assurance that I wouldn't end up doing the same thing to my child if I had one. I'm a pretty happy-go-lucky person most of the time, but the thought of having a baby puts me into the worst kind of depression you can imagine. I cannot do it, and I never will!"

Fortunately, not many of us have fallen victim to such cruel memories, but they are starkly real to the few who have. Considering that from 1957 to 1970 the infanticide rate in the United States rose from 3.1 to 4.7 per 100,000 babies, the existence of genuine fear in certain cases is understandable.

"I wasn't an abused child," a child-free friend in her early thirties confided to me, "but my mother nagged at us incessantly and was very strict. It seemed we could do nothing to please her. Try as I might, I've never been able to conjure up warm feelings about a mother-child relationship. My sister went the other route. She set out with a dogged determination to raise a family 'the way it should be done.' Her little monsters are three and five now, impossibly spoiled. I can't stand to be around them. Yet she thinks *I'm* some kind of freak."

Frequently I listened to fears among child-free women that as mothers they might turn out to be like their own mothers—mean and impatient, cold and unresponsive, emotionally destroyed by their children, ignored by their husbands—I must have heard the gamut. To many proparenthood people, such fears undoubtedly take on the character of excuses, but the accusation is grossly unfair. Our fears, of whatever nature, are a very real part of our psychological makeup and, consciously or subconsciously, they exert a great deal of influence over all that we think and do (or don't do). And where children are concerned, it's not always easy to find a healthy outlet for those fears. A parent may cringe on those ugly days when the youngster turns red in the face and screams "I hate you!", but assuming the said parent is a reasonably mature adult, an enraged "I hate you, too!" is not considered an appropriate reply.

I recently fell into a discussion at a cocktail party with a woman who had decided to remain child-free after having had a miscarriage. "Not because I was afraid of another miscarriage," she explained. "It was what happened while I was pregnant. I was talking with a friend of my husband's one evening, a man quite a bit older with several children—mostly grown or nearly grown. I knew he had a reputation for playing around on his wife, but I wasn't prepared for what he was going to tell me. He just launched right into this great lecture about how I shouldn't worry if Rod didn't always come home at night after the baby was born. That it didn't mean he loved me less, it was just that when women became mothers they just didn't make very good lovers anymore. He said they were always too busy with the baby or too tired or too something and never bothered to look pretty around the house anymore, and all kinds of stuff like that."

"A real chauvinist pig!" she fumed. "If his wife was so busy and so tired, why didn't he go home and help her instead of galavanting all over town with some chick? Trouble is, I'm not super sure how terrific Rod would be in the help department, either. But I'll tell you one thing, I've decided I'm not going to find out! I miscarried about a week after that conversation and I still wonder a tiny bit whether it was because Mr. Chauvinism upset me so badly. Anyway, if I have to choose between my husband and a baby—well, I don't need a baby *that* bad! Nobody's ever going to refer to *me* as his 'old lady.' "

And the fact is that many husbands feel exactly the same way. "I married a beautiful, wonderful woman," one man informed me. "And I want her to stay that way. I watched my sister turn into a screeching hag after her children started coming along. That's not for me. I married Joni because I love her and I love what she is." Another declared, "I have no intention of trading off half of my gentle, loving wife just so I can have a couple of kids."

Then there is the ever-present fear of divorce. "My marriage is wonderful right now," an acquaintance declared recently. "But all around me I continually see how quickly that can change—particularly after children enter the picture. If we were ever to split I know I can perfectly well look after myself, but with a child or two . . . I don't even want to think about it."

It's another very real—and growing—fear. Between 1953 and 1970 the number of children under eighteen whose parents were divorced nearly tripled. And in 1978 Beatrice Marden Glickman and Nesha Bass Springer reported in *Who Cares for the Baby?* the granting of eight-hundred thousand divorces annually, affecting one million children. To make matters worse, the National Commission on the Observance of International Women's Year reveals that only 44 percent of divorced mothers are currently awarded child support, and that only *13 percent* of all divorced mothers actually receive regular child support. That is indeed enough to give one pause.

Just as a less-than-conscious approach to having children can backfire in later years, a less-than-conscious approach to being child-free can also have some negative ramifications later on. Life never issues guarantees against regret.

There may also be something subtle in a child-free couple's background that makes them hesitant about parenthood. As New York University psychiatrist Henry Greenbaum told me, "People usually learn about the desirability or lack of desirability of children from their parents. A man or woman doesn't all of a sudden in adulthood decide not to have children. He or she may tell you, for instance, that it is because of his career commitments or lack of money or whatever, but it is more likely traceable to some subtle, but influential, nonparenthood message—or more likely thousands of messages—he received as a child."

What about the possibility that accepting parenthood is like acknowledging that we're getting older—acknowledging that we are closer to death? There's a German proverb that says, The coffin is the cradle's brother. As Garry Wills wrote in a 1973 *Esquire* article on parenthood and nonparenthood, "In a country that wants to be agelessly young, the baby is a death's-head at the feast." By becoming a parent, you are moving up the generational hierarchy. You have a whole new status. You're no longer a child—and that means you're closer to the end of your life. For some people, at least unconsciously, this fear may provide a basis for the nonparenthood orientation.

Is It Okay Not To?

Given the "sacredness" of babies and the traditional American proparenthood disposition, it's understandable, if unfortunate, that some young couples today still ask themselves if it is really okay not to have children. Until recently, only W. C. Fields ever got away with criticizing children en masse. ("Anyone who hates children and dogs can't be all bad.") Couples don't go around asking if it's okay to have children, to bring another life into the world. Of course it's all right not to have children. It's still controversial, to be sure, but it's okay. And in some cases it's probably much better that way.

In the last decade, we've slowly come to acknowledge that, just as men and women differ widely in their orientation toward life goals, interests, and accomplishments, they differ also in their attitudes about children and parenthood. One couple might see children as a form of enrichment, a way to develop their own potential to the fullest; another might envision parenthood as an undesirable form of self-restraint. For some, children may be a real burden. As Nigel Balchin, an English author and discontented father of five, put it, parenthood is, "on the whole, an expensive and unrewarding bore, in which far more has to be invested, both materially and spiritually, than ever comes out in dividends."

"From the point of view of the man," Balchin continues, before the birth "he was a race horse (with a pretty filly at his side). Now he is shut up between shafts and bidden to pull the family coach." And for the woman, motherhood might be seen as the possible deathblow to a very promising career.

Of course it's okay not to have children. Not everyone is really cut out to be a parent. It's unrealistic to assume that everybody who is fertile is capable of being a parent or will be fulfilled by parenthood. There already exists an abundance of children; society doesn't require every couple to contribute its own share like a tithe. How could anyone actually encourage a couple who have said straight out that they didn't want or didn't *like* children, to have them anyway? What kind of life does an unwanted, unloved child have?

All of us know at least one mother, probably more, about whom we have wondered why she ever had children in the first place. And while no one expects mothers to dash around publicly radiating love for their children at all times, much of their "motherly" behavior is positively unnerving. How often have you witnessed, in the local supermarket, for instance, unmistakable expressions of hate toward a child? I am not referring to momentary anger, but what can only be construed as a distinct dislike. What is the point?

Life is full of choices. We have to consider alternatives, benefits, and disadvantages and decide. We can't do everything. And that is sometimes part of the problem—people try to do everything. "Very few people are graced with the ability to excel in several diverse areas simultaneously," Dr. Robert Gould, professor of psychiatry at New York Medical College, told me. "This is probably why so many outstanding statesmen, writers, scientists, and psychiatrists fail as parents. They spend so much time attaining success that, even if they are not emotionally spent from their exertions, they lack time to meet the needs of a child. Love, of course, may be there; but if a parent does not have the time or energy to communicate that love, his child cannot develop a feeling of security and the sense of positive identification with that parent which is necessary for healthy development."

A 1977 study conducted by Linda Silka and Sara Kiesler indicated that couples planning to remain childless were neither more nor less happy than those intending to have children; that the child-free couples did not appear to be either more or less selfish or immature than the others; and that although the child-free couples tended to place greater value on personal freedom, they were neither more nor less desirous of a "stimulating life" than were the intended parent couples.

In addition, two recent nationwide Institute for Social Research studies offered some statistical evidence that marriages without children survive—and in some cases are happier than those with children. Contrary to the popular myth (the one your mother tells you) that childless marriages are incomplete or unfulfilled, these quality-of-life surveys find that child-free couples do not appear to suffer. "Married couples without children give no evidence in this study that their lives are in any way diminished by the fact that they are not parents," the researchers on one study conclude. On the contrary, the study showed that young couples who have no children describe their lives in unusually positive terms, and that even later in life—after marriage without children has become a definite life pattern—women continue to be as positive about their lives as similar women with children, and childless men are somewhat more positive than men who are parents.

"People with children," the study goes on, "find that parenthood involves both costs and rewards during the years of raising small children; the costs appear to be substantial. The deterioration of perceived relationships with the spouse from the stage of early marriage (before children) to the stage of the small child is quite marked. Parents of young children show a great deal of strain, both personal and economic, which gradually subsides as they pass through the stage of later parenthood."

Before you take these results as infallible reflections, remember that it is possible that child-free respondents were in a position to be more defensive than those who followed the expected marriage pattern and had children. Perhaps they were less likely to give a candid evaluation of their contentment with life. On the other hand, as the results seem to show, maybe they were as positive in their outlook as the parents were—or more so.

A note on the relationship of nonparenthood and divorce: again, contrary to what you may have heard, child-free couples do not have a greater risk of experiencing a deteriorating marriage. If you glance casually at United States divorce statistics, you will see that couples without children *do* have higher divorce rates. But think about that. Since a significant proportion of all divorces occur early in marriage—when there is a higher probability that no children have been born—then of course the divorce rate would be higher among the childless group. Additionally, child-free couples may feel under less pressure to remain in a bad marriage and may more freely terminate it. There is, at this point, no evidence of any cause-effect between childlessness and divorce. Indeed, the opposite might be more true.

No Kidding—Are There Some Psychological Costs of Nonparenthood?

"Psychological costs in the nonparenthood decision? How can there be costs associated with freedom?" a nonparent and NON member ask me as I watched her stuff envelopes that carried non-Mother's Day greetings. "When you decide to be child-free, you escape all the psychological costs. That's the whole point. There aren't any."

Her attitude is somewhat naïve. A decision involves choosing between or among options—each of which presumably has benefits as well as costs, or they wouldn't be in the running. So, for every choice you make, you have to give up something. How easy it would be otherwise!

I talked with other child-free couples who did admit that there were psychological costs involved in choosing nonparenthood. These costs didn't deter them from their decision, but they were there, and they had to be dealt with.

Social Censure

In the *Woman's Day* article mentioned earlier in the Chapter, Marcia Kamien offers this quote from a woman who elected to remain child-free: "If you tell people you've decided against having children you're accused of being everything from selfish to infantile—and by folks who are normally too polite to tell you your lipstick's on crooked!"

"Having a baby," one child-free woman told me, "is like having a society wedding. It's a time of tremendous social approval. You're doing what is expected of you, and, in turn, you're offered rewards. So I guess one of the costs of nonparenthood is being denied that type of approval. Instead you're fighting currents all the way."

She's right. Nonparenthood can be a rocky road—especially if you have relatives and friends who look on child-free individuals as misfits.

Dr. Isaac Asimov has noted that childlessness is perfectly acceptable among priests and nuns, apparently indicating that it's great not to have kids as long as you don't have sex. But to many upstanding citizens the idea of sex without children is abhorrent. Asimov therefore suggests that perhaps children are a punishment for indulging in the enjoyment of sex.

After writer Dan Wakefield received the Non-Parent of the Year award in 1974, he said that one of his friends who had read about this NON event said, "You know what it was like, picking up the paper and reading about your accepting the award as Non-Parent of the Year? It's like picking up the paper and reading that one of your dearest friends has become a Nazi."

Nonparenthood is controversial. And in choosing this alternative, you may be subject to the ravages of social pressure. How significant a cost this is depends on how confident you are about your decision.

Second Thoughts

"Do you ever have any ambivalent feelings about your decision not to have children?" I asked Jeff and Barbara.

"Well, I have to say that there are times when I see particularly well-behaved children," Jeff admitted, "and I have this fleeting thought, Gee, wouldn't it be great if I had a son. But it doesn't last too long—about two seconds, I'd say. When I have those thoughts, I wonder if I'm not thinking of children as baubles—something to decorate me and my wife." He sat back and thought through my question again. "Ambivalence? I really wouldn't call it that. When I think of the word *ambivalence*, I think of something where the odds are forty-sixty—or even seventy-thirty. But here we're dealing with one proparenthood thought out of one hundred. I have second thoughts about not going to medical school, too. But I made a decision not to, and, the overwhelming portion of the time, I am happy with that decision."

"How about you, Barbara? Do you think a woman carries more than her share of the psychological costs—or do you think it's about the same?"

She responded in a serious tone. "No, it's definitely not the same." She laughed and looked over at Jeff. "Blame it all on physiology! He can be a father thirty years from now if he chooses to. My time is going to be up shortly." She looked back at me. Her expression reflected her mixed feelings. "So in that sense, yes, I carry more of the burden. There's this movie played a few times a year on Channel Thirteen that really sets me off. It shows a fifty-five-year-old woman waking up one morning screaming, 'My God! Why didn't I have children! I will never see the face of my child!' And of course she goes insane and lives unhappily ever after. Needless to say, I can't stand that movie, but I think it reflects a little of the fear in every woman who chooses not to have children. But that's my decision at this point—and I'm not changing my mind."

If you make a decision not to have a child, you can have second thoughts. But you can have second thoughts after becoming a parent too, and in that case it may be deeper trouble, because a third person is involved. The decision not to have a child is a major one; specifically, in terms of ambivalence, the psychological cost is likely to be greater for the nonparent than for the parent. Why? A mother, for instance, can play "what if" and imagine where she would be if she had pursued a career instead of raising children; she has also had some time as a nonparent and knows what it's like. It is more difficult for a nonparent to put herself in the corresponding "what if" position, and, since she has never experienced motherhood, she can't compare the two situations. To her the alternative is less clear—and in that sense more capable of provoking a nagging ambivalence.

"I went to a couple of NON meetings," Emily explained, "because I thought I might be able to find some support for our decision not to have children. Given that it was more Stuart's decision than mine, I needed all the support I could get. I wanted to hear how other people had come to terms with themselves." Emily gave me the same wan smile she had had earlier. "The first thing that surprised me was that the majority of the couples at NON had a situation like mine—I mean one member of the couple had a child or children by a previous marriage, and either one or both of them didn't want another child. The other thing was that very few of those I met had fully resolved the issue. We were all looking to each other for reinforcement, and in a sense we got it. It's a difficult question to work out; why not admit it? Of course there are those really militant about being nonparents. But down deep, I bet they too are like the rest of us."

Ellen Willis, writing in *Ms.*, tells of the time she went to a New York Radical Feminist conference on motherhood, hoping to discuss with other women in the same situation her feelings about not having children. She found that, as a group, the women placed a high value on personal freedom, privacy, independence, and self-development, and they generally found motherhood incompatible with their priorities. That would apparently fit the bill for nonparenthood. But these women also worried about being cut off from a basic human dimension—a human experience—and they knew that parenthood had profound pleasures as well as frustrations. And *that's* ambivalence.

Balzac, in his novel *Two Women,* describes the opposing anxieties about parenthood that can exist in the female psyche (undoubtedly a similar range of feelings exists in men, too). He tells the story of friends who relate their experiences through letters. Each expresses the opposite views about love, sex, and motherhood, but, at the end, each discovers in herself the hidden longings for the other's life. Baroness Louise de Macumère is a courtesan, a devotee of love, constantly in pursuit of passion and erotic experiences. Her friend Renée de l'Estorade is described as "always the mother," even in her relationship with her husband. Louise writes:

> We are both women. I a most blissful goddess of love, you the happiest of mothers. . . . Nothing can be compared to the delights of love. . . . You, my dear friend, must describe for me the joys of motherhood, so that I may enjoy it through you.

Yet even in the ecstasies of love, a voice within Louise calls out: "A childless woman is a monstrosity; we are born to be mothers. I too want to sacrifice myself, and I am often absorbed in gloomy thoughts these days: will there never be a little one to call me mother?" Then Louise returns to her passion.

But Renée is ambivalent too, and she expresses her feelings to Louise:

> I have had to renounce the pleasures of love and the sensual joys for which I long and which I can only experience through you, the nocturnal meeting on the starlit balcony, the passionate yearnings and unbridled effusions of love.

Ambivalence. It's there no matter which choice you make, but it may be particularly pronounced in nonparenthood and may occasionally lead to some minor depressions—not the morbid type; just the normal variety that may accompany second thoughts about any major decision. This cost is by no means insurmountable, but it must be reckoned with.

Stagnation?

You've probably heard someone say that people who don't have children get strange. Funny. Maybe weird. Self-centered and eccentric. I talked about this type of evaluation of a childless/child-free couple in Chapter Three when I presented Erik Erikson's dichotomy between generativity and stagnation.

"I have an aunt," Peggy told me, "who is that way. She married but never had children—I don't think she was able to. And she did get a bit strange." She chuckled. "My mother tells the story of how she took me there when I was three years old and Aunt Margie got all upset because I wouldn't eat her spinach soufflé. During our whole visit she was jumping up and down making sure my brother and I didn't put fingerprints on her precious Dior drapes. As I told you before, I've had an operation and can't have kids, but before I did my mother used to threaten me by saying that I would be like Aunt Margie someday if I didn't have children. And since I am conscious of this possibility, I bend over backwards to make sure I'm not like that when children are around. Luckily, we don't suffer from something else I see in child-free couples—the tendency to dote on one another like they were each other's one and only child. We find enrichment outside each other, too."

New York Medical College's Dr. Robert Gould stresses that there are many alternative ways to self-development. "Parenthood is not the only one. The idea that people who don't have children are stuck in one psychological state, destined to stagnate, is not consistent with reality. There are many constructive, fulfilling, and happy ways to live without being parents. It is time to retire the old wives' tale that life without children is incomplete."

But as Peggy indicated, it sometimes takes extra effort to avoid cutting yourself off from the younger generation and to understand the problems and points of view of people who do choose to become parents. The risk of being unable to develop a feeling of understanding with a major portion of humanity may be a cost of nonparenthood.

"Not for me," Andy, the confident nonparent, told me. "We make it a point to keep in touch with children. We are active in our neighborhood day camp during the summer—and we really enjoy the time we spend with my brother's three children. We feel there are ways to experience many of the positive aspects of being with children—but when we've had enough, we just say good-bye."

When I talked to Barbara and others about this problem, I got a different reaction. "A lot of my child-free friends talk about how they are going to spend time doing this and that with children." Barbara shook her head and looked at me quizzically. "I sometimes wonder if they aren't trying to prove to the world that they are normal or something by making these statements. For me, the reality is, I don't know any children, and if I did, I'm not sure I'd have the time to do anything with them. We both work from early in the morning until late at night. The last thing we want to do when we get home from work—or on our hard-earned days off—is to go to the local school to play with someone else's children. I'm just being honest. I don't really *dislike* children, but I don't have the time—and I don't want to make the time—to be with children with whom I cannot develop a permanent association. Our relatives have children, but again, the reality is that we live in the city and they live in the suburbs. We get together on holidays, but that's about it. I really wonder if that talk about spending time with kids isn't a lot of make-believe."

If you are considering remaining child-free, you might ask yourself exactly what you mean by "freedom." Is it, as Janis Joplin sang, "just another word for nothin' left to lose"? Or is it the capacity for exercising the option to apply energy that might otherwise have been directed at children into something that you, as an individual, might find more rewarding and, in the long run, more constructive?

Some of the reasons many couples offer for electing to remain child-free necessarily raise a quizzical eyebrow—simply because they are identical to some of reasons presented by their counterparts for making the opposite choice. The no-child opters may tell you that being child-free binds a marriage more closely, makes it easier to talk and to do things together, keeps life more interesting, keeps you young, keeps you laughing. As we have already seen earlier in this book, a great many parents insist that the presence of children: strengthens a marriage, presents a multitude of subjects to talk about (and ask questions about), invites you to accept the challenge of new discoveries, extends your youthfulness, and keeps you laughing (well, at least *part* of the time). What it all boils down to, of course, is a necessity for the Want Factor we discussed much earlier. If you *want* to have children and stop to consider why, the reasons are easy to find. Conversely, if you don't want to have children and stop to consider why, reasons are also easy to find—even if they're the same sets of reasons.

Dr. E. James Anthony, Professor of Child Psychiatry at the Washington University School of Medicine, feels that "despite their stated motives for not having children, the question arises whether young people really, in fact, lead richer lives today." That's a question you'll want to think about before you do decide to remain child-free. And if mutual careers in lieu of children appear to provide that enrichment, or if there are opportunities to derive pleasure and make a contribution by working with children or young adults who are not biologically yours, the cost of non-parenthood may be minimal.

Sometimes It Hurts

Emily, whose husband Stuart didn't want to start all over again, certainly hurt. She wasn't either willing or able to talk to me about it, but Stuart was.

"That really bothers me a lot. I mean, *really* a lot. Here I set the child-free condition as a requirement of marriage, and now, two years later, I know Emily regrets it. Oh, she'll stick with her part of the deal, but I now see how much she wants a child. And that's a psychological cost I will have to bear—one she will have to cope with, too. What makes the situation worse is the fact that she did not prepare herself for anything but motherhood. She went to college—and took an office job for a few years. Her whole orientation was motherhood someday. And now things are not working out that way. She has a full-time job, but her heart isn't in it. If she just had some kind of career, something to really make her feel creative, I wouldn't feel so bad as I do. But she doesn't."

Emily and Stuart's situation is not unusual. Other child-free couples have less than unanimous feelings about nonparenthood. Perhaps, for instance, a wife is adamant about not having children, maybe even militant. Her husband may go along with her, partly because he feels it is not the man's role to be so interested in having children, or because he wants to respect her views. But he may be assuming the psychological cost of not having children, knowing that in a different situation he would have opted for and enjoyed fatherhood. And it can work in reverse. A man might feel very possessive about his wife, to the point where he insists that they not have children, even though that's what she wants. Just as some men or women use children as a means of influencing others, so it may happen with nonparenthood—for example, withholding the option of children to keep control of, or possibly even hurt, the other individual.

During the past five years a few, very few, preparenthood counseling services have come into being. Their purpose is to help such couples to sort out their feelings and, hopefully, to reach an ultimate conclusion.

And don't forget the psychological cost of realizing that your decision not to have children may hurt your parents—or some other relative, for that matter. It is a personal decision, but it can affect many others.

"We feel very badly about that," Joan admitted to me. For the first time she sounded more like a human being with human concerns than a nonparenthood enthusiast. "We know all the reasons why we aren't going to have children—but that doesn't help in conveying the point to our parents. They really want grandchildren, and it hurts to see how terribly disappointed they are. We're letting them down. Of course, it's not enough to make us change our minds—after all, it's our lives—but the hurt is there." She returned to her normal confident, carefree tone. "On the other hand, it really becomes obvious only a few times a year—you know, during the holidays."

Even the person people associate with the cause of nonparenthood—Ellen Peck—had some of these same feelings. "I was straight from a small town with a Catholic background," Ellen told me, "and yes, it was a difficult decision to make. I was worried about my parents' reaction, but I just hoped they would come to understand why having children wasn't right for us. Eventually they were able to accept this, but for a while it was a source of concern."

What's Your Mutual Focus?

I asked all the child-free couples I met if they had any type of child substitute—anything toward which they directed their mutual time and attention. The response of one nonfather immediately comes to mind: "Well, yes, there's Pinkus. As a matter of fact, right now he is under the couch unplugging your tape recorder." I resisted the urge to get up and look. "And there's Wally. He's currently dancing on the coffee table in front of you, and he just slipped another lump of sugar into your coffee. We've got lots of imaginary children in our lives—and they do impish, devilish, amusing things. No, we're not crazy. We just have very vivid imaginations. And we communicate to each other through these imaginary creatures. Do you think that's strange?"

In the previous year, I had met so many cats, dogs, plants, Teddy bears, stuffed owls, fish, horses, and hamsters in the homes of child-free couples, I had come to expect some type of object—living or otherwise—to provide a base for a mutual interest, a focus, something uniquely theirs, often something they could take care of. A *New Yorker* cartoon once captured the feeling very well. A woman was in a phone booth talking: "You'll be all right, dear. When I get home I'll move you into the sun. Now let me speak to the philodendron."

People of all ages and marital statuses, those with or without children, have animals—stuffed or otherwise—and vivid imaginations, and interests in hobbies and work. But it was my distinct impression that child-free couples had more than their share. More often than not, there was not just one cat, dog, Teddy bear, or whatever—but two or more. ("Muffin was getting lonely when we left her in the apartment all day, so we decided to get another cat.") Or there was a tendency to attribute life and a personality to inanimate or nonexistent things ("Our car's name is Bucephalus"). Frequently the object or animal is a gift from one partner to the other. One couple alternated giving each other plants—contributions to a collection that, at the time of my visit, numbered well over 150. I heard more than one couple refer to each other with nicknames that revolved around the theme "ma and pa."

Maybe the mutual focus is a career. Perhaps the couples write books together or work on the same research project. Or they may both have a strong common interest in music, drama, or poetry. Perhaps there is a need for a means of releasing a type of mutual "love energy," a need to be creative, to care for something or somebody. Obviously this is a need that a child can well fill—but for some couples a child substitute will do just fine, or maybe even better.

Referring again to the Silka and Kiesler study of childless couples, they wrote in *Family Planning Perspectives:* "Whether or not there is a significant increase among young couples in the choice never to have children may well depend on the status of the upper-level job market in the next few years—especially in the availability of rewarding careers for young women." In other words, the degree to which a couple—particularly the wife—experiences successful career development becomes a definite factor in their yes-or-no decision. On the other hand, Silka and Kiesler also note the possibility that in order to fill the child-free void, many couples tend to pour themselves into their work. The result is often greater employment success than might otherwise have been achieved.

Margaret Mead once noted that an unusual thing happens to those women who learn that they can't have children. "Suddenly their whole creativity is released—they paint or write as never before, or they throw themselves into academic work with enthusiasm, where before they had only a half a mind to spare for it."

Similarly, perhaps there is a tendency for the voluntarily child-free couple to intensify some particular joint interest, to give whatever mutual attention that would under other circumstances be directed at their child to another creature, object, or activity. Is there anything weird or morbid about this? "It's so sad," one mother told me, "to see couples without children waste all that love on an animal." But is it sad if they don't want children in the first place? Perhaps, for them, what would be more weird and more morbid would be the decision to create a child—when for them a cat will fill whatever need they have.

The ultimate point of this chapter has been to illustrate that no longer need any kind of stigma be thrust upon couples who voluntarily choose to remain child-free. Many continue to publicly endure their decision with various forms of rationalization and pretense. It is not necessary. No couple owes an apology; they are free to declare, without guilt or shame, the fact that they simply do not wish to have children. And that is far better than creating one more disturbed family of the future.

How do all these decisions about parenthood and nonparenthood turn out? How do nonparents feel when, after a while, they see their friends' children start college, and they themselves are coming home from work to find a sluggish eighteen-year-old cat? And how do people with children feel about their decision and about what they may have passed up? Chapter Eight is a glimpse into the future via other people's pasts.

⪜ 8 ⪝

Looking Back—
Parenthood/Nonparenthood:
Was It Worth It?

"So many of our friends seem to resent their children. They envy us our freedom to go and come as we please. Then there's the matter of money. They say their kids keep them broke. One couple we know had their second child in January. Last week, she had her tubes tied and he had a vasectomy—just to make sure. All this makes me wonder, Ann Landers. Is parenthood worth the trouble? Jim and I are very much in love. Our relationship is beautiful. We don't want anything to spoil it. All around us we see couples who were so much happier before they were tied down with a family. Will you please ask your readers the question: If you had it to do over again, would you have children?"

Letter to Ann Landers, 1976

It was an innocent letter, one out of the huge batch received by Ann Landers every day. She printed it, quite unprepared for the response. "I had struck an unprecedented number of raw nerves," Ms. Landers later wrote in *Good Housekeeping*. "That question unleashed an incredible torrent of confessions—'things I could never tell anyone else.'. . . Motherhood, which always rated right up there with apple pie, Old Glory, and the U. S. Marines was due for a reassessment."

The letter, almost classic by now, evoked over ten thousand replies. But the astonishing fact was that 70 percent of them carried a negative message, some version of "No, if I had to do it over again, *I would not have children.*" Ms. Landers goes on to comment: "Twenty years of writing the Landers column has made me positively shock-proof. Or so I thought. But I was wrong. The results of that poll left me stunned, disturbed, and just plain flummoxed."

Can it be really be that bad—*70 percent?* Well, not quite. This was not a random sampling; it was simply an invitation to followers of a popular daily column to send in their viewpoints. As Ms. Landers herself carefully reminded her readers, persons who are dissatisfied are much quicker to take pen in hand to air their gripes than are those who are happily content, or at least complacent. After all, it would be highly unusual to pick up a newspaper and read that no planes had collided over the Atlantic this week or no banks were robbed in Brooklyn today. As long as life is following its expected course, with no more than its usual number of difficulties, few people see that as "news" and consequently feel little compulsion to write in and say "Everything's fine."

Consider, too, that approximately 40 percent of those who said no did not sign their letters, while almost 100 percent of the yes submissions included names and addresses. Many of the latter asked that their letters be printed and their names included.

Stunned at the results of the Landers poll, the editors of *Good Housekeeping* decided to conduct a poll of its own readership to compare results. The letters poured in, numbering well beyond the ten thousand mark of the Landers poll. Editorial faces brightened as the pendulum swung far in the opposite direction. This time 95 percent said they *would* do it all over again. According to Rosemary Guss and Diane Coleman of the *Good Housekeeping* staff, the responses came from every stage of parenthood.

Guss and Coleman also mention that they received a few queries from women still debating the parenthood issue. They quote one of them:

> After reading the results of the Ann Landers poll I'm afraid to be a mother. If 70 percent of the parents feel their experiences are unpleasant, why should it be any different for me? If there are any positive responses, please print them.

Good Housekeeping did print some of them, and I quote a few excerpts below:

> *From a mother in Sebring, Florida:* From the moment of birth, my daughter and son have been a joy and comfort to me. Their father died of a heart attack when they were four and six, and for a long time they were my only reason for living. I don't feel my children owe me anything; on the contrary, I owe them. They made me laugh when I was down and kept me humble when I got proud.

From Colorado Springs, Colorado: I enjoy my children because I love my husband and he loves me, but it must go much deeper than just *love* because our children are an extension of each of us.

A woman from Pittsburgh: I've also seen the look of pure love and excitement as one of them handed me a dandelion as if it were an orchid. . . . I've been shocked when they did not agree with my values, but I am pleased with the adults they have become.

Flushing, New York: Yes, my grocery bills are outrageous, as are my fuel bills, utility bills, medical expenses, etc., etc. But my children do not hand me these bills. . . . Our hope for a better world lies with our children. It is my job and every other parent's to bring up these children into adults of tomorrow. I cannot think of a more rewarding (or more difficult) position in life.

And finally, from Sparks, Nevada: We shouldn't expect to live our lives through our children. A rose is a rose and a child is a child, to be valued for his or her unique existence.

In fairness the article reporting the survey also included a few negative responses. These tended to be less interesting, however; for the most part they expressed a general venting of anger rather than concrete criticisms. One ended with "nothing stops a screaming kid." (When all else fails, my next-door neighbor recommends adhesive tape.)

"But," you may logically be asking, "what do I have in common with the readers of *Good Housekeeping?* Maybe those who read the magazine regularly tend to be contented mothers in the first place." Good point. And again, it is still a readership survey, not based on a legitimate random sampling.

The year before the Landers poll was published in 1976, *McCall's* magazine commissioned the Gallup Organization to ask a representative sampling of American parents the same question: "If you had it to do over again, would you have children?" Respondents for the Gallup poll *were* scientifically selected on a random basis; therefore the results could more reliably be expected to approximate actual current trends. Yet this study never received anywhere near the publicity of the Landers poll.

The results? Ten percent of parents in the Gallup survey said no, they would not do it again. The *McCall's* editors found even that figure alarming in view of the fact that only ten years earlier a similar study at Princeton University revealed that less than one mother in a hundred regretted having children. While the 90 percent-pro figure is not quite as optimistic as the 95 percent-pro figure of the *Good Housekeeping* survey, it certainly is far less frightening than the 30 percent-pro figure of the Landers poll.

What does that 10 percent mean when it's translated into numbers? According to the U. S. Census Bureau, the Gallup poll suggests that approximately 5.5 million American parents of children under eighteen wish they had not had children. Put that way, pessimism tends to creep back into one's thinking again.

There were two distinct factors uncovered in the poll: (1) Parents with annual incomes of less than $10,000 were far less likely to want to repeat parenthood than those with higher incomes; and (2) a very high percentage of regretful parents were divorced or widowed, thus in most cases, they were raising or had raised their children alone. Respondents were also asked to choose the reasons that best explained their negative feelings. Fifty-two percent selected as an answer "the uncertainty of the world," the truthfulness of which I personally question in view of the fact that so few Americans are very much involved in either political or civic activities, not to mention the deplorable voting records at election time. Thirty-nine percent indicated that children are too expensive, 26 percent that they are too much responsibility. Other reasons included loss of personal freedom, overpopulation, and "too much hard work." Only one person gave as a reason that children were a disappointment, a fact commented on by sociologist E. E. LeMasters, author of *Parents in Modern America*. LeMasters believes that disappointment is probably a far greater reason for not wanting to repeat parenthood than most people are willing to admit: "I liken parenthood to military service. If you don't get killed or disabled, you don't regret having done it." I am inclined to agree with him. Even as a little girl I knew parents who were obviously disappointed with their children.

What of the indicated rise in rueful parents from less than 1 percent to 10 percent over the short span of ten years? More than simply an attitude change, the figures probably reflect among parents of the seventies a greater willingness toward honesty and openness. Dr. George W. Goethals, a clinical psychologist at Harvard University's Health Services, feels that about 10 percent of parents have always regretted having had children, but simply refused to admit it.

A crystal ball would come in handy in making decisions about parenthood. Barbara and Jeff would probably love to glimpse into it to see if, when they are in their sixties, they would feel as comfortable with the decision not to have children as they were in their thirties.

And Ann and Richard, who elected to have a child? They would certainly like to know if parenthood actually will bring them closer and provide for a family base in the future, or whether instead they will be wishing technology had advanced to the point where birth control was retroactive.

I could locate no such crystal ball, so I turned to the next best source: men and women who were near the end of or past their reproductive years and bound to whatever decision they had made. I'm going to tell you about five different circumstances. In three of them the decision was to have children; in two the child-free option was selected. Are these couples representative of the way people look back on decisions about having and not having children? Probably not. But at least they give you a view of the diversity of feelings hindsight can evoke—and how you get the whole gamut of responses when you ask the deceptively simple question, Was it worth it?

Peter and Meredith

"You mean, would we have children if we had to do it all over again?" Meredith asked me. She and Peter both appeared to be in their mid-sixties. We were sitting in their living room talking while she deftly weaved a knitting needle in and out of two masses of yarn. "Of course we would. There is just no way that we could imagine a life without children."

I was particularly interested to hear what Meredith and Peter had to say, because earlier they had told me something about their lives and the problems they had encountered; it appeared at least possible that there might be some second thoughts. They were married in the early 1930s, and they had two sons and a daughter during the first five years of marriage. Making ends meet for five individuals on Peter's salary—he worked on an assembly line in a toy factory—proved tough enough. But just after the third child was born, Peter was laid off, and Meredith, who told me she had never before seen the inside of an office, was forced to take a job as a clerical worker. Eventually Peter did find something more stable, but, because of severe respiratory problems, he was unable to work full time. So Meredith kept her job to supplement their income.

"It was difficult, let me tell you—especially for Meredith," Peter explained. "I was in bum health most of the kids' high school years, and the burden fell on her. I know now that it was the beginning of this emphysema. Looking back on it, it was a real struggle, but we didn't look at it that way at the time." He smiled broadly. "You know, things were different back then. You expected difficulties and problems. Things just didn't come as easily as they do for you youngsters today. We felt that children gave a real meaning to life. We were just thankful we could have them. I wouldn't trade anything in the world for the Christmas days when the kids were young. We didn't have much, but we had a lot, if you know what I mean. Watching them grow into adults—it's just great. And today, my sons are a real joy. For a man, there is nothing like that feeling of closeness you get from being with your boys. And I know Meredith feels that way about our daughter. No friend in the world can fill the same role. Yes, it was all worth it. Our children and grandchildren are terrific." He paused for a moment and his eyes lit up. "Have I shown you the album we have of our kids when they were just toddlers?" Peter went off to find it. It was about the only one I hadn't seen.

Meredith looked up from her knitting and spoke thoughtfully. "We didn't have money for fancy colleges. Both our sons went to the state university, and they both graduated near the top of their classes." She was obviously proud, and she took the opportunity to brag a bit. "One won a scholarship to law school, and the other is taking graduate courses at night. Neither Dad, here, nor I went to college, so it was exciting for us to follow them." She put her knitting aside and gave her full attention to what she was saying. "My daughter got married right after high school, and she and her husband now have three little girls. And are they ever adorable." She leaned forward and spoke firmly and sincerely. "I can't tell you how much happiness our children have brought us, how proud we are of them. Of course there were sacrifices. But what is life all about, anyway? It can't be fun all the time. You have to invest some of yourself if you ever want to get dividends. Right now, I feel I have only things to be thankful for. I have three normal, healthy children who have enriched our lives more than any amount of money possibly could have. What more could I ask for?"

So you're thinking, as Euripides put it, "How sweet to remember the trouble that is past." They can only remember the good parts. Maybe. Or, you might add, the real reason they are so enthusiastic about parenthood is that the children filled a void that for someone else could have been taken up by an interest in a job or hobby. Could be. But for some parents the good parts *do* far outweigh the disadvantages. And it is not just "career parents" who insist that parenthood was definitely worth it and that they would certainly do it over again. As we have seen, national surveys indicate that perhaps 10 percent of American parents feel they would have no children at all if they could return to "go." This may reflect rationalization of behavior that has already occurred, but the great majority of parents are probably sincere.

"I didn't have children just because there was nothing else for me to do," one mother of two grown sons told me. "I had them because I wanted them—and I managed to run a small but fairly lucrative business here in town, too. I had both a career and motherhood, and there is no doubt that, for me at least, it was the children who gave me the greatest pleasure. Parenthood is the most incredible maturing process. It changes people—almost invariably, I feel, for the better. The enforced responsibility and selflessness that it brings tend to make you a more interesting person, more aware and considerate and understanding of life and life's problems. Perhaps some people don't need this type of maturity—or maybe they have it to begin with, but I know that I am a much broader, happier person as a result of raising two children. I was busy—okay, sometimes harassed—but I vote yes for doing it over again!"

This mother's reaction reminded me of what *Ms.* magazine's Letty Cottin Pogrebin said when her child asked her, "Did you ever wish you never had us in the first place?"

She gulped and responded, "Sometimes my life is a little too full because I have you, but for me, it would be much too empty if I didn't."

Betty and Joe

"I bet I would really shock you if I told you that I wish I'd never had my two kids," Betty began. She had told me earlier that she was fifty-seven years old and had never before been part of a survey or opinion poll. She was enthusiastic about the opportunity to tell her story. She paused for a moment to see if she could interpret my reaction. Then she softened her tone. "You know, I don't *really* mean that, but the thought has crossed my mind, I mean about what life could have been for me if I hadn't been so tied down with them. I'm only being honest when I tell you that for every moment of joy parenthood has brought me, there has been an hour of anguish."

Her husband, Joe, was sitting next to her and had turned his head sharply when he heard what she had to say. He obviously felt she was overreacting.

"But maybe our situation is unique, Betty." He turned to me. "You see, we had some serious problems with the boys. Both of them required specialized medical help from the very beginning. One needed orthopedic surgery to straighten out his hip, and the other had severe asthma. We didn't know if the younger one was going to make it. Betty was tied down for ten straight years. For her, everything revolved around the children. At least I had my job."

"The health problems certainly made things worse," Betty went on, "but even without them, I know my life would have changed drastically. Both Joe and I were getting our master's degrees when our first was born. The pregnancy was fully planned, and I somehow had the idea that life would continue with just some minor changes. I thought being a mother might slow me down a year or so in my degree program. Boy, was I naïve!" Betty looked bitter as she spoke. "I had to drop out of school—I thought just temporarily. Then I thought it would be efficient if we had our second son as soon as possible so I could get on with my career. Well, we had the second—and after that, everything is a blank. Would you believe that right now I hardly remember the first twenty years of my married life? The kids are out on their own now, and sometimes at dinner I look at Joe and say, 'What happened?' It's like we were just married again, except twenty years of my life are gone. I'm back working now, but I've lost all the sense of ambition I once had. Now I'm just waiting for Joe to retire, and then I will, too."

Joe was getting increasingly uncomfortable about Betty's depressing assessment of the situation. "You shouldn't get the idea that all aspects of our parenthood years were negative," he told me. "We do now enjoy getting together with our sons, and we've come to accept them as individuals. You know, before you have children, you have an image of what they're going to be like—about what they will do in life. I'm a lawyer. I've got my own firm. But nothing came easy for me." Now he spoke intently. "I worked my way through college, graduate school, and then law school and earned every cent I've ever spent or saved. I was in the position to give my sons things I never had—like carte blanche at the colleges and graduate schools of their choice. I had great plans for them. So when my oldest son announced that he didn't want to go to college, I was—to say the least—distraught. I insisted he go anyway. He did, and dropped out after a year. He's now doing some free-lance photography work. That's always been his love. I still had high hopes that my younger son would be a lawyer—and possibly join my practice. But he too has other ideas. He's in college now—and tells us he wants to pursue some environmental or ecology issues after graduation." Joe sighed. "I realize now that you can guide children, but you ultimately have to accept what they are as individuals. If I had known that in the beginning, I think I would have enjoyed parenthood more—I could have relaxed more—and I think we would have avoided the strain that the conflicts between me and the boys put on our marriage." He turned to his wife with a slight smile. "But now that they're on their own and we're beyond the crises, we really enjoy them. Don't you agree, Betty?"

"Of course I do. Everything wasn't bad." She appeared to have cheered up significantly. "And I do look forward to their calls and letters and am always planning for their next visit. But the point I want to make is that if I had known what parenthood was—how it was going to change my life—I think I would have at least considered the option of not having children. Or maybe I would have waited until I had the education and career experience I think I needed. But, in fact, we didn't really think about realities. And that's where I feel cheated."

It's all right for a child to say, "My parents are such a *drag!*" Or "Boy, I just can't take my father anymore," or even, "I really can't stand my mother—she bugs me." But for parents to utter similar exclamations about their children? Never. Well, hardly ever.

In August 1937, *The American Mercury* carried a story by a mother entitled "I Do Not Like My Children." Part of this mother's message (which was reprinted in a National Organization for Non-Parents Newsletter) is as follows:

> I am the mother of four children. For twenty years I have squeezed myself dry for them. I have shed my own life—which was dear to me—without having time to be sorry, and given my life, bit by bit, to four individuals for whom, viewed objectively and not possessively, I do not care. Today, for the first time in twenty years, I have been left at home without them.
>
> "It must be terribly lonely in your house," neighbors say to me.
>
> "It's really rather restful," I reply cautiously. But what I want to do is dance, to crash cymbals, to praise the Lord.
>
> For twenty years I have done the impossible. Crisis after crisis has come up in our family and I have managed to avert, to heal, to work miracles. And now I have had enough. I want a respite from children.
>
> Not that I regret having had them. I know the experience of bearing children is the ultimate experience for any woman. Without this, a

woman is only half a woman and knows it all her life. Nor do I regret the years in which I have poured myself out for them. That is part of motherhood. It is the cycle of destiny into which a woman moves the instant her first-born is laid upon her arm. I shall continue to pour—and try not to pour unwillingly. What honors come to them come, vicariously, to me. I shall help them to be honored.

But—*I don't like them.*

Undoubtedly all parents feel this way at some point. But there are mothers and fathers out there who really mean it, who really wish they'd never had children, or at least wish they could free themselves of the direct burden of raising a child.

One of the first mothers I interviewed about the why's of parenthood reacted incredulously: "Who says I *wanted* them? Oh, I know I probably seem like one of those 'perfect' mother types, but I suspect it's mostly because I feel guilty all the time."

She began to explain more fully, her gentle voice constrasting strangely with the bitterness of her words. "I've been married and divorced twice and I have a child from each marriage. I practically never talk about this to anyone, but you seem to really understand that not all parents are one hundred percent in love with their children. I like mine okay. But they're always there as a constant reminder of my two really unhappy marriages. Every day I think about how I didn't do any of us a favor by giving birth to them. I'm a single woman again, but with none of the freedom. I try not to let them know that sometimes they're in the way, just by existing, but maybe they sense it. And I know they often blame me for the fact that they have no father at home like most of their friends do. So I try to be mother and father both. I've been both to my older kid most of his life. Yet their attitudes seem to be that I'm not doing a very good job at either one.

"I don't suppose I'd feel this bitter if at least one of my marriages had worked. Neither child was planned, but I don't think I would feel any worse or have any more problems than most parents if I were still married. I can't say I'd recommend *not* having children, but I'm sure it must be a whole lot easier in a good marriage.

"Would I do it over again? You can figure out the answer to that one. Can I make a suggestion? Please put in your book that couples should be really sure they've got a good marriage before they start producing kids. Separation and divorce are hard enough for adults to understand; children never quite do."

Judy Sullivan, in her book *Mama Doesn't Live Here Anymore*, tells of how she transgressed one of our strongest cultural taboos: she left her eleven-year-old daughter and husband and moved from Kansas to New York City. Why did she do this? Why did she run the risk of being labeled a monster? For her, marriage and motherhood were imprisoning her emerging self and threatening her sanity. As she described her decision to leave, "I saw it then . . . and see it now as something incredibly ruthless . . . and something absolutely necessary."

"No, I would never have dreamed of leaving them," another previously discontented mother told me. "I think that once you've undertaken the responsibility of bringing another life into the world, you have got to stick with it. But what I regret is that I stuck with it during one hundred percent of my time. Now that's what I feel made me resent my children. When I was raising children during the 1940s and 1950s, you just didn't hear much about women's lib. You would get strange looks if you announced that while motherhood was important to you, other things were, too. Children were supposed to be fulfilling enough. I know now that both my family and I would have had it easier if I had had some outlet, say even a part-time job and day help. Looking back on it, things would have been so much smoother that way. I think my daughter realizes this. She's expecting her first child next month and plans to go back to work as soon as possible."

In a lighter vein, humorist Erma Bombeck recently satirized parenthood opinion polls in her syndicated column. "In a recent poll," she writes, "teenagers admitted they were dissatisfied with their parents and would replace them if they could." Further along in the column she mentions that what the hypothetical teenagers did not know was that a hypothetical closet poll had been conducted among their parents with these results:

> Of two million parents polled, 97 percent said they were not happy with their children and would replace them if they could. An overwhelming number of mothers headed their list with Paul Newman, while fathers voted for the NFL. Two percent were undecided and one percent was under sedation and unable to comment.

Ms. Bombeck then proceeded to list the major reasons for parental dissatisfaction with children. Among them were: nagging ("Children always wanted to know where their parents were going and what time they would be home") and lack of privacy ("Every time a parent closed a door, a kid from the other side would yell, 'What are you doing in there with the door closed?' ").

The upshot of the mythical poll uncovered the fact that in spite of unhappiness with their parents, 95 percent of the teenagers said they wanted to get married and have children of their own. Ms. Bombeck's final comment: "It would serve them right."

Philip

"I just recently moved in here," Philip told me as I entered his suburban apartment which was cluttered with unpacked boxes and furniture. "I used to have a house about three blocks from here, but my wife died six months ago, and I realized that with my daughter married and with my working every day, there was no way I could keep it up. All I really need is a bedroom for myself and a guest room for when my daughter and her husband come to visit." Philip disappeared for a moment and came back with a picture, obviously taken many years before, of him and his daughter. He told me that he was sixty years old. His one daughter had been married for four years and had no children.

He had chosen this apartment because it was right near the railroad station he used to get to his downtown real estate office.

"Do you see your daughter often?" I asked.

He put the picture on the television set next to a more recent one of his daughter and her husband. "They're about a four-hour drive from here, so we hardly get together every weekend. But ever since Ann's death, we have been more closely in touch. We talk by phone about twice a week." He sat up straight and began to sound more animated.

"You're interested in children and why people have them, so let me tell you a little about my situation. My wife and I would have had more than one—but that's just the way it worked out. For us, children were a part of being married. We didn't ask as many questions as you young people do today. My daughter, Sue, brought us only happiness. She even married a man we really liked. And don't think that didn't worry us. So many of our friends suffered floods of tears over what they thought were unacceptable marriages for their children. So we were lucky." He was staring at the pictures again. "I'm alone now."

I started to ask him another question, but he evidently didn't hear me.

"And my daughter means even more to me than when Ann was alive." He looked up at me. "I don't want to sound melodramatic, but the truth is that it can be very lonely being by yourself at night, after having spent your whole life surrounded by other people. Sometimes when I come home from the city, make my dinner, and do some office work before I go to bed, it really hits me how alone I am. Oh, of course I've got friends, and they've been particularly good in these months after Ann's death. But friends are different from family. You can't always count on them in the same way. Take last month. For years, Ann and I had been invited to our neighbor's New Year's Eve parties. It was kind of a special event for our group. This year I wasn't invited. Why? Maybe the host and hostess thought they were doing me a favor by not putting me in the awkward situation of going to a celebration party alone. Or maybe they thought my presence would make them feel awkward. I don't know. But family is different.

"I know I can count on Sue and her husband—I don't mean financially—I've got all the money I could possibly want—but I mean emotionally I can be sure she is there. Does that make any sense to you?"

Philip told me more about his daughter, where she lived, and the kind of job she had. He obviously had much to be proud of, but something bothered him here, too. "She told me about a year ago that she and her husband might not have any children. Of course, I'd love a grandchild now. But it's more than that. I think by cutting yourself off from a personal family experience, you're missing a lot, and risking the possibility of being very alone someday. Now, I'm just telling you my feelings. I wouldn't want to have to go to the Golden Age Club for Thanksgiving dinner. On family occasions, you want family, not strangers, or even good friends. You get old faster than you think, you know. It kind of sneaks up on you. And you see life from a totally different perspective than you did when you were young and newly married."

After talking with Philip, it occurred to me that he, single-handedly, could make the birthrate go up. It is often said that there are two great human motivating forces: love and fear. More often than not, fear can be the stronger of the two. For Philip, as a widower, his one child—even though she is not living with him—provides a welcome emotional cushion. For a man and woman, the fear of not having that cushion may be an important element in the drive for having children. But to lend some balance to this, I must tell you that not all those I spoke to who had lost their spouses felt the way Philip did.

I asked Lynn Caine, author of the well-known book *Widow,* if she could relate to Philip's feelings about children being a comfort when you are left alone, even though her circumstances were very different. Lynn was in her forties when her husband died, leaving her with two small children, and, as she put it in her book, "I felt like one of those spiraled shells washed up on the beach. Poke a straw through the twisting tunnel, around and around, and there is nothing there. No flesh. No life. Whatever lived there is dried up and gone."

"Did you turn to your children for comfort? Did they in some way alleviate your grief?" I asked her.

"When Martin died I looked to my friends, not to my children. I needed adult relationships, not hours of 'I need this or that.' I adore my son and daughter, but I must say that I have earned every pleasure I have derived from them. Motherhood can be a one-way street for a long time, you know, and when I was left alone with them, the burden was even more intense. I wouldn't give up my children for anything in the world, but I can't say that they made my adjustment as a widow any easier. People shouldn't look to their children to alleviate loneliness. I'm really fierce on this subject. It's not fair to the kids to attempt to drain them in that fashion. It can only make them feel guilty for not being able to do enough."

Sandra and Bill

When I located Sandra and Bill and was invited to their home to do an interview, I felt as if I had isolated a rare breed of buffalo. "We're your token child-free-by-choice couple and we're over age fifty," Sandra said in a cheerful voice as we chatted by phone, "so come on up and ask your questions. We've answered them for years now, so we're getting pretty good at it."

We sat around their pool and caught the afternoon sun.

"All right, first you want to know why we didn't have any children, right?" Bill began. I had a feeling they were going to know all the questions. "We were married in 1940. I didn't know what my draft status was to be, so we decided to wait on having a family until we were more secure about the future. Two years after we were married I was drafted, and I spent four years in the navy. While I was in the South Pacific, Sandra finished college and got a job in publishing. We talked about having a baby a few times when I was home on leave, but we both thought about what would happen if I never came back. We decided to wait until that mess of a war was over with and then see where we were."

"When the war was over," Sandra broke in, "I was well established in my job and I was really enjoying it. When I was around thirty, we turned from talking about having children of our own and began to discuss adoption. When I think back on it, all the adoption talk was just our way of ruling out having children of our own, but at the same time leaving the door to parenthood slightly ajar. Just to give you an idea how serious we were about that, I never called one adoption agency."

"Okay. Now you want to know if we have regrets, right?" Bill said. "No, I can't say we do. I've seen so many unhappy parents, have heard endless sagas about the sadness children can bring you. And I see lots of very lonely people who have three or four children. We have a great life. Money has never been a problem; we travel and can afford luxuries like this pool and a small cabin cruiser. No, at least I have no anxieties about not being a father. What about you, Sandra?"

She shook her head. "No real regrets, but I have had thoughts about what a child of ours would be like—what it would look like now. Sometimes when I see a youngster in a store I can't help thinking about that. On the other hand, I never felt that I wanted to share my life with anyone else but Bill. And we have had a great life." She winked at Bill and turned to me. "When we were in our thirties, I recall that we got a great deal of criticism. Everyone—but everyone—we knew had children, and we were constantly being labeled selfish. You know the expression, marriage breaks up the old gang? For us it was the arrival of babies that had that effect. Our supply of friends dwindled there for a while—and we turned even more to each other. But now that most of our friends' children are grown, we have more in common with them again."

"For us nonparenthood has worked out just fine," Bill continued. "Our marriage is probably much stronger than it would be if we had run the risk of the dissension that children can add. Of course, because our marriage is so good, one thing does worry us. It will be really rough on the one who's left. We have been very independent; we haven't gotten really involved in anyone else's family. We are our own unit. If I could change something, it might be that. In the long run I think we might be better off if we had turned a little bit more of our attention outside of our twosome—as an insurance policy. But that's easier said than done. We both work long hours and want to spend our leisure time alone together. It is an effort to cultivate other relationships, but maybe it's worth it—we'll see, I suppose."

Mary

I waited for about twenty minutes in Mary's office. I had never met or talked with her before; her secretary had set up an appointment for me. All I knew was that she was a psychiatrist, divorced, and in her mid to late thirties. I also knew that she had no children. She was aware of what I wanted to talk about, so when I sat down on the couch in her office, she got right to the point.

"Yes, I regret not having children. I really feel that, despite my educational and work experiences, I have missed something—a basic life experience. I'm thirty-eight and have a great career, but I'm ready for something else now. Maybe for me generativity came late. Let me tell you how it happened. I sort of feel as though I should be on the couch!"

She leaned back in her chair. "I was married when I finished my residency—I was just turning twenty-nine. My former husband is a radiologist, and as committed to his work as I am. He felt very strongly about not having children, primarily because I was a career woman." She paused and thought for a moment. "But no, there was more than that: he didn't have the qualities of a father, either, and I think he knew it. So we decided no, and we turned to our work. A few of our colleagues were making the same decision, and for us it seemed like the thing to do, too. We were divorced about a year ago—and that is when I began to feel as though I really had missed something by not having a child." Mary frowned and looked toward the ceiling. Then she leaned forward. "It has become clear to me that the reason I really didn't choose parenthood was because of my husband and what he was like. If he had been a different man—more flexible, warmer—I think we could have managed it. In other words, if I had had someone to share the emotional and practical burdens as they came up, I would have opted for motherhood. If I had married someone else, I would probably have a child now." She looked troubled by that thought. But she went on.

"About ten years ago, when my friends' kids were young, my husband and I would say to each other, 'Aren't we lucky not to have to be doing *that*?' But now those kids are like little adults, and they've become interesting to me."

"Do you think about this often? Does it get you down?" I asked.

"Yes, I have thought a great deal about it recently. I've been dating a number of men in my first year of 'freedom,' but even if I get married again, this time to the right type of man, would I have enough time to squeeze in a baby? Probably not, unless I get married tomorrow, and I don't have any immediate prospects. That part gets me down. I've toyed with the idea of just having a baby, married or not, maybe being artificially inseminated to keep it anonymous. But I come back to my original problem. I would not want to be the only participating parent. I think a child needs two dedicated people. Well, I'm not going to dwell on the issue, but I think you should know that as the parenthood decision doesn't always work out, neither does the nonparenthood one. I wish now I had thought more about it. If I had realized five or ten years ago what having a child would mean to me now, it might have awakened me. I might have left my marriage earlier."

Can people find out too late that they made a mistake in choosing nonparenthood? Yes, but you can find you made a mistake by becoming a doctor instead of a lawyer, too. There appears to be just one remedy for reducing the I-made-a-mistake anxiety later on. And that's thinking about the decision and its ramifications before it becomes irrevocable. As Mary pointed out, the decision to remain child-free can backfire if it isn't well thought out. Especially in an age when being child-free is considered the new and "in" thing, and the stigma against voluntarily childless marriages appears to be diminishing, a bandwagon approach to nonparenthood could mean trouble later on.

As Eric Hoffer put it in *The Passionate State of Mind,* "When people are free to do as they please, they usually imitate each other." And imitation or fad following does not make the basis for a good decision.

I decided to contact Gael Greene to see if, more than twelve years after her historic article on nonparenthood, she was still as enthusiastic.

"Absolutely," she told me. "I have never regretted it. At the time I wrote the article I felt I could not successfully divide myself into writer, lover, mother. Other women do it, but few succeed without incredible acrobatics and great measures of guilt. So I chose the two roles that were most important to me. Nobody I knew ever sat down as we did and said, 'Shall we have children?' They simply had them. But my husband and I looked at the lives of our friends and found them tyrannized by the real or imagined demands of their children. I was depressed seeing all my friends' dreams of glory drowning in pools of dirty diapers. My husband and I felt close and full of needs and unwilling to share each other with anyone. We treasured our privacy and our freedom from responsibility. Mine was not "A Vote against Motherhood" as the *Saturday Evening Post* titled it. It was a vote against motherhood for me. And my life has been so full of adventure and fulfillment, I have never felt anything was missing. There is a good life—a beautiful life—without children. Oh, yes, people still ask, 'What will you do when you're old with no children to love and care for you?' But parenthood is no guarantee of love. I've seen too many old people sitting abandoned on park benches and in nursing homes waiting for children who never came. Anyway, if I'm lucky, I will have a husband when I'm old, or a lover, and certainly good friends, nieces and nephews, and perhaps if I've the energy, a protégé. If I'm cranky, I'll have tropical fish and a cat."

In response to her would-you-do-it-again question, Ann Landers found that the letters she received fell roughly into four different categories. First were the ecologists, those who were deeply concerned about global hunger, overpopulation, and nuclear weapons. Second were those who felt that children had ruined their marriage, that their happiest years were the prebaby ones. The third category included those from parents whose grown children had left home and were seemingly too busy to give much attention to mom and/or pop. And fourth were the letters from parents of teenagers in trouble. Ms. Landers, too, mentions the disappointment factor: "Every mother wants her daughter to be beautiful and popular, especially if *she* wasn't. When the daughter turns out to be neither, the mother feels let down." The same holds true for a father whose son chooses not to follow him into the same line of work: "So Dad is disappointed and Junior feels inadequate and rejected."

Do you notice a recurrent theme here? Apparently, too many parents start out with a preconceived notion of what they want their children to be and to become. In the *McCall's* report of the Gallup poll, a complaining father of two boys is quoted as saying: "You raise them, you go through the hard times, and then you find out that what you've created are two independent people who go off and leave you alone." I get the impression that he must have preferred to raise two mindlessly *de*pendent people who were willing to hang around the house indefinitely.

And, too, it hardly seems fair to blame "the kids" for so many of life's misfortunes, as though a child were a kind of built-in scapegoat. It's conceivable that children can contribute to the problems of a situation that is already less than ideal. What is *not* conceivable is that a child or children can all alone cause the collapse of marriage, career, or personal identity. If kids wield *that* much power, perhaps we ought to consider the instigation of a juvenile State Department.

Perhaps you can identify with the feelings of some of the individuals and couples mentioned in this chapter. Maybe parts of what they say are relevant to your thoughts. But ultimately it is you who have to decide, on the basis of your own circumstances, needs, and priorities, after asking yourselves all the questions necessary to find out who you are, what specifically it is you want, and how much you are willing to compromise in return. Maybe Chapter Ten will help on that. But first, we deviate for a moment to consider some of the practical aspects of the parenthood question. After all, you can't make a decision without knowing these facts.

The Baby Brochure: Questions about the Logistics of Parenthood

This chapter deviates from the general path we've been following. Some of the questions raised were on my mind as I was making a decision about the if and when of parenthood, and others were asked by couples I spoke with. An intelligent decision can't be made without some practical information. We need to know how old is too old to have a baby; how much it now costs to have and raise a child; what the chances are of choosing in advance a prospective baby's sex; how to go about deciding your own ideal family size; and the facts about the alternate path to parenthood—adoption. Sobering though it will be, you should have the facts about what can possibly go wrong during pregnancy and what types of risks you face. Whether you're leaning for or against parenthood, you need to know what's involved one way or the other. Because of biological realities, the questions and answers below are directed at the female of the species, but certainly the subject matter should be of interest to prospective fathers.

When Is the Ideal Time to Have a Baby?

If you *are* going to have a child, there are a number of questions you will probably be asking yourself: Is there a time that will be convenient in terms of juggling parenthood and a joint career? How late can you postpone childbearing and still hope for a problem-free pregnancy? How do you know when you are emotionally ready to accept the responsibilities that go with raising a new human being? In short, when is the best time for you to have a first or later baby?

Death, taxes, and childbirth. There's no convenient time for any of them. So goes the proverb. Shortly after her marriage, Annie in Betty Smith's *Joy in the Morning* finds that her period is two weeks late and prays, "Please, God . . . don't let it happen yet. Not right now. Give us a year of grace. Just one year. And I'll never ask you for another favor as long as I live." As most couples do, Annie and her husband wanted some time alone before the two of them became the three of them. So the first factor that might go into determining your ideal time to have a baby is how long you've been married.

Given the current high divorce rate, it is neither pessimistic nor impractical to assess your marriage, making sure it is well grounded before deciding to turn a twosome into a threesome. Certainly every couple has some problems, some source of conflict; however, a significant disagreement or general lack of communication may well be reason enough to postpone parenthood.

As we've already discussed, having a child to fill in a gap in one's own life, possibly to patch up a deteriorating marriage, is hardly an admirable motivation for creating a baby. Parenthood can offer a new dimension, a new type of richness to a marital relationship, but it certainly cannot make up for shortcomings that existed beforehand. Indeed, the reality is that the first child brings many psychological changes to marriage, producing a negative impact within people who are highly immature, secretly dependent, and who themselves wish to be children. For some women, motherhood might complicate domestic problems; a young child demanding time and attention leaves little opportunity for resolving marital difficulties that may exist.

Having a baby very soon after you are married (even if the child is conceived after the wedding) may not be ideal because most marriages take some time to "settle down." Yet it can be argued that there is such a thing as waiting *too* long after marriage to have a baby. You may get too used to having things your way, too accustomed to it being just the two of you, and the transition to parenthood may be more difficult to make.

You probably are not surprised to learn that couples who have a baby soon after they get married—say, within a year—have a highter-than-average divorce rate. Given that it can take some time to adjust to married life, it is understandable why pregnancy and parenthood might add an additional strain.

There may be no completely convenient time to be pregnant and care for a newborn infant but, on the other hand, if you really do want a child, there are times which are less inconvenient than others. The key to handling the practical questions is in being both realistic and flexible.

Take your career plans into account. You may not want to miss a great opportunity in your chosen profession or feel that you have to take a leave of absence before you are at the least somewhat established. Were you to do so, you might harbor some resentment that would interfere with the development of the intimate emotional relationship you'll want to develop with your child. By assessing the current and future situation at your office, you may be able to find a logical time for "intermission." But on the other hand, you should attempt to avoid being unrealistic in your evaluation. Ask yourself if your job will really be less demanding a year or two from now, if you will be traveling less, having a more regular work schedule. "I have been saying for the past two years that my job was just too hectic right now to take time to have a baby," one thirty-nine-year-old advertising executive told me, "but all of a sudden I realized that my job was *always* going to be hectic. So now is as good—or as bad—a time as any to take off some time."

Being realistic here will help you avoid postponements which may result in your having a child when it is actually less, rather than more, convenient. Similarly, if it is finances that concern you, do some calculations to predict, to the extent that you can, what your future economic situation will be. Yes, it is expensive to have a child, and it is nice to have some money put aside before starting a family. But if you do some careful thinking and predicting, you may find that, given the inflation that is likely to be with us for the next few years, the difference between right now and three years from now in terms of how much money you have available might not be all that significant.

In coping with practicalities, be flexible. Don't lock yourself into thinking there is just one way of doing things. For example, having a baby doesn't mean that you have to leave your apartment and move to a house, or to a larger house. There are ways of managing, either by getting larger living quarters or by doing some clever rearranging in the place you have. And becoming a mother doesn't automatically mean that you have to sever all ties with the business world. Of course, life will change if you have a baby. If you are currently working nine or ten hours a day at an office job, something will have to give if the child is to get the attention he or she deserves. But there are ways of working out part-time assignments, or taking a limited leave of absence during the first few months or year of a child's life.

Obviously, you can't count on postponing parenthood until you've achieved what you believe to be complete success in your career. First, that time may never come, and second, if it ever does, you may be past the reproductive years. But you can get yourself established and get a feeling that you know your own nook in life. A marriage should be a combination of two complete individuals, not a man and a woman who are looking to each other for mutual completion, and the approach to parenthood should be the same. Prospective parents should try to establish their own identity before they participate in creating a new, separate one. Most important, you should guard against creating a child as a means of filling an otherwise empty life.

The benefits of postponing parenthood until you really know yourself and where you are going in life are multifold: you'll feel more comfortable with your decision to have a baby; you'll be likely to welcome the child more enthusiastically, with fewer reservations, fewer second thoughts; you'll have more to offer a newborn child if you, yourself, are a complete person.

Ibsen's Nora, heroine of *A Doll's House,* demonstrated this by noting the importance of being a whole person, one who has been able to come to terms with her own shortcomings before assuming the responsibilities for someone else's. Once more the message is, Know thyself.

Can You Be Too Young or Too Old to Have a Child?

In *Future Shock,* Alvin Toffler notes that once childbearing is detached from its biological base, nothing more than tradition will suggest that having children at a relatively early age is good. He suggests that men and women over sixty might prove to be ideal parents. They would have had their careers and made their contributions, and they would be in a position to spend a considerable amount of time with a growing child. That is, if they could buy their embryos and have them grow at that point. But we still have to deal with the biological limits placed on childbearing.

The past twenty years have introduced a definite trend toward later childbearing. In 1960, 20 percent of women under age thirty who had ever been married were still childless; by 1975 that figure had risen to 32 percent. According to Linda Silka and Sara Kiesler in *Family Planning Perspectives*, even accounting for those women who were not childless by choice, by 1977 approximately three million American women under age thirty had intentionally postponed motherhood. Nevertheless, the data indicated that only 4.6 percent would remain childless. And while only about 5 percent of them would delay giving birth beyond the age of thirty, the figures reveal a distinct trend toward later childbirth. (Further proof of the trend toward "older" mothers is found in the changing maternity fashions. Many styles are now being geared to the tastes of somewhat older women.)

Of course I had been only too well aware of my own reasons for having delayed thoughts of motherhood, but I was curious about other women's reasons. The same answer, and sets of answers, came back at me over and over: "I wanted to become established in my career first." "We couldn't really afford a baby sooner; we wanted to get a little money saved." "I just hadn't met the man I wanted to be the father of my children." "There were too many things to do, places to go; I didn't want to be tied down with a child right away." "I needed to get myself together, find out who *I* am first." "I wanted to be free to travel." "I wanted to be sure my marriage was really solid."

One mother, a temporarily "retired" public relations executive was waiting in line ahead of me at the supermarket late one afternoon. She was quite pregnant and had a three-year-old boy in tow. She told me she was thirty-five, though I would have guessed her to be younger. "I wanted to feel comfortable about taking a few years out to raise my own family," she said. "Right now I know I can go back to work anytime I want to. I was reasonably successful at what I did, and I have a scrapbook to prove it. I handled some good PR programs. It's good for me to know that I can do that; I'm not plagued with that locked-in feeling so many of my friends have."

She began unloading her shopping cart as she continued: "Quite a few of my girl friends got married right after college—or sooner. Babies started arriving almost immediately and I've watched what's happened over the years. As soon as the novelty of a brand-new baby wore off, a lot of these mothers began feeling antsy. All the time they were convinced they were missing something, and I'm sure they probably were! But most of them stayed at home because it was the traditional thing to do, or because—would you believe?—because their husbands insisted. Some got involved in affairs with other men, just out of boredom, I think. I watched marriages disintegrate, and children grow into young tyrants or, just as bad, little puppets afraid to open their mouths or wiggle their feet unless specifically told to do so. And I saw some of these friends almost destroy themselves in a desperate attempt to bring some kind of meaning into their lives."

"For me," she went on, as my own groceries were being checked out, "I'm perfectly contented right now. My family provides more than enough meaning and pleasure. But I know a lot of the reason for that is because I did the other things first. I have a pretty realistic notion of exactly what I am and am not missing. I don't have to sit at home stewing and wondering. What I'm doing right now is exactly what I want to be doing. I heartily recommend later parenthood!"

Before further pursuing the pros and cons of delayed childbirth, let's first take a look in the opposite direction. Can you be too young to have a baby? Definitely, yes. For instance, high-school-age mothers run greater risks than older ones of complications such as toxemia, anemia, and prolonged labor, and their emotional adjustments to pregnancy and parenthood are often more difficult. In addition, even though younger teenagers are adequately equipped for pregnancy and birth, their reproductive systems may continue to be somewhat immature for a time, increasing the possibility of birth defects due to imperfect cell division.

And further, women who begin having sexual intercourse before the age of eighteen have two to three times the frequency of cervical cancer as do women who experience their first coitus at a later age. (Women who have both early sexual experience *and* multiple partners are at even higher risk of contracting this disease.)

But the more common concern among couples trying to make up their minds about the yes or no of parenthood is on the other end of the age gamut. A familiar question is, when do I become Old Mother Hubbard?

Maybe you've heard some old wives' tales (or more appropriately, old mothers' tales) that could cause a woman at age 29.9 to act as nervous as a turkey in November. But before you panic, consider the facts. Most gynecologists feel that, generally speaking, first pregnancies in the early thirties, and subsequent pregnancies in the late thirties, present no significantly greater risk than do those that occur when the mother is in her twenties. With increasing medical knowledge and advances in prenatal diagnostic techniques, some gynecologists have even upped the relative safety level into the forties. In the majority of cases, the timing of parenthood is a socially rather than a medically oriented decision.

There are some specific medical facts you should know about what could possibly go wrong and how a woman's age may increase the risk. Before I say anything else about possible pregnancy-related problems, I am going to acknowledge again that this is hardly the cheeriest topic for discussion with potentially prospective parents, but it does reflect reality. However with one major exception that you will read about later, problems related to pregnancy and childbirth at *any* maternal age are very rare.

Although it has not been thoroughly documented, there is a strong probability that a woman's fertility—that is, her chances of conceiving—does decline as she gets older. Indications are that the decline is fairly slow during the thirties, but very rapid during the forties. Babies born to women in their fifties are rare. "We don't really know for sure if a woman's fertility decreases gradually during her thirties," Dr. Allan Rosenfield, Director of the Center for Population Sciences at Columbia University told me. "One thing that is obvious, though, is that a woman who waits until she is thirty-five or so to seek a first pregnancy is going to have less time to work out fertility problems if they do come up."

At birth a female baby's ovaries contain all the eggs, or oocytes, that will ever be produced during her lifetime. As the years go by, the supply gradually becomes depleted. Eventually, as a woman approaches menopause, she ovulates less and less frequently even though she continues to have normal menstrual periods. Estimates vary, but a woman between the ages of forty and forty-five probably ovulates in only about 75 percent of her menstrual cycles. After that the figure drops abruptly to nearly 60 percent, gradually approaching zero as she nears the age of fifty.

Not only is ovulation affected by age, but patterns of hormone secretion also tend to alter, leading to disruption of normal processes even when the woman does ovulate. Hormonal changes can result in "overripening" of the eggs, rendering them either infertile or genetically defective. Given that approximately 15 percent of any woman's eggs are "duds" to begin with, and that another 25 percent will spontaneously abort after being fertilized, it's clear that advancing age could reduce a woman's fertility considerably. In addition, age tends to bring on certain medical problems such as fibroid tumors or endometriosis. Both conditions contribute to lower fertility.

Male fertility is subject to the effects of aging as well, but to a much lesser degree than in the female. Nor are men hampered by the biological cutoff date as females. (Even men in their nineties have been known to father children.) Nevertheless, male fertility does begin to decline after the mid-twenties, though very gradually. If a couple is in their thirties, problems of infertility could be very slight in either partner alone; but combined, the ability to conceive could be substantially lessened.

Other things being equal, and unless a known fertility problem of a more drastic nature exists, there is no particular danger in delaying childbirth until the thirties if a couple so desires. What you should take into account in your scheduling, however, is the fact that conception may take longer than you would normally expect. You should also add in a few extra months if you've been on the Pill. A woman's body needs some time to begin proper functioning on its own again and, in fact, most gynecologists recommend that you avoid becoming pregnant for at least three months after the Pill is discontinued. Many women take as long as six months to begin ovulating on a more or less regular basis again.

When a pregnancy does occur, the risk of having a miscarriage may be slightly higher among women who have their first child after age thirty—and even greater among those who wait until after thirty-five.* Although at any maternal age the overwhelming percentage of pregnancies that proceed as far as four months lead to a successful birth, a substantial number of them do end in miscarriage: about 15 percent of pregnancies are known to terminate this way. It is estimated that up to 50 percent of all conceptions end naturally during the first week or so when most women may not even suspect they are pregnant. Perhaps the woman thinks she is just having a rather late and heavy menstrual flow, but conception may indeed have taken place. Again, these are depressing statistics, and a woman who experiences an early miscarriage is of course disappointed. But she is likely to interpret the event more as a lost opportunity than as a lost baby, and she is eager to start a new pregnancy as soon as possible.

If the pregnancy is successful and a live birth occurs, there is a very small chance that the baby will die in the first year of life. When deaths do occur, they are often related to congenital malformations, premature delivery, poor nutrition during pregnancy, low birth weight, or a contagious disease. There is no reason to believe that babies of older mothers run a higher risk of infant deaths. Generally, the percentage is under 3 percent for all babies.

In the abstract, it's easy to brush aside infant deaths as just another statistic. But when it does happen, it is an almost unbearable tragedy

*The percentage of reported miscarriages rises from about 9 percent among mothers whose first pregnancies occur when they are 20-29 years old, to 15 percent for those 30-34 years of age, and to 28 percent for those over age 35.

for a couple who have been planning a pregnancy for months, and anticipating for nine more. What is 3 percent of a national statistic becomes 100 percent if it happens to you. In Sinclair Lewis's *Cass Timberlane,* young Jinny marries Cass, an older, staid divorced judge. They are both thrilled when Jinny learns she is pregnant, but the happiness is marred by the discovery that she has diabetes. After a safe delivery, the baby soon dies. Lewis writes that Jinny "lay with her face deep in the pillow, whimpering like a sick and frightened kitten." She goes into seclusion for many weeks, before emerging one day with an uncontrollable desire to give a party every night.

It's not pleasant to acknowledge that infant deaths do still occur in this country; however, it is encouraging that we have one of the lowest infant mortality rates in the world, and today the chances of losing any baby are very slim.

Does age at pregnancy have any effect on the mother's health? As with most of the problems we're discussing here, serious maternal complications during labor and birth are unusual anyway—and maternal deaths these days are exceedingly rare. There is some evidence that women over the age of thirty-five develop more than their share of problems, but the differences aren't significant. If you want to have your first child in your late thirties, your physician will consider you in a high-risk category and will generally see to it that you receive special handling. (He even has a special label for you: elderly primipara.)

In *You're Not Too Old to Have a Baby,* Jane Price cites a study of labor and delivery problems that was conducted by Sidney Kane on twenty-six thousand women aged twenty-five and over who were pregnant for the first time. The findings revealed that compared to the younger mothers, babies of women over age thirty-five more frequently tended to be in abnormal fetal positions, and/or to require the use of forceps or the procedure of Caesarean section. With reasonable medical attention, none of these is considered dangerous. And while it's a generally accepted medical fact that older women tend to spend approximately 25 percent more time in labor, there are no indications that their labor is particularly difficult. On the general subject of first-time older mothers Ms. Price writes:

> I found no pattern among the older women I interviewed that distinguished their childbirth experiences from those of women much younger. What stood out was their attitude toward having a baby. These women all appeared to have gone through pregnancy with a

remarkable degree of composure, even the ones who ran into trouble. In their descriptions of pregnancy, labor, and delivery, I didn't discern a single note of hysteria or complaint.

There is one other factor to consider at this point. Evidence exists that a woman's age at her first pregnancy is an important factor in determining her chance of developing breast cancer. We've long known that women who don't have children are more likely to develop cancer of the breast than are those who do become mothers. Presumably the hormonal changes that occur during pregnancy offer some protection against this particular form of cancer.

But recently we've learned from a series of international studies that women who have their first child after thirty-five run about a 20 percent greater risk of breast cancer than do those who never have children at all. And post-thirty-five first-time mothers are even more likely to develop this disease than are those whose first child was born earlier. This relationship between mother's age and breast cancer appears to apply only to the first birth. Having subsequent children after thirty-five appears to have no effect on breast cancer risk.

These statistics should be put in perspective. A 20 percent increase in probability of disease is not really all that alarming. People who smoke a pack of cigarettes a day are ten times more likely to develop lung cancer than nonsmokers—that's a 1000 percent increase in risk. So if you are planning a pregnancy, the breast cancer risk factor will probably be only one of many you will want to think about.

What about Genetic Problems?

About 1 in every 200 to 250 pregnancies is affected by a chromosomal abnormality of some type; 88 percent of these pregnancies end naturally, usually in the first few weeks after the missed menstrual period.

Probably the best-known genetic defect is Down's syndrome, or mongolism. Children with this disease are usually physically and mentally deformed and have a reduced life-span. Mongoloids usually have an IQ ranging between thirty and fifty (though occasionally it may be slightly higher), and tend to be born with a greater number of heart defects than average, as well as an increased susceptibility to colds and other respiratory infections. Mongolism is generally easy to diagnose because of the unique physical characteristics presented: slanting eyes, small ears, slightly pro-truding lips and tongue, and short hands, feet, and trunk. Sometimes an unusual crease appears in the palms of the baby's hands.

What is of interest here is that there is a definite association between increasing maternal age and increasing risk of mongolism. (This is the exception I mentioned earlier. Unlike any of the other problems we've mentioned so far, the relationship of a mother's age and the risk of mongoloid birth is definitely significant.) A woman under age thirty runs about a 1-in-1,500 risk of having a mongoloid child; the chances are 1 in 750 births, and 1 in 280 births, at ages thirty to thirty-four and thirty-five to thirty-nine respectively; and the risk goes up to 1 in 130 (or, according to some sources, a 1-in-100 chance) between maternal ages forty and forty-four. At forty-five and over the risk increases to an unsettling one in forty births. This correlation between advancing maternal age and mongolism applies to both first and subsequent births.

To everyone's frustration, the exact cause of mongolism and the underlying reason for its increased incidence after maternal age thirty are still obscure. We do know that mongolism is a chromosomal disorder. A mongoloid baby has forty-seven chromo-somes in the cells of its body, rather than the normal forty-six, with the extra one being attached to the twenty-first pair. That is, pair number twenty-one contains three chromosomes rather than two; thus the reason this disease also bears the name of Trisomy twenty-one. Presumably, the effects of aging in some way alter cell divison, but just *how* or *why* is still open to speculation. Some researchers have proposed that this "mistake" in cell division can occur in either the egg or the sperm, but the close correlation with rising maternal age tends to indicate that the error is most commonly, if not always, associated with the egg.

I have already mentioned that a woman is born with her lifetime supply of eggs (as opposed to a man who is constantly manufactur-ing sperm). Thus when a woman has been around for thirty-five years, so have her eggs. Not only are the eggs subject to direct effects of aging (malfunctioning hormones, for instance), but they have had a great many years in which to become exposed to various types of physical or chemical forces, such as radiation, that might have damaged the genetic material.

In terms of what has been established about mongolism, it is obviously better not to postpone pregnancy too long. Also, conception can be timed so that you reduce the probability of fertilizing an old egg. (See the Appendix on pregnancy planning for tips on this.) Still another resource is *amniocentesis,* a medical procedure whereby amniotic fluid is drawn from the sac surrounding the developing fetus in the uterus to determine in advance if the child is a mongoloid. If mongolism is detected, there's the option of terminating the pregnancy.

There are a number of other chromosomal problems, all of which are relatively rare. I'm going to mention three serious ones, simply to give you some idea of how they are transmitted. The purpose of this discussion is not to depress or discourage you, but to emphasize the desirability of seeking genetic counseling services if you have any reason to believe you might be at risk of passing on a genetic disease (specifically, if any member of your family is or was affected).

A number of hereditary diseases are known to be concentrated in certain races or ethnic groups. *Sickle-cell anemia,* for instance, a painful blood disorder, is common among blacks. Some one in ten or twelve healthy American Negroes carries the sickle-cell trait. Ironically, what is now viewed in the United States as a defective gene once helped the African forefathers, for the *trait* provides protection against malaria; blacks thrived in malaria-infested areas that became known as the "white man's graveyard." Having the trait does not mean that the individual carrier of it necessarily has a serious problem, although the carrier will be told to avoid situations where oxygen is limited (for instance, high mountain climbing, unpressurized airplanes, alcohol intoxication, or deep-sea diving).

The *disease,* however, is usually totally debilitating. Tragically, children affected with sickle-cell anemia rarely survive to young adulthood. There is currently no known treatment for this affliction, though research is in process. Thus it is vital for you to know whether or not you are a carrier. If one prospective parent is a carrier of the sickle-cell trait and the other is not, none of their offspring will have the disease. Their children will have a fifty-fifty chance of being carriers. If both parents are carriers, the chance of having a completely normal child is reduced to 25 percent: 50 percent of the children will have the trait, and 25 percent will have the disease itself.

Tay-Sachs disease, an enzyme deficiency that invariably kills its young victims, is widespread among Jews whose ancestors came from eastern or central Europe. About 90 percent of Tay-Sachs babies born in the United States are of Jewish heritage. The baby at birth may appear perfectly normal and indeed may be exceptionally beautiful. But after six months, development slows down and the brain gradually deteriorates. The chance that two carrier-parents will produce a child with this disease is one in four for each pregnancy.

Cystic fibrosis, a generally fatal glandular disease that affects between twenty thousand and twenty-five thousand Americans, mostly children and young adults, appears to be almost entirely confined to Caucasians. An individual carrier, on a random basis, has about a one-in-four-hundred chance of marrying another carrier. (If a carrier chooses a first cousin as his bride, the chances are one in eight that she also is a carrier.) If two unaffected carriers do marry and plan to have children, the chances are one in four that the baby will inherit the disease.

There are a great number of other hereditary, or chromosomal, diseases, including some which are related to the advancing age of the father. The incidence of all of them, however, is so exceedingly low—even for parents in their twenties—that there is little point in including them here. To do so would only paint an unnecessarily gloomy and distorted picture of the risks involved.

In addition to genetically caused disorders, there are a few other conditions often associated with maternal age. Compared to younger mothers, older ones tend to have babies who are born prematurely or have lower birth weights, and who are more likely to be victims of such conditions as cleft palate, congenital heart defects, and hydrocephalus (excessive buildup of fluid in the brain). Again, the statistics here are of no great significance since the overall incidence is so low.

It is not uncommon to come across medical advice advocating that the risk of birth defects at any age can be minimized by spacing children at least two years apart and by limiting family size. The reasoning behind some of this advice is a bit obscure. Presumably, a mother's body should ideally be allowed to fully return to it's prepregnant state before she takes on another go-round, but the waiting period is probably at least as necessary for her mental stability as it is for her physical health.

What I question is the logic in proposing that family size is associated with birth defects. Realistically, it appears that the only correlation would be due to the fact that the more children there are in a family, the more times a couple is tempting the odds. Then there is the additional fact that if a mother gives birth to a large number of children, she's likely to be older by the time she bears the later ones. Other than that, the only foreseeable risk is of being placed under siege by the Zero Population Growth faction.

To return to seriousness, how does one go about assessing the probabilities of giving birth to a normal, healthy infant when the mother is over age thirty? Unless a known genetic defect is present, in which case genetic counseling is imperative, the one major threat is mongolism. There is no way to completely rule out the risk of a myriad of other disorders, but the odds are too low to worry about.

If you are under age thirty-five (or thirty-seven in some medical circles) and have no medical history to suggest that this genetic problem might occur, then you probably will have to cope on your own with any anxiety you may have about mongolism, reminding yourself regularly that you are not in a high-risk group. For you, amniocentesis—the procedure whereby a bit of fluid is removed from the amniotic cavity—is probably not necessary. It is a procedure that is complicated and carries at least some small risk of its own, although the past year or two have seen the safety level raised enormously. Since few medical laboratories are equipped to perform the fluid analysis, and your odds of carrying an affected child are so relatively low, your physician will probably not recommend it, and may discourage you from seeking someone to perform it.

But if you are over thirty-five and pregnant with either a first or later child, your fears about mongolism may have more basis. As the middle months of pregnancy begin, you will want to evaluate carefully the question of whether or not to undergo amniocentesis. The procedure is generally performed between the twelfth and sixteenth weeks of pregnancy. A local anesthetic may be administered, after which a needle is inserted into the uterine cavity and a bit of fluid removed. Several weeks may go by before you receive the results, but hopefully when they indicate "everything okay," your concerns will be relieved about mongolism or other birth defects.

On the other hand, if the word you get back is that everything is *not* okay, you may wish to consider a therapeutic abortion. The operation is legal in a number of states; should it happen that you reside in a state that does not allow abortion on such grounds, you may have it performed in a neighboring state without problem. There are no residency requirements.

In *You're Not Too Old to Have a Baby,* Jane Price offers a checklist of conditions that most obstetricians consider high-risk. Particularly if you are over age thirty-five, this list may help you evaluate your odds for a healthy baby.

MOTHER'S AGE
  Under 16
  Over 40

BIRTH NUMBER
First child to woman thirty-five or older

Rh FACTOR
Rh incompatibility when the wife is Rh negative
and the husband is Rh positive

MOTHER'S HEALTH PROBLEMS
Anemia
Heart, circulatory, or kidney disease;
high blood pressure
Diabetes
Malnutrition or obesity
Urinary tract infection
Rubella infection of mother during pregnancy
(sometimes requires therapeutic abortion
before pregnancy)
Emotional instability
Tuberculosis
Syphilis or gonorrhea
Toxoplasmosis (an infection carried by animals,
especially cats, but most frequently
contracted by eating rare meat)

ANATOMICAL DEFECTS
Android (manlike) pelvis
Incompetent cervix (where the mouth of the
uterus doesn't remain closed enough to
hold the developing fetus)

GENETIC PROBLEMS
Relatives or ancestors with genetic defects
such as Down's syndrome or Tay-Sachs disease

OTHER HIGH-RISK CATEGORIES
Drug addicts, heavy smokers, heavy drinkers
The unwed, separated, or divorced
The poverty-stricken
Anyone under unusual stress

Undoubtedly, you've heard of a great number of problems that
can affect a newborn, or appear later in life—allergies, diabetes, and
others. If you have a family history of any type of genetic disease or if
genetic abnormalities have occurred in previous pregnancies, tell

your physician and inquire about genetic counselor services in your area. If you have no family history of such problems, there is no reason to suspect you are a carrier. If you do want a child, the odds are overwhelmingly in favor of a successful pregnancy and delivery of a healthy baby.

How Long Will It Take to Conceive?

It doesn't happen overnight. Considering that a woman's egg is available for fertilization only some twelve to twenty-four hours a month, and a sperm may be able to live and retain its ability to do what it does best during the forty-eight hours before ovulation, you're talking about a period of seventy-two hours per month during which sex can lead to pregnancy.* (The rumor is that it's easier to get pregnant if you're not married.) You'll still hear, "Oh, we decided on Monday we wanted a baby, and on Tuesday I was pregnant." But in the great majority of cases, it just doesn't work that way.

If you have sexual relations five times during a month, the probability of conception occurring in the first month is about 16 percent. Obviously you can increase these odds by having intercourse more frequently, especially during the most fertile portions of your cycle. Keep two points in mind. First, as I've mentioned, as a woman approaches thirty-five, her fertility may decrease, and she may need a few more months to become pregnant. Second, there is evidence that fertility may not return instantaneously after you stop taking an oral contraceptive. It might take several months for your body to get back on schedule.

What Are the Current Odds in Sex-Predetermination Roulette?

In 1350 B.C. the Egyptian papyruses, our oldest known medical records, offered the first historically documented advice on sex predetermination. Years of careful, empirical observation had led to the undeniable conclusion that the sex of an unborn child was reflected in his or her mother's face. Egyptian mummies-to-be who wanted a son right away would pray that they would develop an

*Some physicians believe that sperm can remain capable of fertilizing an egg for more than 48 hours, so the fertile period may actually be longer than this.

excellent, flourishing color; that would indicate they were carrying a member of the superior sex and as a result could not help but flourish themselves. Prospective mothers of sons would also always be cheerful, untroubled, and generally pleasant to be with, although they were sure to have more vomiting spells, since they were "carrying something foreign" inside them.

But clues to the *determination* of the sex were not enough. What man (and woman) have historically wanted is *control* over this mysterious natural secret.

Practically every decade has had its book on the "newly discovered" ways of human sex selection. In 1970, for instance, Landrum B. Shettles, an American physician, announced that he had found a truly scientific way to influence the sex of the yet-to-be-conceived baby. His boy recipe called for a couple of tablespoons of baking soda mixed for douching (this had been recommended for years; it was nothing new), infrequent intercourse until the time of ovulation, and early and frequent female orgasm. His girl recipe called for a vinegar douche, frequent sex until the time of ovulation, and avoidance of female orgasm. It all sounds about as easy as baking a cake, but there is one problem. It doesn't work.

This recipe was based on the experience of women who were artificially inseminated. It is known that women who are artificially inseminated prior to ovulation are more likely to have girls, and those inseminated at ovulation are more likely to have boys. *We now know that just the opposite is true when babies are conceived the natural way.*

At the time, however, and in the absence of any other more established advice, couples eagerly tried the Shettles method. The results were somewhat less than satisfactory. For example, one respected gynecologist in Texas began advising his patients to follow the procedure for having boys. When I spoke with him later he was so upset over the results that he had given up recommending it. The first thirty couples who followed Shettles' advice and had sexual intercourse as close to ovulation as possible had girls! One of his patients, an artist, had taken the formula so seriously that she put it into a cartoon depicting the Y spermatozoa leapfrogging the X ones.

From the time the Shettles method was first introduced to the public, scientists had several reservations about it. First, the advice contradicted all animal studies and earlier human studies which showed that it was *early*, not late, insemination that favored a male birth. Second, the method relied on cases that were based almost exclusively on artificial insemination. In the majority of cases Dr.

Shettles had not tested his methods on couples who conceived as a result of sexual intercourse.

Third, and potentially more serious, concentrating intercourse relatively late in the cycle—that is, on the day of or the day after ovulation—may carry with it some undesirable side effects. There is reason to believe that an egg begins to deteriorate soon after it is released from the ovary. If a couple is avoiding intercourse until they feel ovulation has occurred, they may be increasing the probability of fertilizing an "old egg" and assuming an increased probability of miscarriage and possibly other problems. For that reason, it is generally a good idea to avoid sexual intercourse on the day or two immediately following ovulation or, if you prefer, to use a mechanical form of contraception.

The Appendix presents some of the latest findings in this area, but here is one relevant conclusion:* Following to the letter the most modern sex-predetermination recipe, you can only count on raising your odds on having a boy baby from about 50 percent to up to 68 percent with early-cycle insemination. Manipulating events to improve the chance of having a daughter are more difficult, but you can raise the odds to about 56 or 57 percent when insemination takes place near ovulation.

If you describe this method to parents who claim to be familiar with the exact timing of their children's conception, a good proportion of them undoubtedly will contradict you and the method. They and I could both be right. Remember, if in early-cycle inseminations 68 percent of the babies are male, that means that 32 percent are female. This method sways the odds in your favor. It does not rule out the possibility of the other sex. One thing is clear. *Don't* follow the recipe given in pre-1975 books because the timing advice is backward and might actually *reduce* your chances of having a baby of the sex you want.

What about Adoption?

"Where have all the babies gone?" Since the late 1960s there has been an uninterrupted decline in the number of "highly desirable" (otherwise defined as "infant, white") adoptable babies.

The relatively new and widespread availability of birth control and abortion services has contributed a continuing decline in the

*You may also want to consult my book *Boy or Girl?* New York: Bobbs-Merrill, 1977.

number of out-of-wedlock births—traditionally, the source of supply for the pool of available babies. And, although there are still a substantial number of births outside marriage, more and more single mothers are keeping their children instead of offering them for adoption. Furthermore, the Zero Population Growth philosophy has stimulated more couples than ever to think about adoption. You might agree with the widespread but mistaken belief that if you are willing to take a child, you will be immediately eligible to set the specifications for your new son or daughter. Sorry.

Mrs. Arlene Nash, Director of the Adoption Resource Exchange of North America of the Child Welfare League of America, told me that she regularly receives letters from couples who indicate that, for ecological or demographic reasons, they have decided either not to have children at all, or to have just one and then adopt, preferably a white infant. But the process does not work this way.

Policies on eligibility differ from agency to agency (and they can be different when you turn to private adoption services); however, some general points can be made. Most agencies today do require some evidence that the prospective parents have tried to have a child of their own but have been unsuccessful (in some cases, a year or more of medical infertility documents may be required). Next, the home situation must be "right"; that may mean religious and/or ethnic compatibility with the child's biological parents.

What comes as a shock to many prospective adoptive parents, particularly when the wife has a career and decides not to have children because she "could always adopt," is the fact that *many agencies will not place a child in a home of a wife who works full time.* This is not just the case with those healthy white infants who are in demand. The Holt Agency (headquarters in Eugene, Oregon), a major intercountry agency working to place Korean and Vietnamese orphans in American and European homes, includes the following among its requirements: "the mother must not be working, particularly during the initial period of adjustment." Undoubtedly you can find some exceptions to this rule, but don't take for granted that you can have an adopted child *and* joint full-time careers outside the home.

The general feeling seems to be that the adoptive parent should be willing to sacrifice something, and the woman's job is at the top of the list. With an overabundance of prospective adoptive parents and the drastic shortage of babies, agencies can be very selective about who gets a child. A few agencies, however, will place a child with a single parent if she (or he) is able to provide financial support, which for most such parents means that they hold a job. Practically none, if any, of these adoptions are from the "infant, white" category. Most are older children who are either physically handicapped or mentally deficient.

There are other requirements. Financial requirements are not stringent, but income should be solid enough to avoid money worries. Apartment living is acceptable but a separate room must be provided if you already have a child of the opposite sex. Both prospective parents must take a medical examination and must be able to produce references of character and stability.

Once these basic requirements are met, there begins a process usually known as "home study" wherein a caseworker schedules a series of sessions with you and your husband. Most of these meetings take place in your own home but some may be held at the agency. This investigation lasts for at least several months, sometimes as long as a year. During that time the caseworker attempts to discern any instability in either one of the prospective parents or in the marriage itself. The investigation is extremely thorough, attempting to uncover all of your basic desires, expectations, and motivations for wanting to adopt, and to establish whether or not you have the capability to love and nurture a child successfully.

If you do meet all of the eligibility requirements, the waiting period for an agency placement may well be three or four years for a white infant. In view of the fact that some agencies now have such long waiting lists and that no new applications are even being accepted, more and more parents are turning to "less desirables": children between ages three and eight who are being cared for in foster homes; multi-siblings, that is, brother-sister groups that must remain unbroken; and handicapped children whose difficulties may range all the way from cleft palate to mental disorders and cystic fibrosis. (Children above age eight are also available, of course, but few parents are inclined to start a family with a child older than that.) Adoption requirements tend to be somewhat less stringent among these groups; some agencies, in fact, refuse to set any firm criteria at all. Generally speaking, waiting time is shortened considerably.

A few years ago the above statements might also have applied to interracial and transracial adoptions, but this subject has led to so much controversy that today it can hardly be construed as a solution. In the late 1960s and early seventies, quite a number of white families adopted black infants. The black community has since created such an uproar that few adoption agencies will any longer even consider the possibility. And while in past years, couples frequently adopted babies from other countries—Mexico, the Philippines, Greece, and Colombia, for example, in addition to

Korea and Vietnam—national leaders of these countries have grown reluctant to sanction such adoptions. While it is difficult to comprehend the rationale, there is little room for argument.

What about the "gray market" babies encountered so often on television shows and other media? The practice of buying babies has been growing tremendously and is now a lucrative field for both doctors and lawyers who generally work in tandem to arrange the "independent" purchase. These costs—both financial and emotional—can be exceedingly high. The average price ranges between $10,000 and $15,000, and may go up to $25,000 or even higher, depending on what the traffic will bear. (High fees tend to be more common when a couple insists on a Jewish infant.) But the potential heartbreaker is that the adopting parents have no protection should the biological mother decide at some future time that she wants her baby returned. Surprisingly, gray market procedures are legal in most states although a recent report in *Changing Times* indicates that many of these states are now drafting legislation to control independent baby-buying.

The cost of adopting through an agency seems almost small by comparison, but it's not exactly cheap. Generally, an agency fee ranges between $600 and $2,500, plus the additional legal fees that might range between $250 to $600. The amount is determined in part by your income and circumstances, sometimes being calculated as a percentage of gross annual income. Most states have some form of subsidized adoption but qualifications tend to be limited. Often the subsidies are given only to foster parents who wish to adopt a child who has already been living with them for some time, or in cases where a couple wishes to adopt a brother and sister, for instance, but can only afford one of them. Subsidies may also be offered to those couples who elect to adopt a handicapped child who requires considerable medical expense.

Just to give you an idea about how desperate the adoption situation is, and to what extremes and expense some couples will go to get a baby, *The New York Times* described one lawyer in the business who sends out pictures of attractive men and women, complete with a questionnaire that asks the prospective adoptive parents, "Which ones do you want to make a baby for you?"

How Much Does It Cost to Have a Child?

You may think that it is unfeeling, and perhaps irrelevant, to boil down into dollars and cents something as personal and sacred as the birth of a baby. Unfeeling because you shouldn't relate a new life to economics, and irrelevant because once a couple decides to have a child, and their Want Factor is really strong, they will somehow swing it. You might argue that if you stopped to calculate the cost of breakfast every day, you would be so horrified you'd give it up. Even though it most likely won't affect your decision on the "if " of parenthood, you probably do want an idea of what is involved financially to get a better idea about the "when." One thing a new baby does not need is a set of worried, harassed parents, and advance planning can help.

Table III gives you some idea of what can be involved from the moment you discover you are pregnant to the day you walk with your bundle of love into a modestly prepared nursery. When you see these figures, don't panic! These represent the *maximum* amount you'd ever spend in having a baby (assuming that inflation doesn't send prices soaring *too* far out of sight during the next few years). There are many inexpensive ways of entering parenthood.

For instance, there are ways of cutting down through insurance payments, clinics as opposed to private medical care, borrowing, improvising, and buying wisely. Don't forget about baby gifts, either. Keep in mind that *particularly with regard to doctor and hospital fees, there is dramatic variation from state to state,* and even within the same state. (The medical fees here are based on a random survey of East Coast hospitals conducted in the late 1970s by the Health Insurance Institute and the United States Department of Agriculture.)

You can adjust these medical costs to reflect the reality in your own town, and scale down the furniture, clothes, and other supplies so that they are more consistent with your own taste, ingenuity—and pocketbook. And don't feel reluctant to take advantage of what's already available among friends and relatives. That's standard procedure.

TABLE III
Costs of Having a Child in 1980
Hospital and Medical Fees

Obstetrician	$900.
Semiprivate hospital room (4 days @ $150)	600.
Nursery (4 days @ $60)	240.
Delivery room charge	250.
Anesthesia	150.
Laboratory work	100.
Pediatrician's newborn service	50.

Circumcision setup	25.
Circumcision	55.
Medication, etc.	75.
SUBTOTAL	$2,445.

Maternity Clothes

2 daytime dresses @ $30	$60.
1 long party dress	40.
1 short "out to dinner" dress	30.
3 smocks or caftans for at home @ $15	45.
2 skirts @ $11	22.
2 slacks @ $15	30.
3 tops @ $16	48.
3 bras @ $8	24.
6 panties @ $2	12.
6 panty hose (stockings) @ $2.50*	15.
SUBTOTAL	$326.**

*If you plan to go to business every day during the latter part of your pregnancy, you'll want to budget some extra dollars here.

**The $326 does not include a roomy coat (if it's winter) or a bathing suit (if it's summer) or a girdle (if needed). Nor does it include a larger pair of shoes, if you need to accommodate swelling feet late in your pregnancy.

Nursery Furniture and Equipment

Crib	$110.
6 fitted crib sheets (knit or permanent press) @ $4.50	27.
6 waterproof lap pads @ $1	6.
5 waterproof sheets @ $4	20.
1 crib blanket	7.
2 blanket sleepers @ $7	$14.
1 quilt/comforter	18.
1 crib mattress	48.
2 mattress pads, fitted, @ $4.50	9.
Crib bumper set	11.
Musical crib mobile	18.
Toy chest	32.
Dresser/diaper changer	65.
Bassinet or infant carrying basket or infant seat	20.
Vaporizer	20.
Baby carriage	100.
Nursery lamp	20.

Stroller (carry-and-fold)	30.
Car seat/bed	45.
Playpen	35.
Highchair	40.
SUBTOTAL	$695.

Baby's Wardrobe
(1 dozen diapers plus a case of disposable diapers,
or 5 dozen diapers; 6 shirts, 4 gowns, 4 kimonos, 4
stretch coveralls, 2 sacques, 5 receiving blankets, 3
sweaters, 3 waterproof panties, one bunting, one
towel, 3 washcloths)

SUBTOTAL	$165.

Baby Care Needs and Miscellaneous

10 8-ounce nursers, 4 4-ounce
    nursers, sterilizing kit, nipple
    and bottle brush, etc.
	$17.

Heated baby dish	15.
Bottle warmer	7.
Diaper bag	15.
5 bibs @ $1	5.
Bathing table	40.

Health products (vitamins, baby
    lotions, oil, cream, powder,
    cotton, shampoo, petroleum jelly,
    zinc ointment, baby-care books,
    rectal thermometer, etc.)
	40.

Brush and comb set	5.
Birth announcements	15.
SUBTOTAL	$159.
GRAND TOTAL	$3,790

In planning and budgeting for pregnancy and parenthood, you might be able to take a pencil and cross out just about everything on my list. Again, hand-me-downs, borrowing, and candid requests when friends and relatives ask you what you need can considerably reduce that "bottom line" of having a baby.

The costs in Table III do not take into account the expense of a child's living space. If you have a large home, your additional costs may be a little more than a can or two of paint. But if you live in an apartment or a small house, a new child could force you to spend more for larger quarters. It's been estimated that in high-rent cities, the extra baby room will add about one hundred dollars a month to the rent.

Then you've got to raise and educate the child. A few short years ago the President's Commission on Population Growth and the American Future concluded that the average American couple pays out about forty thousand dollars in direct costs in raising a first child to age eighteen. Today, most estimates raise the figure closer to sixty thousand dollars. That doesn't include any unusual expenses; for instance, if you have to fix the child's teeth to prevent him from looking like a werewolf. That does not count college or take into account the unprecedented rate of inflation since that study was done in 1970. You'll have to budget all that in.

But wait. We're not finished yet. There is another important and expensive service component that goes into raising a child: the mother's time (or the father's, if he is the major caretaker).

If you have never worked, or have no desire to work after starting a family, the "opportunity cost" on your time is not such a vital factor. But if you enjoyed working, were a successful money-maker before the birth, and elect to be a full-time mother afterward, money is lost—and that can be considered another major cost of parenthood. The amount of lost income depends largely on your education and the type of work you can do. It has been estimated that a woman with a high school education forgoes about $59,000* in salary by staying home and raising a child. For the woman who went to college and perhaps has a master's degree, the estimate of the average loss is $103,000.* Again, these are 1970 preinflation figures. That bundle of love costs a bundle.

You say you're going to work after you have a baby, so your expenses won't be quite that high? Maybe you can cut down somewhat by taking a full- or part-time job, but remember there are costs involved there also. Sometimes these costs strike a fatal blow to postpartum working plans. To get an idea of what your economic situation will be, first find out the going rate for child care in your neighborhood. (The average weekly mother's helper fees at the agencies I called in Manhattan ran around $175, and they suggested budgeting at least another $20 for someone to do the laundry and to prevent the house from looking as if Hurricane Betsy had just

*Before federal, state, and local taxes.

passed through!) In small towns and suburbs you may be fortunate enough to find someone for about $90 a week, plus meals and transportation. But in any large city you can expect to pay the minimum wage per hour—and up. Second, calculate your itemized deductions, child-care deduction, and expenses associated with working. Subtract all of these from your joint income and compare the results to what they would be if just one of you worked and you did not need to make other child-care arrangements. Sometimes the results can be depressing, particularly when it becomes apparent that it may be *costing* money for the wife to work.

But the economic forecast need not always be a gloomy one. It is very likely that you could find some child-care and household help for considerably less than $200 a week. Again, we are dealing here with estimates of the "upper limits." Possibly you can get someone who will take a significantly lower salary and still do some housework while the baby is napping.

(One mother I talked to ran just one advertisement in *The New York Times,* specifying that she wanted a child-care person who would work five days a week from 8:00 A.M. to 6:00 P.M., *and* one evening until midnight, would do light housework, including laundry, could produce references, and would be willing to accept $125 a week. She had 103 respondents from whom to choose.)

If you have only one child you may wish to consider using a good day-care center. Weekly costs range between $40 and $75 per child, but are somewhat higher for infants and toddlers. If you have more than one child, you may well find it more economical to stick with an at-home sitter.

Perhaps you can make arrangements for the days when the person you hired calls at 8:30 A.M. to tell you she isn't coming in. Most cities do have agencies that deal in child-care day help. Maybe you have a relative who lives nearby—or a neighbor with whom you could make a more economically realistic arrangement. Or your husband may have a flexible enough employment schedule so that he can work part time. Let's not forget that parenthood responsibilities should be shared whenever possible. Perhaps you could be successful with the share-a-baby plan: four or five working mothers taking turns watching children so they can all work part time. Or perhaps you can wait until the child is three and eligible for group care, which can cost considerably less. Even *with* full-time day help or some other type of arrangement, most couples I spoke with pointed out that working a nine-to-five day and coming home to play mother and father from 6:00 P.M. until 8:00 A.M. can be rough.

What's the Ideal Number of Children to Have?

There's an English proverb that says, When you've got one child you can run; when you've got two you may go, but when you've got three you must bide where you be. This is one of the many factors you might consider in deciding how many children, if any, you're going to have. I'm going to raise two specifics here.

First, there is the prevailing view that it is a curse to be an only child, or as one early-century psychologist put it, "Being an only child is a disease in itself." "If you are going to have any, then have at least two," the traditional advice goes. Interestingly enough, the available evidence does not support that view.

Research has shown that only children have a distinct edge over those with one or more siblings. A disproportionate number of both firstborn and only children are National Merit Scholars or doctors or are listed in *Who's Who*—if that manifestation of accomplishment is of interest to you.

Margaret Mead, who had one child, felt that someone should write about the advantages of stopping at one, both from the parents' and from the child's point of view. Only children are typically less dependent and get along better with their peers than those from large families, who may seek in school the attention they fail to receive at home. This all makes sense when you consider that the only child has more of his parents' time—and spends less time in a children's world than does the boy or girl who is constantly relating to his brothers and sisters. People assume only children are spoiled, but they needn't be. It depends on the parents' approach.

If you're considering stopping at one and are challenged with arguments like "One child? How could you do that to him/her?" you might raise the population issue and how it influenced your decision. And you could point out that you are not aware of any scientific studies that suggest that there is validity in the traditional belief that a child needs a sibling. Indeed, you know of evidence to the contrary. Tell them you prefer to concentrate on one child instead of dividing your limited resources between two or more, but that you understand that other parents with greater time and money, or a greater devotion to the joys and travails of parenthood, prefer larger families. If the arguments persist to the point of the old standby, "Your baby is spoiled," just shake your head, laugh, and say, "No, all babies smell that way."

Second, in planning your family size, consider the effect it will have on you and your homelife. Before the first birth, there was just one interaction to think about, that of you and your mate. Afterwards, there are four different relationships with which to contend: mother and father, mother and child, father and child, and the trio together. With each family addition, the pattern becomes more complex. One sure way of documenting the extent of that complexity is to use a noise meter. You will quickly become convinced that there is an exponential increase in commotion associated with each subsequent child. Contrary to what Frank B. Gilbreth and Ernestine Gilbreth Carey suggest in *Cheaper by the Dozen*, a happy family does not necessarily have to be a large one.

What about the children? Are they affected by the number of siblings they have? Dr. E. James Lieberman, Chief of the Center for Studies of Child and Family Mental Health at the National Institute of Mental Health, points out that a number of studies, even taking into account differences in social class, indicate that intelligence measures progressively decline with family size. Subsequent studies indicate, however, that this phenomenon tends to be confined to children of borderline intelligence; that is, a child with either a high or low IQ is usually only minimally affected.

The reason behind this observation is not fully clear. Perhaps the parents' time is so divided that each individual child gets relatively little attention. Or perhaps it is because having a large number of young brothers and sisters limits a child's contacts with adults. A child talking baby talk all day with his three young siblings may have poorer verbal development than the only child, who is more likely to be communicating with his mother or some other adult.

However, there are opposite factors to consider, too. Many youngsters learn a great deal from their older siblings; in many cases, more than they do from their parents. As many adults are aware, children almost seem to possess a communication system all their own. Frequently an older child, or even a young friend, is better able to interpret a baby's request than can the baby's own mother.

A large national study of American men between the ages of twenty and sixty-four found that the more siblings an individual had, the less likely he was to have advanced education and the lower his probability of getting a high-paying job. Again, only children and firstborns seemed to be best off in this respect, perhaps partly due to the fact that parents tend to be more ambitious for their firstborn. Individuals who came from a family of four or more children appeared to be handicapped in their competition for job success.

Do these studies suggest that having three or more siblings can have an adverse effect on a child? Not necessarily. It is likely that many of the large families studied were the victims of unwanted fertility. *Wanted* children in large families would certainly have better odds of success; even so, there would probably be a point in the family expansion when the pie that represented the parents' time and money was sliced too thin for the good of all concerned.

What about spacing children? There is only one answer here: beyond some consideration regarding your age, it's a personal matter. For some couples, "two under two" is fine. For others it would represent a domestic disaster. There are compelling arguments on all sides of the timing question. From a practical point of view, you might want to get the early childhood years "over with" as soon as possible, and this might mean having babies one right after another, as soon as nature permits. Many reports indicate that children with an age difference of two years or less play with each other more, are lonely when they are apart, have fewer hostilities, and are more likely to unite when parents become "intolerable." In other words, they are friends. But then it can work the other way. Children very close in age may develop an unhealthy form of competition, not to mention the unhealthy form of exhaustion that may develop in their mothers.

There can also be advantages to having three or more years between children, giving one child a chance to be toilet trained before the next child arrives, and giving the parents a chance to catch their breath. You might also consider costs of overlapping years of college.

Why a Second Child?

For parents who were undecided about having a first baby, the idea of a second may seem particularly surprising—even to yourself. After all, you've now experienced pregnancy, delivery and the what-it's-like of infancy and beyond. You've learned many new things and watched your baby learn many others. The pluses and minuses of parenthood are no longer foreign territory to you—by now you *know* what it's all about.

The fact is that however reluctant a couple may have been before they took the first giant step into parenthood, the majority of American families do want more than one child. And as with a first child, they tend to be motivated by reasons that may be either good or bad depending on one's viewpoint. Let's take a brief look at some of those reasons:

Probably the most common one has to do with The Myth of the Only Child. You have to be careful with this one. A second child deserves the right to be wanted and loved for his unique self, in just the same way that your first one has been. It would be grossly unfair to consider a second child in terms of what he or she could provide for the first.

Many parents still assume that a first child needs the company of a sibling. A child *does* need the company of other children, but not necessarily that of a sibling. Understandably, that statement may carry little weight if either you or your husband happens to be an only child. Many an "only" parent has made statements to me similar to the following: "I really envied my friends with brothers and sisters. I was so lonely. I would never let that happen to my child." It's too easy to provide playmates for a child today; you don't really need to create a new one from scratch.

And, as I have pointed out in the last section, an only child tends to fare considerably better than does a child from a larger family. Lest that discourage you, however, I should mention another very large study of first- and second-born children that was reported in *Science* a few months ago. The findings revealed: (1) practically no difference in the intelligence potential between first- and second-borns, and (2) that the number of years between them appeared to have no effect on their intellectual development. (Spacing between births probably *does* contribute to children of larger families, however.) What is particularly interesting about this study was that the three researchers set out expecting to prove just the opposite. It is logical to assume that with reasonable attention on your part, a second child has just as much chance to achieve as did your first.

Another oft-mentioned reason for a second child is that a couple wishes to try for a child of the opposite sex. Obviously, even when applying the latest sex preselection techniques, there are no guarantees. If that's the *only* reason, better skip it. In a recent survey conducted by *Redbook* of eighty-thousand women, it was interesting to note that a definite new trend is emerging: daughters are gradually becoming desired just as much as sons. The survey also disclosed that women are currently giving increasingly serious thought to family planning—whether for their first, their second, a later child, or none at all.

Less common reasons include a fear of losing a child who's an "only." Risks are comparatively low today; yet if the fear exists, it can be very real. Still another reason is occasionally voiced by women who were "asleep" during their first delivery. Some of them continue to feel they've "missed something" and want to try it again while they're awake enough to know what's happening.

Only you and your husband can judge the legitimacy of your reasoning. Just as the decision to have your first child was a very intimate and individual one, so should be your decision about a second. The Want Factor is no less important the second time around.

What if There's a Conflict with My Spouse?

The major part of this book has assumed that most of the "maybe" puzzle found wife and husband on the same side. While ideally you should both be in agreement as to the "if and when" of parenthood, in reality it doesn't always work that way.

"We both are very positive about having a family," Molly, a thirty-year-old actress, told me, "but my husband wants to wait another four or five years. He says he will be ready then. But I'm ready now, and I just think it would be foolish to postpone having a child just because he has a vague feeling that he needs more time."

In some cases, of course, the man is not only hesitant about having a baby when his wife suggests this, but he is hesitant about having one at all, perhaps even adamantly against it. "We talked about having children before we were married," Emily, a thirty-three-year-old scientist expecting her first child, told me. She looked a bit depressed as she spoke. "Every time I raised the subject he would say, 'Someday, later, maybe.' I finally realized that this postponement could go on so long that we might never have children. And I knew I wanted at least one. Finally, I had to confront the issue head on and say, 'Look, I don't want to wait any longer.' And I did conceive. But I would hardly say he was a willing participant in the whole process. I'm hoping that he will come around as the pregnancy progresses."

Perhaps it is because a woman is more vividly aware of the biological limits on her childbearing potential, but whatever the reason, it is more common for her to bring up the topic of the "when" of having a baby. Very often a man *is* hesitant. Often he *does* need to be nudged some. Indeed, after speaking to dozens of couples about this specific issue, I have concluded that if we all waited to have our husbands sing the glories of parenthood before we conceived, children would be on the list of endangered species.

Of course it can work the other way too—the husband being eager to start a family, the wife stalling for more time. "I'm a grammar school teacher," a young father declared, "and I simply love kids. I think I saw having a child as a means of consummating our marriage, making it really forever. And I wanted one right away. But my wife had other things to do with her life, so she kept me on a string for a while."

"My husband is the born father type," another mother explained, "and has been for years asking me, 'Are you ready now?' Well, until recently I wasn't ready. Why? Because, quite honestly, I didn't want to compete with a child. I was so lacking in self-confidence that I thought he would prefer the child to me. Only when I began to feel better about myself did I come to the point where I could say, 'I'm ready.' "

What we are talking about here are differences of opinion between husband and wife on the issue of *when* to have children, not more serious conflicts about whether or not to have them at all. Obviously, if the conflict about the question of parenthood is more fundamental than simply the timing of it, you might want to seek outside professional help, either through a carefully chosen preparenthood counseling specialist, marriage counselor, psychiatrist, or psychologist.

I will mention here a few preparenthood counseling services in the event that you might wish to take advantage of one of them. The first one in existence in this country is my own A Baby? . . . Maybe Services, founded shortly after publication of the original version of this book. The address is 1995 Broadway, 18th Floor, New York, New York 10023 (212-362-7044).

Other services, both in New York City, are: Pondering Parenthood, 405 West 118th Street; and Parents By Choice, 110 West 86th Street.

You will need to keep in mind, however, that counseling services can only help you raise and clarify the issues; they cannot make decisions for you. Where a conflict exists with your spouse, all facets must be considered and weighed even more carefully than if the dilemma were a mutual one. This is not the time for a stubborn holdout. Each of you must give as careful thought to the opposing partner's wishes as to your own.

The ultimate question is: Will a baby make one of you more happy than it will make the other unhappy? Not an easy problem to solve, but few truly important ones ever are.

Now that you have some of the basic, practical facts, let's move back to the decision-making process—and how to resolve your own parenthood puzzle.

What Kind of Birth Control Should I Use?

"You have the right to become pregnant when you think the time is right" states a pamphlet put out by the Office of Economic Opportunity's Family Planning Program. The pamphlet continues: "Babies should have some rights too . . . like the right to be born to a mother and father who are looking forward to taking care of it."

The fact that contraception is so popular tends to refute the "instinctive" theory of motherhood. Of course there are those cases of half-hearted vigilance that end up as "unexpected" pregnancies. They *might* be regarded as expressions of instinct, but they're more likely to be a subtle form of decision making.

Contrary to popular opinion, the use of mechanical and chemical contraceptive methods is far from new. Cervical plugs, douches, sponges, and abortion date back at least as far as 850 B.C. Many of the devices were mentioned in the writings of Plato, Aristotle, and Hippocrates, and examination of the detailed procedural instructions for some of these methods could lead one to believe they were lessons in witchcraft. The list of substances that have been used in the past for birth control seems amusing to us today: among them were lemon juice, parsley, camphor, opium, seaweed, olive oil, and foam from the mouth of a camel. Perhaps the earliest known contraceptive was a cervical plug made from honey and crocodile dung, a concoction that should ingratiate women and men alike to the progress of modern medicine. Condoms and diaphragms made from animal stomachs and other organs were used for centuries. Even oral contraceptives had their day: American Indian women used to chew certain roots in the hope of avoiding pregnancy. The effectiveness of all these devices is no doubt obvious. Those that worked at all were downright dangerous.

The past three decades, however, have seen the advent of new birth control methods that for the most part are both highly effective and reasonably safe. The risky part is that many women have only an incomplete knowledge about the method they are using.

As of 1975, 26.3 percent of *all* married women under the age of forty-five were using the Pill, making it easily the most popular method of contraception available today. *Oral contraceptives* work by raising the body's hormonal levels which in turn prevent ovulation. The most common form in use today contains a combination of both estrogen and progesterone, but there are various types and dosage levels. (The so-called sequentials, however, were removed from the market in 1976.)

When taken as directed, pregnancy is virtually impossible for a woman on the Pill. For maximum protection each pill should be taken at about the same time every day, preferably within a two-hour time span. If a pill is forgotten, it should be taken as soon as remembered, with the next one taken at its regularly scheduled time. Manufacturers of at least one brand warn that a forgotten pill requires some additional means of contraception for at least seven days. If two or more consecutive pills are skipped, another contraceptive method is needed for the rest of the cycle (but *don't* discontinue the pills; you must take the entire month's supply or your body will become unmercifully confused). If spotting should occur at any time during the cycle, you must also continue taking the remaining supply, but if it becomes a continuing problem, consult your doctor.

Besides almost 100 percent effectiveness, the Pill also has the advantages of being easy to use and does not interfere with sexual spontaneity.

But the Pill does have its drawbacks. Many users suffer a variety of side effects, although most of them tend to disappear after the first three months. Symptoms of early pregnancy (morning sickness, weight gain, and swollen breasts) are common among first-time users. If these or other symptoms—such as dizziness, headaches, depression, and yeast infections—persist, your doctor may modify your prescription in some way, or he/she may recommend a different method of birth control.

Additionally, Pill users are subject to a much higher risk of thromboembolism (formation of blood clots in the veins) than are non-Pill users. Still worse, what is too often ignored is the potentially deadly combination of the Pill and cigarette smoking. The effect is of a synergistic nature; that is, the two factors compound each other. Women who smoke moderately or heavily *and* use the oral contraceptive run significantly higher risks of heart disease than do nonsmoking Pill users. According to recent medical reports, this may be bad news for smokers, but it is good news for nonsmokers in that the Pill appears to be much safer than previously thought, since some of the effects attributed to its use can actually be explained by its use in conjunction with cigarettes.

As if that weren't enough, over fifty metabolic changes occur when you are "on the Pill,"—including a number of nutritional effects. However, with reasonable attention toward eating a well-balanced diet (as you should be doing anyway), this should be no cause for alarm among most women.

There is one last caveat here for those who are contemplating parenthood at some time in the future. Since the Pill works by blocking the production of ovarian hormones, a woman who has been taking it for many years may find herself having a great deal of difficulty reestablishing ovulation when she is ready. It is now an established fact that after an extended period of time on the Pill a few women never again have a menstrual period once they stop taking it. In other cases, fertility may be greatly reduced, either temporarily or permanently. Doctors are in general agreement that five years is probably the maximum time that oral contraceptives should be used consecutively. Periodically replacing the Pill with some other form of contraception will greatly reduce your risks of future difficulties, and in most cases ovulation will resume within a few months, perhaps sooner.

Many women and/or their physicians take a dim view of oral contraceptives, feeling that unnecessary meddling with normal body chemistry is asking for trouble. They may choose instead one of the newer *intrauterine devices,* or *IUD*'s, that have come into vogue in recent years. Modern types are usually made of plastic and come in a whole variety of shapes and sizes. No one is quite sure precisely how these devices work, but apparently their movement around the uterus continually irritates the uterine lining just enough to prevent a fertilized egg from becoming implanted.

At first thought the IUD would seem to be the ideal means of birth control: there's nothing to do, nothing to remember; they're highly effective (only very slightly less reliable than the Pill); and although the initial insertion (by a doctor) is expensive, long-term cost is extremely low, given that the device theoretically never needs to be replaced (although most gynecologists do every few years). In practice, IUD's are not always so satisfactory. Some women cannot use them because of severe cramping which may begin within half an hour after insertion, or may develop after several years. Probably the most common complaint is unusually heavy menstrual bleeding, sometimes with bleeding or spotting between periods, which may worsen (or lessen) with time.

In 10 to 12 percent of users, the IUD is spontaneously expelled, usually within the first year, and most often by younger women who have had no children. As a precaution the devices have an attached thread (or threads) which extends through the cervix down into the vagina. Thus a woman can regularly check to be sure the IUD is still in place by feeling the thread.

Various types of IUD's, most of them highly dangerous, have

been in use for over two thousand years. (Camel owners reportedly have their own variation. To prevent their animals from becoming pregnant during long desert trips, they insert small stones into each female camel's uterus.) As with oral contraceptives, IUD's are not recommended for unbroken long-term use if you are planning a future pregnancy. Studies now indicate that the constant irritation to the uterus over a period of years tends to inhibit conception.

The *diaphragm*, used in conjunction with *spermicidal cream* or *jelly*, remains the choice of many women. Invented in the late 1800s, the basic design has changed very little. The device works by covering the mouth of the cervix so that sperm cannot enter the uterus. If you choose this method you should know that a diaphragm can only be obtained by prescription and must be very carefully fitted by a physician if it is to function effectively and comfortably. The fitting must also be checked every two years, as well as after any bodily change that might affect the shape of the cervix (childbirth, abortion, weight gain or loss). A few women are so constructed that it is impossible for them to use this method of contraception.

A diaphragm cannot be inserted more than two hours before sexual intercourse and must be left in place for at least six hours afterward. The major drawback here is obvious: there simply is no room for spontaneous sex. As Jane Price writes in *You're Not Too Old to Have a Baby*, "Before [the introduction of oral contraceptives and safe IUD's] successful practitioners of birth control were those who either resisted the sweep of passion or had a high degree of luck."

While side effects of diaphragm usage are virtually nonexistent, the device is only relatively reliable. Theoretically, it should have an effectiveness rate of 97–98 percent during a year's time; that is, two to three unplanned pregnancies can be expected to occur among every hundred women each year. But because of incorrect insertion or inaccurate fit, the actual statistics place the effectiveness rate between 90 and 95 percent (thus the relatively large number of "diaphragm babies").

Condoms were first used during the sixteenth and seventeenth centuries by the Chinese and the Italians for protection against venereal disease. During the following century, as the devices spread throughout Europe, their contraceptive properties were gradually recognized. Early condoms were made from animal membranes, but during the late 1800s the less expensive rubber variety came into use. Since the beginning of the century "rubbers" have afforded an inexpensive, easily available, simple-to-use birth control method to billions of Americans (although the latter versions are not nearly as fancy as some that were reputedly in use during the last century).

As with diaphragms, condoms interfere with spontaneity and have the added disadvantage of diminishing sexual sensation. When properly used—and too often they are not—good quality condoms have an effectiveness rate of 85 to 90 percent. Probably the most usual cause of unexpected pregnancy with this method is due to the frequent temptation to skip it entirely.

The four birth control methods just described are by far the most common, yet they may be unsuitable for some women because of religious or cultural practices, lack of knowledge, or other reasons. Many women still rely on the rhythm method, a highly ineffective procedure whereby sexual intercourse is avoided during the fertile phase of the woman's menstrual cycle. For those with highly irregular cycles, the method is particularly unacceptable. However, it is commonly used by Roman Catholics, since that religion prohibits any other form of birth control.

Still other means of contraception are now available but most are too new to accurately assess either their effectiveness or their safety. I mention them mainly because I feel they are of interest. One type is an injectable form of progestin (a progesterone-like compound) that remains effective for three months. After using the method for a minimum of a year, most women find their monthly period entirely eliminated. Unpredictable bleeding in the uterus can be a major problem, however, as well as long delays (one to two years) in the return of regular menstrual periods after the injections are stopped.

A certain amount of publicity has been afforded to the "morning-after" pill, but its safety is still questionable enough that its use should be restricted to emergency situations only (as recommended by the Food and Drug Administration). The pills contain extremely high doses of estrogen and are taken for five consecutive days following unprotected intercourse. High-level estrogen dosage tends to result in nausea, vomiting, and certain metabolic changes. Additionally, the form of estrogen used is diethylstilbestrol, or DES, a compound now known to be carcinogenic when administered in large amounts over a period of time.

Still other of the novelty contraceptives are: Implants under the skin (a capsule of a progestin compound that may last for five, ten, fifteen, or more years, and which causes side effects similar to the injectable progestins); the vaginal ring (resembling the rim of a diaphragm and containing progestin, the device is worn for three weeks, removed for a week, then a new ring is inserted for the next three weeks); spermicide barrier (a suppository that effervesces into a dense spermicidal barrier across the cervix, effective for two hours); and copper IUD's known as the copper *T* and copper 7 (differing from the usual all-plastic IUD's by having copper wiring wound around the stem. The copper very slowly dissolves, acting as an infertility agent. To date, effectiveness is lower than for other IUD's but so is the incidence of side effects).

And still in the research stage are a "male pill" and contraceptive immunization. In the latter, theory has it that a man can be sensitized to his own sperm cells, thus producing antibodies that will inactivate the sperm. Similarly, a woman could be sensitized against either her own eggs or the sperm of her partner.

The two most drastic birth control methods I have saved for the end: abortion and sterilization. I strongly feel that *preventive* birth control is far superior to relying on abortion procedures to undo what has already happened. Nevertheless, no contraceptive method is 100 percent foolproof (though the Pill is close with a 99.7 percent) and "accidents" do happen.

The decision to have an abortion should be approached with caution, however. Recent studies indicate that two or more abortions tend to increase a woman's risk of problems in later pregnancy. Under some circumstances, even one abortion may up her odds of having a later miscarriage, premature delivery or low-birth-weight infant. According to Deborah Maine in *Family Planning Perspectives,* the increased risks most commonly occur when the D&C (dilation and curettage) abortion procedure is used. Risk is substantially reduced when the abortion is performed by means of the newer vacuum aspiration technique.

Sterilization carries a note of finality with it. If you and your husband have definitely and unequivocably decided to remain nonparents, sterilization for one or both of you is certainly the safest and most effective means of contraception. Sterilization in the male is called a *vasectomy,* the procedure whereby the two tiny tubes (vas deferens) that transport the sperm are severed. Sperm continue to be produced but they are absorbed into the body. In the female, the usual sterilization technique is a tubal ligation in which the Fallopian tubes are tied so that the egg cannot reach the uterus and sperm cannot enter the tubes. (There is some variation in the way the operation is performed.) Attempts to reverse sterilization in either the male or the female fail more than 50 percent of the time; thus neither technique can be regarded as a temporary form of birth control.

One last caveat: whatever contraceptive method you may now be using or would like to use, I suggest you discuss the subject thoroughly with your physician. And remember—maximum effectiveness and safety can best be achieved by carefully following instructions and having regular medical checkups.

I shall close this section on birth control with a quote from Margaret Sanger, founder of planned parenthood:

> No woman can call herself free who does not control her body. No woman can call herself free until she can choose consciously whether she will or will not be a mother.

~§ 10 §~

"Very Interesting. But Now How Do I Make Up My Mind?"

By way of a grand finale, this is the shortest chapter in the book. The only way it can help you is by raising questions. It cannot give you answers. The answers are where you come in.

Davy Crockett's motto was, "Always be sure you are right—then go ahead." Unfortunately, even if you are the most diligent thinker and evaluator, you must accept the fact that any decision about pregnancy and parenthood involves ambivalence. Even some of those who have positioned themselves on the extremes of the parenthood-nonparenthood controversy will admit that.

Stewart R. Mott, a principal supporter of the National Organization for Non-Parents, refuses to have a vasectomy. He understandably does not want to rule out the option of parenthood.

Anna Silverman, who with her husband wrote *The Case against Having Children,* says, "We just don't want any children right now . . . we might change our minds later." Even those who have passed the fertility point-of-no-return without children will tell you, if they are honest, that there are some second thoughts.

Conversely, the most perfectly planned, desperately sought after conception can elicit a reaction of "oh my gawd what have I done to my life" at least once during the pregnancy. Dr. Niles Anne Newton, in *Pregnancy, Birth and the Newborn Baby,* emphasizes that all women have this ambivalence:

> If the pregnancy was a "planned" one, the expectant mother sometimes feels that she is obliged to feel glad. Psychiatric interviews in depth have

221

shown, however, that this is not always true. In fact, one study showed that about one out of every eight women with planned conceptions developed very strong regrets about being pregnant.

Margaret Drabble succinctly described this ambivalence in her novel, *The Millstone*. She tells the story of Rosamund, an unmarried girl, who after her first act of sexual intercourse discovered she was pregnant. She was gloomy and very unenthusiastic about being an expectant mother, and she recalled a do-it-yourself abortion method that involved lots of gin to be drunk, and lots of hot water in a bathtub to be soaked in. (This method is not recommended unless you are partial to hangovers.) As she started to drink her potion, guests arrived and helped themselves to her bottle. By the time she started to repeat the procedure a few hours later, the gin supply was much depleted. Rosamund's reaction was: "There was not very much left. Not enough, I thought. Not enough, I hoped." (For Rosamund, the child turns out to be the joy of her life.)

But how do you separate natural ambivalence from genuine indecision?

Judge Ben B. Lindsey wrote a book in 1927 called *The Companionate Marriage* in which he proposed two types of wedlock: "companionate marriage," in which the expressed intention of the couple would be companionship without children—in other words, a type of trial marriage either before or instead of marriage with children—and a more permanent union with children that would require a more solemn ceremony.

Margaret Mead expanded on this idea and suggested that couples also enter into some type of trial parenthood arrangement to "explore thoroughly their aptitudes and mutual capacities before they elect to have children." She recommends spending a great deal of time with other people's children, taking the kids of a relative while they are on vacation, and assuming the responsibility of children during *your* vacation some year.

Maybe for some people that would work. But keep in mind Harlan Miller's oft-quoted statement: "Genuine appreciation of other people's children is one of the rarer virtues." The experiences you have with your cousins may be very different from those you would have with your own offspring. You may find yourself getting lots of the bad part and none of the good part of parenthood. Necessarily, there will not be the kind of closeness as between a child and his own parents; in most cases, you simply don't know each other that well. Without even giving it a thought, the mother of, for instance, a seven-year-old substitutes a chunk of lettuce when the rest of the family is having tossed salad. She already *knows* he dislikes salad and automatically sidesteps a hassle. On the other hand, an extended period of time with someone else's kids could be enlightening. It might give you a better idea of what children are really like.

As Alvin Toffler has pointed out, "Parenthood remains the greatest single preserve of the amateur." Almost every other task or assumption of responsibility involves some selection—the necessity on the part of the applicant to show some competence. But not parenthood. So perhaps contact with other people's children can do something in terms of providing that screen test.

Almost surprisingly, people *do* solve their conflicts and ultimately reach a decision. On one side of the coin are mothers like Linda Matthews who writes in *The Balancing Act*:

> My adjustment to motherhood has been strenuous, undeniably, because I am involved with my work as well as with my child. But what [my daughter] has taken away in freedom she has replaced in richness; my life is fuller and deeper because of her.

And in the same book, Sharon Ladar writes:

> I want it all: marriage and freedom, son and career. I am willing to struggle, because the rewards nourish me. How can I compare my delight in avocados to my anticipation of ripe strawberries? So it is with my commitments to [my son] and my career. They are not comparable; they are simply different.

The other side, however, is rather neatly summed up in a recent study at the University of California in San Francisco by Drs. Nancy Kaltreider and Alan G. Margolis. The recent study of thirty-three voluntarily childless women was reported in *Woman's Day*:

> The doctors found them all aware of "their inability to mother adequately," making it a rational, responsible choice. In other words, even though they gave quite different, perhaps selfish-sounding reasons, such as "I don't want the responsibility," or..."I need my freedom," what was really at the bottom of their decision was that they *knew* they wouldn't be good mothers.

There is no secret formula for deciding about having or not having children. There are no shortcuts to making any important decision. Can you get some professional counseling? Maybe. But few areas of the country are fortunate enough to have professional parenthood counseling services. There are, of course, other psychiatrists, psychologists, and counselors to consult, but the ones I spoke with all seemed to push one point of view or the other—to be either pro or against parenthood—and that type of bias you don't need. Even with a preparenthood counseling specialist the decision is so personal that about all anyone outside the immediate circumstances can do is to help you explore the questions concerning the to-be or not-to-be of parenthood. The big caveat here is in making sure that whomever you may turn to for help will be truly objective about this highly emotional issue.

You've seen some "Are you the parent type?" quizzes in women's magazines, but they are of limited help. Such questions as "Are you calm on the whole or nervous?" "Do messes bother you?" "Do you tire easily?" "Are you sensitive to noise?" "Do you have a good sense of humor?" "Are you sensitive to unpleasant odors?" "Do you like to take risks?" and "Can you control your temper when you are annoyed?" have frequently been asked to separate the parenthood from the nonparenthood type. One of the newest collections of quizzes is offered in *The Parent Trap* by Ellen Peck and Dr. William Granzig. But inevitably, still another question is raised: What do these questions mean? As with most other kinds of "psychological" tests, their chief value is probably in serving as an indicator of how well you're able to take tests.

Consider a question like "Would you enjoy taking a small group of seven-year-olds to the zoo?" No matter how proparenthood you may already be, a query like that is enough to send many a would-be mother (or father) into a slight state of hysteria. An antiparenthood second-grade teacher, on the other hand, might view such a trip as a shoo-in. That kind of question is very close to nonsense because it ignores the factor of experience. A woman who has never worked as a nurse doesn't start out in charge of a whole floor; a man just entering the banking business doesn't begin as a trust officer. Likewise, novice parents need to become accustomed to their new roles gradually. A couple attempting to begin parenthood with a group of seven-year-olds at the zoo could hardly be blamed for deciding to throw in the towel right then and there. Even an experienced mother who sincerely enjoys children is not likely to include a zoo trip on her list of Ten Most Favorite Things to Do.

(To check out my theory I actually put this question to a few happily well-adjusted mothers I know. Here are a few of the answers: "I might enjoy a small group of two." "Yes, as long as a small group, of mothers came along, too." "Are you kidding? My four-year-old is a small group all by himself.")

Implicit in all of these preparenthood quizzes is the notion that a no answer to the majority of the questions would put you in the nonparent category, and a yes indicates you are mother or father material. I don't think that holds—either way. As the parents I talked to pointed out, the birth of children unfolds in you capacities you never knew you had. In answering no to those questions before the conception, you may be underestimating yourself. On the other hand, getting 100 percent on a preparenthood quiz may have little relevance when the real pediatric chips are down. The analysis of parenthood decisions is too complex for quizzes. But there are some guidelines.

First, think about who you are—and who your spouse is. The critic Malcolm Cowley once observed that, in any marriage, one person takes care of the other more than the other takes care of him/her. Which are you? If you are the one taken care of, how will you feel if the balance changes? What is it that you would like to get out of life? Or, more specifically, how, ideally, would you like your life to be, when, say, you are fifty-five or sixty? What is it about life that you find rewarding? Is parenthood compatible with your answer?

Second, consider all options. Don't be pushed by tradition in one direction or by a fad in the other. And don't assume that just because you have one child, you must automatically have a second. Think through each decision about parenthood individually.

Third, sort out real concerns from smoke screens. Career and life-style factors and doubts about parenting ability may be authentic concerns, or they may be cover-ups for more serious qualms about having children, ranging anywhere from hostility toward a spouse or a miserable childhood experience of one's own to a possible fear of childbirth. It may help to spell out the pros and cons in writing, or free associate into a tape recorder. Ask yourself if you'd still be undecided if your life circumstances were any different, say if you suddenly became very wealthy. By doing so, you may be able to separate deep psychological conflicts ("I do not like children" or "I am too insecure in my marriage to invite children") from logistical problems ("We can't afford a baby right now" "Having a child would require us to move to larger quarters" "There is no way I could keep my job and have a baby, too").

Fourth, if you're leaning toward having a child, consider seriously what impact it would have on your life. Keep in mind the theme "life will change" which I heard from every new parent I talked to. Think about how you will handle those changes and how you might react to them. Be specific. For instance, write out in detail the business, social, and personal events that occur in your life over the next two weeks. Then go back and see which would have to be altered—or how you would juggle things—if you had a child. Be honest about how you feel about rearranging or modifying your life-style. Don't expect miraculous new forms of cooperation from a husband who has always left everything to you. If it's nonparenthood you're seriously leaning toward, take a good look at the type of activities you are currently involved in—your work or social life, for instance— and ask yourself if it is likely that those activities will always be present and as rewarding as they are now. Will they be enough to fill your life and accommodate all your energy and creativity?

Fifth, look at other couples of all ages—preferably those somewhat older than you, or at least out of the parenthood quandary. Find a few with whom you most closely identify, the ones with whom you share ideals about career, education background, political and social interest. How are they responding to their decisions about parenthood? Maybe you could even talk with them about it.

Sixth, in setting guidelines for your decision, use human criteria, based on human needs and wants, not some meaningless rhetoric that tells you there is only one good reason for this or one good reason for that. Decisions about having or not having a child are based on a series of very personal and highly variable circumstances. Consider your own, not someone else's.

Seventh, if you are close to a decision to have a child, remember that you will be assuming, as Simone de Beauvoir described it, "a solemn obligation." In thinking about this human life you may create, don't focus on your image of a baby. Children remain babies for a very short period of time. You will need to think *person,* not baby. The concept of *baby* may discourage couples who envision parenthood as an endless sequence of bottles and diapers; or it may encourage people taken by the image of an angelic cherub, but horrified by the continuous responsibility for someone who will be an infant, a toddler, a school-age child, and a young adult.

Eighth, spend some time wrestling with this question: How do you view parenthood—as more of an enrichment or as more of a burden? Would you like to create an individual who reflects qualities of you and your spouse? Do you look at parenthood as a means of understanding yourself—and others—better? As a means of emotional growth? Or do you feel that the responsibility of caring for children will stunt your growth? Do you agree with this: "The more people you love, the richer your life is, even though you're more vulnerable to pain?" Jane Johnson, associate executive director of Planned Parenthood of New York was once quoted as saying: "I know of nothing that takes more talent than being a good parent. I'm convinced that some people have oodles of it, and others have almost none of it. . . . People have to recognize that . . . you have to be able to love your child unconditionally."

Ninth, can you accept the inevitable ambivalence that will come with whatever decision you make? It's a fact of life. Robert Frost understood that:

> Two roads diverged in a yellow wood,
> And sorry I could not travel both
> And be one traveler, long I stood
> And looked down one as far as I could
> To where it bent in the undergrowth . . .

It's fine to plan, to talk about parenthood, to go through all the pros and cons of having a child. But after digesting all the facts, doing elaborate cost/benefit analyses, going through a myriad of other intellectual exercises, you must realize you're dealing with an *emotional* decision. Perhaps for the first time in your life, you will have to admit to yourself that you can't have all the answers—you simply do not know what the future will bring. In deciding to have a child, you are taking a leap of faith.

Epilogue: After I Wrote This Book

As I was completing the research for this book, strange things began to happen to me. I'd come home from a day of interviews or an afternoon at the library to find some messages on my telephone-answering machine: "Hi, just wanted to give you a ring to see if you'd made up your mind yet." And I'd find notes in my mailbox or under the door: "Hey, we're dying to know! Is all that research going to *produce* something?!" When I asked a colleague if she would be willing to read a draft of this book, she agreed, but added, "Send on the ending first. I always like to read the solution of a mystery story before I turn to page one."

Did I reach some conclusions as a result of my investigation into the question of whether or not to have a baby? Indeed I did.

Most important, I clearly saw that my seemingly contradictory feelings about parenthood were both normal and healthy. And I learned that when people are honest in talking with you about parenthood and nonparenthood, their ambivalent feelings also become evident.

Do you remember my aunt who resorted to plug-in gimmicks to encourage my husband and me to reproduce? At the time, she was the prototype of the individual who says, "Don't think about it, just do it." But in the course of subsequent conversations, even she began to see that there were two sides to the question. When I took the time to explain calmly why so many young couples were pondering the question, her position shifted dramatically. She began to relate personally to my dilemma.

When I asked why she had initially exerted so much pressure in favor of parenthood, she said, "Well, I never really thought seriously about the question before. I never realized that there is another point of view. It's almost an established social custom to tease young couples who haven't had kids yet. You sort of assume that eventually they will, so your comments are really part of the game."

We're living in an age of transition. Contraceptive technology, an awareness of population growth, and widespread interest in dual full-time careers are all very new. Indeed, the word revolution applies. Social attitudes, however, change painfully slowly. But I learned that with patience and an understanding of the feelings of individuals who lived—or still live—in an earlier age, I could succeed in leading people to understand my point of view.

I even found that the forces of grandparenthood can be dealt with effectively when you gently but persistently present your thoughts, while making sure you don't ridicule theirs. My mother, for instance, slowly began to see that, at least in my husband's and my case, the decision about whether or not to have a child was a complex one, one that might take time to resolve. With some regret, but with a great deal of newly acquired understanding, she put her plans for my "maternity boutique" on hold and began to purchase smaller patterns, more appropriate for the wife of my newly married brother.

Were there other conclusions? Yes. I gained some perspective about why my husband and I—and so many other couples like us—found ourselves in *the quandary* in the first place.

We had never really thought much about becoming or not becoming parents. We always assumed that we would have children. We took it for granted. When we were in school, no one ever discussed with us the alternatives to parenthood or various options in family size. We moved through life and prepared for marriage, thinking, Oh, yes, we'll have children someday. We never for a moment stopped to think about the appropriateness or consequences of that decision for ourselves as individuals. Instead of trying to know ourselves and what we wanted to get and give in life, we subscribed to goals, parenthood among them, set by others.

Then, almost overnight, the pressure was on. Time began to run out, and the approach to the decision became a panicked one. Some members of our generation jumped blindly into the waters of parenthood, for better or for worse. But many of us evaluated the prospect of having a child as we would consider the pros and cons of buying an expensive piece of furniture. We smothered ourselves with rational reasons why we couldn't afford it, but we still had to cope with a persistent vague uneasiness. We were on the spot without benefit of a gradual evolution of inner reasoning, a process that would have allowed the decision to unravel more slowly, more comfortably, and above all more naturally.

My approach—making an official project, a meticulous scientific investigation into my personal parenthood question, complete with a tape recorder, calculator, file cards, and a big eraser—is not what you would call a natural one. The fact that I was driven to this technique as the only way I knew to work out our questions reflects how confused we were, how committed we were to reasonable, as opposed to emotional, decision making—and how novel the whole subject matter was.

There is no doubt that I was coping with new questions. No wonder people looked oddly at me when I asked them if they would comment on how one decides whether or not to have a child. No wonder I got blank stares after asking. "Why did you become parents?" People were confused by the nature of my whole investigation. For instance, when a well-meaning hostess introduced me as "the lady who might have a baby," one startled man gasped, "You mean right here, now?"

Perhaps ten or fifteen years from now prospective parents won't feel the pressure my husband and I felt. Perhaps they will have had the opportunity to arrive at their decision slowly, gradually, naturally, without marching to the beat of someone else's drum. We might all be better off for it. But right now we must learn to deal with the conflicting pressures that always accompany sudden social transition.

Throughout this book I have strived to maintain balance, addressing each side of the quandary with equal candor. That I evidently succeeded was illustrated rather neatly after the original version of the book went to press. Two editors from a well-known women's magazine each reviewed the book with the result that one commented that it was too pro-baby, while the other that it was too anti-baby!

The vast amount of mail I have received since A Baby? . . . Maybe was first published in 1975 lends credence to the fact that there definitely are two sides to the baby question, and I did succeed in presenting both of them. A letter received only recently chided me for my "excellent job of sitting on the fence." It was my careful scrutiny of all the issues that eventually led my husband and me toward The Decision. We decided yes to the question A Baby? . . . Maybe.

I first became aware that my own pregnancy experience had begun while I was on a publicity tour for this book. One morning in a hotel room as I prepared to go on the television program "A.M. Chicago" to discuss whether or not I was going to have a baby, I felt about as nauseous as a seasick ocean voyager. Fortified by five glasses of ginger ale, gripping the arm of the chair, and taking in deep breaths between questions, I managed, without throwing up, to explain to about two million midwesterners why my husband and I were in a psychological quandary about the pros and cons of parenthood—without revealing the fact that we had actually made our decision a couple of months earlier and that the results of that decision were soon to be very obvious.

My pregnancy experience ended with me exhausted and exhilarated at New York University Hospital when our eight-pound, two-ounce daughter was placed on my stomach.

In between there was turmoil: fears (particularly early on about having a miscarriage. Later on my fears focused on the possibility of multiple births, having become convinced that after asking so many questions I'd be blessed with three or more at once); worries (particularly about how I was going to keep my professional life intact after the baby was born without sacrificing an emotional bond with our child); conflict (my husband was not enthusiastic about the possibility of joining me in the labor or delivery room. When the time came, he was with me during labor and watched his daughter's birth through a glass door—an alternative which, although not right for everyone, was for him and perhaps others); self-doubts ("Why am I not bursting with enthusiasm?" I would constantly ask myself throughout pregnancy. "What if I'm a terrible mother?").

And there were thrills too: my husband's proud Christmas dinner announcement to his family that we were to be parents; rewards (the first time that he, too, could feel the movement of our child); the wonder (that after this was all over, a real-life baby would emerge); the excitement of late pregnancy (despite my lingering fears that "something could go wrong" we couldn't quell the feeling of anticipation we had the day the crib, chest of drawers, and changing table were set up in the baby's room).

At first I thought my ups and downs were unique, ones which only I and perhaps a few other emotionally confused women had to deal with. I know now, of course, that all prospective parents—but particularly those of us who had postponed having children in favor of careers—have these feelings. And it was for that reason that I then went on to write *The Pregnancy Experience: A Psychological Guide for Expectant Parents.*

Yes, *A Baby? . . . Maybe has* also been a personal book and yes, for a long time there was a loose thread. Today my husband and I are experiencing a life enriched by the presence of Christine Barrett Whelan, the new human being we created together. But in spite of our own decision, we both continue to recognize that not everyone is cut out to be a parent—the same as not everyone is cut out to be a teacher, an artist, or a football player.

Having written this book I was able to come to terms with many of the conflicts about parenthood that were puzzling me. Having now read the book, I hope you also will come to know yourself better, will feel more comfortable with your own decision-making situation, and will reach a solution that satisfies you. What's at stake, after all, is (just) the rest of your life. And maybe some unborn person's life, too.

Appendix: After You Decide

Once you do make up your mind on the parenthood issue, you'll have another whole series of questions. If you decide parenthood is for you, the first thing you'll want to do is to choose a physician, preferably an obstetrician-gynecologist, and tell him or her of your plans. He will answer specific medical questions. I've included in this Appendix some of the more general questions that may occur to you, but obviously you should ultimately depend on the advice of your own doctor—even if he suggests you throw away this book.

If you've chosen nonparenthood, you'll have your own questions, so I've included some discussion for you, too.

For Prospective Parents

Q. How can I plan for a healthy pregnancy?

A. Ideally, you should find a physician *before* you become pregnant. Ask if there is any particular medication either of you should avoid while you're seeking a pregnancy. (The doctor might advise for starters that you omit the Pill!) There is evidence, for instance, that certain drugs can interfere with spermatogenesis or can have an adverse effect if taken during the early months of gestation. It's best to check on them.

Q. What about immunization for German measles?

A. Of utmost importance during your preconception physical exam is a rubella (German measles) evaluation. Rubella is a common mild infectious disease of childhood. For many years it was assumed to be an atypical form of measles or scarlet fever. But in the early 1940s it was discovered that, unlike either of these two other diseases, exposure to rubella during the first three months of pregnancy can have disastrous effects on the developing child. Cell division is somehow inhibited, and the child may be born with such congenital defects as deafness, cardiac malformation, and/or cataracts. Be sure you are immune to rubella! The chances are over

80 percent that you already are. You were most likely exposed to the disease while you were a child. It's highly infectious, yet also very mild, so you may not have even known you had it. Ask for a rubella screening test. It may take a couple of weeks to get the results, so plan accordingly. Do not try to conceive or do not allow conception to occur until you get the results. If you do *not* have rubella antibodies in your system, or if there is some doubt, you should get the vaccination as soon as possible *and* postpone conception for at least three months after the immunization (which actually gives you a mild case of the disease).

Q. What about the Rh factor?

A. Your Rh status really has nothing to do with conception or early pregnancy, but it can be significant at childbirth. For that reason, your blood must be tested for the presence or absence of the Rh factor, now generally a routine procedure.

Some 86 percent of the population have Rh positive blood; the remainder have Rh negative blood, which is not at all compatible with the positive variety. If your blood is Rh negative, your husband's blood will also be tested. If he, too, is Rh negative, or lacks certain of the Rh subfactors, in all likelihood your baby will also be Rh negative and there will be no problem. If, however, your husband is Rh positive, there is a good chance your baby will also carry the Rh factor.

During the process of delivery, a small amount of fetal blood may be released into your bloodstream. If you are Rh negative and your baby Rh positive—and *if* any mixing of blood should occur at birth—your body will immediately begin producing antibodies against this "foreign" substance, much as it would against a bacterial invader. This presents no problem for your firstborn child—and possibly not for your second, or even later children. But should your body have built up these anti-Rh antibodies to any great extent they *could* effect a subsequent baby by reacting against its red blood cells and causing the condition known as erythroblastosis fetalis—or what is sometimes referred to as an "Rh baby." A simple blood test performed on the baby immediately after birth, and repeated during the early weeks of life, assures prompt detection and treatment.

None of this, however, need be any real source of concern today since a drug treatment administered to the mother right after birth can prevent formation of the Rh antibodies, thus virtually eliminating the complication just discussed. But it *is* important that your doctor know ahead of time if you are Rh negative.

Q. Should I give up smoking during my pregnancy?

A. Yes! Smoking isn't smart at any time, but during pregnancy it's really unforgivable. Your unborn baby shouldn't have to share the assaults that cigarettes inflict on your own body.

Both epidemiological and experimental studies unanimously support the view that smoking has a retarding effect on fetal growth. Analyses of hundreds of thousands of births have shown that the average birth weight of babies born to smoking mothers is a full 6.1 ounces less than those born to mothers who don't smoke. Also, significantly more babies under five pounds are born to women who smoke, and they are subject to the same afflictions as babies born to mothers who are undernourished: mental retardation, cerebral palsy, epilepsy, hyperactivity, learning disabilities, respiratory distress syndrome, and sudden infant death syndrome.

Recently the *New England Journal of Medicine* added a new item to the already long list of cigarette-induced tragedies: Women who smoke are at least twice as likely to suffer a miscarriage as women who do not smoke. The number of stillbirths is much higher among smokers. In England, children of smokers followed through their early years were found to be significantly shorter, to have low ratings of social adjustment and greater frequency of reading retardation. In fact, almost every kind of learning disability has been associated with the cigarette factor. Additionally, parental smoking has now been linked with childhood respiratory problems. (And that means that it's not just the mother-to-be who should kick the habit; the prospective father should, too.)

Two theories have been proposed about the way in which cigarette smoking affects the growing baby. One is that the nicotine is responsible directly; the other that smoking constricts the blood vessels in such a way that adequate nutrients do not cross the placenta to the baby's blood supply. Degree of involvement to the fetus appears to depend on how much the mother smokes—a pack or more a day being considered "heavy" smoking and exposing the baby to a very high degree of risk.

Risk tends to become almost totally eliminated if smoking is stopped before the end of the third month. Do yourself and your baby both a favor—kick the habit now!

Q. Is alcohol harmful during pregnancy?

A. It can be if its use isn't restricted to very moderate amounts. "When you drink, your unborn baby does too!" is the title of a pamphlet published by the March of Dimes. If you also keep in mind that such a tiny creature is affected much faster than you are and that his liver is too immature to metabolize alcohol as quickly as yours does, you should have a clue that your drinking is harming your baby.

A substantial number of children born to women who drink excessively exhibit a pattern of physical and mental birth defects collectively referred to as the "fetal alcohol syndrome" or FAS. Growth deficiency is one of the most prominent symptoms. Affected babies are abnormally small at birth, especially in head size, which persists into early childhood—or in some cases, throughout the child's life. FAS babies usually have narrow eyes and low nasal bridges with short upturned noses. Almost half have heart defects, which may be severe enough to warrant surgery. Investigators continue to document a host of other abnormalities associated with fetal alcohol syndrome, including mental retardation and signs of central nervous system impairment. In addition, they are now beginning to observe that brain lesions may exist in offspring lacking any outward features of the syndrome.

FAS is not a minor problem. An eighteen-month study conducted at the Seattle Harborview Medical Center demonstrated that while a degree of growth failure occurred in less than 3 percent of all pregnancies, its occurrence in cases of recognized alcoholism was 83 percent! Another study reported in the *Archives of Disease in Childhood* showed a 17 percent mortality rate among FAS babies, and 44 percent of the others had an IQ below 80. Consider, also, that there are an estimated one million alcoholic women of childbearing age in the United States today.

If you have a drinking problem, right now is the time to get help—for your own sake as well as your future baby's. If you are simply a regular "social" drinker or occasional "binge" drinker, you need to think about cutting down during your pregnancy, if not abstaining altogether. No one knows for sure just how much alcohol is too much, but a glass of wine or an occasional one to two ounces of eighty-proof liquor a day will probably produce no harmful effects. (You may have this problem solved for you if cocktails suddenly lose their previous appeal during pregnancy, perhaps tasting very bitter or even causing nausea.)

If you're not yet pregnant but planning to be, this is still a good time to begin cutting down on the amounts you drink. The first three months are a critical period of fundamental structural development. This does not mean you can resume your "old habits" after the first three months, however. Brain development takes place throughout the entire pregnancy, and that organ must be kept carefully protected. Especially to be avoided are episodes of binge drinking, since it now appears that occasional high concentrations of alcohol at certain critical periods are even more deleterious than the average amounts consumed on a regular basis. Heavy drinking near the end of pregnancy may cause the newborn to suffer withdrawal symptoms and he is almost certain to display a somewhat stuporous state and decreased activity.

Women have consumed alcohol during pregnancy for years, and we have no reason to believe that small amounts will prove to be harmful. But large amounts of alcohol and pregnancy definitely do not belong together.

Q. What do I need to know about nutrition during pregnancy and how much weight should I gain?

A. To start off in the right direction, you need to know not only what but how much you should be eating. Nutrition is a field almost everyone is interested in these days—but perhaps no one quite so much as the mother-to-be. Your baby's future health and mental development are at stake here—and, of course, *you* want to be in peak condition, too.

The subject of weight gain during pregnancy has been a subject of controversy and changing trends for centuries. The average woman of two hundred years ago had a much narrower pelvis than is usual today; that, combined with frequent general malnutrition and rickets, indicated small babies in order to preserve the mother's health. But then the high infant mortality and disability led toward larger babies. As women and their doctors became more concerned about weight control, the trend again shifted somewhat. Even as recently as ten years ago it was not uncommon to hear a doctor pronounce his rule of "no more than two pounds a month." For the most part, this admonition was out of concern for *your* general health and the knowledge that for many American women, lifetime weight problems begin with pregnancy.

Today experts generally agree that a gain of twenty-two to twenty-seven pounds is ideal—and that most of it should be gained during the latter five or six months of pregnancy. *But* you don't need significantly more calories—what you need are calories that are more judiciously selected from the Basic Four Food Groups. The National Academy of Sciences recommends that a typical woman 5'5", normally weighing about 128 pounds, requires approximately 2100 calories a day when she is not pregnant, or one to two months pregnant; 2400 when she is three or more months pregnant; and 2600–2800 when she is breast-feeding. You can get your 2400 calories in a well-balanced form by each day having two to four glasses of skim milk; two servings of meat, chicken, or fish; one egg; four servings of fruits and vegetables (including citrus, dark green, leafy, or yellow vegetables); and four servings from the bread and cereal category.

Admittedly, it is difficult to follow the variety-and-balance rule and stay within the calorie limit if you attempt to include nonnecessary food items like rich desserts, salad dressings or—although they are not technically foods—cocktails. The last two months of pregnancy are a time of very high weight gain for baby. Too often a mother reaches her upper weight limit about this same time and attempts to compensate with a sudden cut in food intake—just when her baby is needing her to eat more. This could lead to some unhappy results.

If you were more than slightly underweight before pregnancy, your doctor may recommend a weight gain of as much as thirty or forty pounds. But if you were *over*weight before pregnancy, now is *not* the time to attempt any kind of reducing diet. You will have plenty of time to work off those extra pounds after the baby arrives. On the other hand, overweight or not, this *is* a time to muster up all the motivation you possibly can to avoid the well-I'm-pregnant-so-I-should-indulge-myself pitfall. Pregnancy is a time when you want to pamper yourself and have other people show you special considerations. But those considerations should not include extra rich desserts and two helpings of everything that precedes it.

From the moment you conceive, your baby begins to feed on the nutrients already stored in your body. So even if you're not yet pregnant, *now* is the time to correct those eating habits.

Q. Is it dangerous to gain too little weight during pregnancy?

A. If you gain fewer than the recommended minimum of twenty-two pounds, it usually means that your baby will be smaller than average, and that could spell trouble. Studies indicate that newborns weighing less than five and one-half pounds are all suffering from malnutrition, however mild, and that they face greater likelihood of mental retardation, epilepsy, cerebral palsy, hyperactivity, learning disabilities, respiratory distress syndrome (RDS), and sudden infant death syndrome (SIDS). There are also indications that too little weight gain may contribute to malfunctioning of the uterus.

In the United States, severe undernutrition is not generally as great a problem as a more subtle—and insidious—form of "imperfect" nutrition that hinders development of the baby's full potential. In 1965, the Department of Health, Education and

Welfare reported almost one million pregnant women (roughly one-third of all pregnancies) suffering some degree of malnutrition. Almost all of it is preventable.

The idea that a baby is a parasite and will take whatever it needs from its mother is strictly a myth. It may get enough calories, but if the mother is eating improperly, her baby will not get enough vital nutrients for proper growth and development. Thus, even an average-weight baby can fall victim to any of the above disorders. Specifically, the brain is frequently affected. This organ continues its cell growth throughout pregnancy and up to the age of about one year, although the rate is much greater before birth. If a nutrient deficiency exists, there is a chance that some brain cell formation is lost forever.

Q. Do I need vitamin supplements during pregnancy?

A. Although your doctor will probably suggest vitamin supplements, you should be aware that these are more likely an "insurance policy" rather than a necessity. The National Research Council recently concluded that such supplements are of questionable value with the exceptions of iron and possibly the B vitamin folic acid, both of which are difficult to get in sufficient amounts from a normal diet. Extra iron must be stored by the baby for use during the first few weeks of life when his food intake is usually limited to milk (which contains no iron at all).

You'll want to take your own doctor's advice on the subject of supplements and feel comfortable with the knowledge that while they may not help a great deal if you are eating properly, they won't hurt you or the baby. But beware of self-prescribing your own megavitamins. Those *can* be hazardous to your health and to your baby's health. Additionally, you do not need any so-called health foods. There is no reason that you need avoid artificially flavored or colored foods, or products artificially sweetened with saccharin. Moderation here, as with all food products, is the key.

Q. Are there specific drugs that should be avoided during pregnancy?

A. Discriminate use of medical drugs is only common sense at any time, but particularly for women who are pregnant or who are contemplating pregnancy. (I am not referring here to "street drugs"—heroin, cocaine, amphetamines—which are destructive to anyone's health at any time.) As with other substances, drug use tends to inflict its most severe tragedies during the first six weeks of fetal growth. That six-weeks rule is by no means absolute; however, some preparations are more dangerous later in pregnancy than in the beginning.

The effects of drug use vary enormously and can result in both physical and mental defects. Additionally, the extent of risk for a specific defect varies not only with the time during pregnancy that the drug was ingested, but also with dosage level, genetic predisposition of the fetus, and the mother's metabolic processes. Apparently, the altered physiology of pregnancy can modify the rate of metabolism as well as the transfer and excretion of any drug. Animal studies are of limited value in this area since their physiological systems do not necessarily parallel those of humans— as was tragically discovered in the case of Thalidomide.

Most drugs are much more insidious than Thalidomide. It is almost impossible at this time to guess even what all the effects of drugs or combinations of drugs will ultimately be on a baby as he grows older. Indications are that many kinds of behavioral and learning problems in school stem from drug use during pregnancy.

It should be obvious, then, that *no* drug can be assumed harmless. This includes medication you may have been taking over a period of time for a chronic condition, such as insulin (oral forms are particularly dangerous!) or certain anticoagulant preparations. And it also includes such familiar over-the-counter drugs as aspirin and cold remedies, among many others. Caffeine is also suspect, with some sources suggesting that excessive consumption tampers with the central nervous system. However, to date caffeine studies are still inconclusive. Apparently, the hazards of most of these substances are enhanced because they're not easily excreted by the baby. Even at birth the kidneys are not fully developed.

For safety's sake, until further research and evaluation are completed, do not take *any* drug without your doctor's knowledge. Any minor discomforts of pregnancy can usually be alleviated in alternative ways. Additionally, to be on the safe side you would be wise to limit yourself to not more than five cups per day of caffeine-containing beverages (including coffee, tea, and most cola drinks).

Q. Are X-rays dangerous during pregnancy?

A. The amount of radiation exposure in a diagnostic X-ray is extremely small. From a practical point of view there is nothing to be concerned about from one or even a few such X-rays during pregnancy if they are medically necessary. But caution is advised. Abdominal X-rays during early pregnancy are probably unwise. In addition, be sure to tell any physician or dentist you visit that you are pregnant and, if possible, postpone the X-ray until after your baby is born.

Q. What kinds of exercise are allowed during pregnancy?

A. Any moderate exercise that you have been used to doing is certainly worth continuing during pregnancy. This may include such activities as swimming, tennis, dancing, gardening, golf, cycling, or hiking. Walking is perhaps one of the best exercises of all—a minimum of a mile a day—to aid both digestion and circulation.

If you have chosen the natural childbirth method of delivery, you are undoubtedly attending classes where special exercises are taught that will aid in the birth process. If you are planning medicated childbirth, your doctor should still be able to provide you with some simple exercises that will, among other things, help relax the pelvic floor for easier delivery of the baby, or alleviate backache by allowing your spine to become more flexible. If no such exercise plan is available, check your local library. An excellent book on this subject is *Essential Exercises for the Childbearing Years* by Elizabeth Noble (Houghton Mifflin, 1976). In it, Ms. Noble, a physical therapist specializing in obstetrics and gynecology, describes an array of illustrated exercise techniques, and indicates which common exercises should be avoided during pregnancy and why. Included also are ways for achieving relaxation and good breathing habits. Throughout, the emphasis is on prevention of future problems and discomforts.

Whatever form your exercise program takes, it is important not to become overly tired. This is not the time to take up a new sport, and most experts agree that sports like horseback riding or any others that jolt the pelvis should be avoided.

Q. Should we leave some time between discontinuing the Pill and seeking a pregnancy?

A. Yes. Most doctors agree that it is a good idea to discontinue the oral contraceptive for at least three months before trying to become pregnant. You could use a mechanical means of contraception—a condom or diaphragm, for instance—to give your body a chance to return to its normal schedule. As you probably know, the Pill is as effective as it is because it interrupts the normal hormonal feedback between your ovaries and the pituitary gland in your brain. Naturally, your body may get somewhat confused when you stop taking the drug and may require a few months to get back on the track. It's also a good idea when you are pregnant to know about how far along you are and to have reliable information on due dates in case there are any complications and your doctor has to calculate the safest earliest time to deliver. Furthermore, there is some preliminary evidence, although it is not documented fully at this point, that the incidence of chromosomal abnormalities is higher during the first ovulation after the Pill is withdrawn. So you'll want to budget some time for a Pill break.

Q. *What is reverse rhythm?*

A. In seeking a pregnancy, you have the choice of two styles: in the first you would simply omit contraception and see what happens. If you have intercourse about five times a month, you would have about a 16 percent chance of conceiving during the first cycle. There would be, then, on the average, some five to six months between the decision and the conception. Again, if you were using the Pill, it could be a little longer.

If, however, you are in somewhat of a hurry to conceive, you might want to try the second style: *reverse rhythm;** that is, concentrating sexual intercourse near the middle of the menstrual cycle (see below) in order to increase the probability that conception will occur.

Q. *How do you go about identifying your fertile period?*

A. For a few months before you try to conceive, take your temperature each morning (except during the menstrual flow) immediately upon awakening. Record the temperature reading on graph paper. You can use any type of thermometer, but it's easier if you use a *basal body temperature* type, because it allows the detection of small changes. The reading during the preovulatory phase will be relatively low. As ovulation approaches, there will usually be a dip in this already low temperature. Immediately after the low point is reached there may be a sharp rise of a degree or more. Ovulation probably occurs right around the time of this upward shift. You'll find an example of a menstrual-cycle temperature curve in the following section on sex predetermination.** As you can tell from the graph, the most fertile portion of the cycle precedes the shift in temperature. Once the temperature goes up, the probability of conception's occurring drops to zero.

Concentrating intercourse just before the time of the upward temperature shift will lead to a high probability of pregnancy. All of this could be thwarted if a cold or other type of infection makes the temperature rise. But generally an awareness of your temperature changes should help you to conceive more quickly.

---

* A word of caution must be added here. Reverse rhythm does not suggest that reversing this advice would necessarily lead to successful application of the rhythm method.

** If you are using the oral contraceptive, since ovulation is inhibited, you will not notice any significant temperature shifts.

If the temperature method sounds too complicated, try the calendar technique. Figure out your range of cycle lengths over the last year or so. Subtract eleven days from the *longest* cycle and eighteen days from the *shortest* one. This is your likely "pregnancy period." For instance, if your shortest cycle was twenty-six days, your longest was thirty-one, your fertile period would be days eight and twenty and the days in between.

Reverse rhythm doesn't do much for sexual spontaneity and can be difficult if you take it seriously. You could, as an alternative, get one of those buttons that read, "I can be very friendly now", and wear it on the appropriate occasion. One eager prospective mother I talked to used to leave the "schedule" on her husband's dresser each month. Another would-be father told me he would carefully check his wife's temperature curve chart as he made the bed each morning; he found it very puzzling, since you have to make sure the temperature has really dipped and that it is really going up to stay before you know ovulation has occurred. "It is worse than buying stocks," he told me. "Some mornings I didn't know if we were past the fertile period or just experiencing a technical rally."

But reverse rhythm does increase the odds on pregnancy occurring quickly, and it may help you avoid some serious pregnancy problems by minimizing your chances of fertilizing an old egg.

Q. What determines the sex of a child?

A. The sperm determines the sex of the child at the moment of conception. The sperm and the egg carry twenty-three chromosomes each. Twenty-two of these join forces to determine all the bodily characteristics of the offspring—except for sex. The remaining two (one from the sperm, one from the egg) decide the course of sexual development. The female egg always carries an X sex chromosome, but the male sperm may carry either an X or a Y. If the X sperm is successful in fertilizing the egg, a girl will result; if the combination is XY, the baby will be a boy.

Q. Does the timing of intercourse influence the odds on your baby's sex?

A. The latest clinical work in the area of human sex predetermination has been conducted by Dr. Rodrigo Guerrero of the University of Valle in Cali, Colombia, South America. It was Dr. Guerrero who determined that, although the timing of intercourse within the woman's menstrual cycle is important (as had been previously noted by others), the *type* of insemination is also important. Women who are artificially inseminated produce offspring with different sex ratios than those who conceive by sexual intercourse. Writing in the *New England Journal of Medicine,* Dr. Guerrero concludes that "The sex ratio was found to change significantly during the menstrual cycle, both in natural and artificial insemination, although the trends were opposite." Dr. Guerrero's advice is to have sex four or more days before ovulation if you want a boy.* Have sex the day before ovulation if you want a girl. The chart below gives an example of how to locate these days on your basal body temperature curve. You would not want to place bets on either of these methods; on the other hand, particularly with regard to a boy baby, they give you a slight edge on nature.

Identification of the "Boy Days" and the "Girl Days"

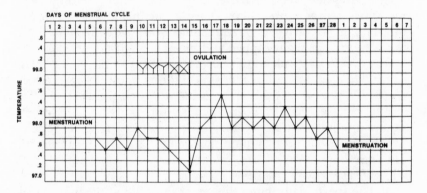

Y = intercourse on these days should increase your chances of having a boy. Your odds might increase from about 50 percent to 60-68 percent.

X = intercourse on these days should increase your chances of having a girl. Your odds might increase from about 50 percent to about 54 percent (sorry).

Q. Does the alkaline/acidic nature of the vagina affect the odds on your baby's sex?

A. For many years, some doctors have recommended baking soda douches for planning boy babies, vinegar ones for girl babies. Statistics in support of this theory are hardly convincing, but it is possible that the two types of sperm have differential tolerance for acid or alkalinity. Researchers from Yale Medical School who attempted to test this recipe raced Y and X sperm through fluids of

---

* How-to-have-a-boy books in the past five years have given exactly the opposite timing advice, but we know now that advice based on artificial insemination statistics is incorrect with regard to natural insemination.

various acidity and alkalinity and reported that there just didn't seem to be any difference between the two at all. Both did better in the alkaline mixture, a solution very similar to the type of secretion present in a woman's body around the time of ovulation. But as we saw with the sex ratio resulting from artificial insemination, laboratory experiments are not always fully applicable to everyday life. So there does remain the possibility that changing the chemical nature of the body could make a difference in sex outcome. Again, it probably wouldn't hurt to try. You can prepare a douche by mixing two tablespoons of white vinegar or two tablespoons of baking soda in a quart of water.

Baking soda or vinegar douches are not the only way to try to change the chemical balance: it is possible that female orgasm can bring about an alkaline response. Early Jewish writings suggested that male babies would result if "the woman emits her semen before the man," meaning, of course, if she has orgasm first. The scientific data on this subject are conflicting, but again, it wouldn't hurt to try.

We really need more research into the relationship of the nature of vaginal secretions and the sex outcome of the baby. Some preliminary evidence suggests that interesting discoveries might be derived from such inquiry; in a recent study of the sex outcome of thirty-eight pregnant women, it was found that 90 percent of those who reported they consistently had orgasm before their husbands—and 73 percent of those who "usually" achieved early orgasm—had male babies. All four of the women reporting no orgasm had girls. When this study is repeated a few times using larger numbers of couples, there might be some pretty strong evidence. Now, however, we're left with only the possibility that early (and frequent) female orgasm favors male births, and avoidance of female sexual climax may favor girls.

Does sex predetermination sound easy? I asked one woman who was desperate for a boy to tell me how the method worked for her. She was pregnant at the time, so I didn't know the final results. "It was unbelievable. Definitely not what you'd call romantic. I bought six boxes of baking soda and mapped out my cycles perfectly. Unfortunately, they did not coincide so perfectly with my husband's business trips. And other times when I was all set in my sexiest negligee, with my thermometer in my mouth to double-check, he was asleep in front of the television. And then the orgasm part—well, there are some things in life that just *can't* be planned!"

Q. How often does infertility occur?

A. For most couples, pregnancy will occur within six to eight months after contraception is omitted. Statistics indicate that 80 percent of couples seeking a pregnancy conceive within a year, and another 10 percent do so within two years. But the stork is not always responsive to a summons. About 10 percent of couples have problems serious enough to cause them to seek medical help.

In an age when a primary focus is put on technology to prevent births, it comes as a particular shock for a couple to learn that they are physically unable to have children. The clincher is that you can never really be sure that infertility is going to be a problem until you try.

Q. Why does infertility occur? And what can be done about it?

A. Many pitfalls can occur between the time sperm are produced and a successfully fertilized ovum implants in the lining of the uterus. Beyond that, there are problems in maintaining a pregnancy once it has occurred. Modern medicine's tests for pinpointing infertility problems are diverse and technical. But generally a physician will seek answers to four initial questions:

1. Is there a normal egg being released from the ovary at regular intervals?

2. Are there sufficient sperm available to fertilize an egg?

3. Is there an open passageway for the sperm and egg to pass up to or down the Fallopian tubes?

4. Is the endometrial lining of the uterus sufficiently prepared to receive and nourish a fertilized egg should one arrive?

To learn if an egg is being released from the ovary at regular intervals, the infertility counselor will probably ask the woman to take her temperature for a few months. If she has been using reverse rhythm, she can supply him with her temperature charts right away. It's a good idea for all women seeking infertility advice to arrive at the first session with at least three months of basal body temperature records. If significant inflections in temperature can be noted in these graphs, ovulation may indeed be occurring, and the infertility problem may lie elsewhere.

In a situation where there is no major shift in temperature throughout the month, and if other tests on both the wife and husband indicate that *anovulation,* the failure to ovulate, may indeed be the probable cause of their inability to conceive, the physician may recommend hormone treatment to stimulate ovulation.

A second common infertility problem relates to insufficient sperm availability in the Fallopian tubes. There are a number of ways this can happen: if a couple is not having intercourse frequently enough, the chances of having an adequate sperm supply around when the egg emerges from the ovary are pretty slim. The Rx for this type of couple may be two or three nights of wine and candlelight each week. But it could also be a low sperm count in the semen, or the inability of the sperm to make it up into the Fallopian tube neighborhood because the woman's cervical secretions are too thick and impenetrable.

If an egg is released from the ovary, and a sufficient number of sperm are matured in the testes, released into the vagina, and able to make the trip up through the uterus toward the oviducts, fertilization may occur. Then again, maybe it won't. If the tubes are blocked in some way, the egg may not be able to pass through and the sperm may have difficulty getting at the egg; or if the two sexy cells do find a way of getting together, the newly formed zygote may not be able to pass through to the uterus. Tubal blockage often results from pelvic inflammation that may follow untreated gonorrhea. But it could also be related to another fairly common disease: *endometriosis*, a condition in which portions of the uterine lining travel to and attach to other parts of the pelvic region. And often these cells don't just sit there, they grow—possibly on the back of the uterus, around the Fallopian tubes, in the Fallopian tubes (thus acting as a roadblock), or around the ovaries.

If everything goes well until the time a fertilized ovum enters the uterus, there can still be failure if the endometrium is not adequately prepared. Both estrogen and progesterone should have made the lining of the uterus the ideal place for a fertilized egg to implant and grow. But sometimes that just doesn't happen. A physician may wish to take a small sample of the endometrium for analysis. If he finds the lining not so prepared as it should be at that time of the cycle, he may feel that some form of hormone treatment is in order.

So many things can go wrong, that conception and pregnancy may present an unanticipated challenge to some couples. But most of those who do have problems manage, with the help of a competent infertility or gynecology specialist, to achieve the pregnancies they are seeking. A small segment, however, are never able to have children of their own. Some infertile couples turn to artificial insemination, a simple and painless process where semen is artificially introduced into the vagina shortly before or at the estimated time of ovulation. If the husband is producing some sperm, his semen will be used in artificial insemination. If his sperm count is extremely low—or if no sperm at all can be detected—a donor, selected by the physician, can contribute a semen sample which might be mixed with the husband's semen. The donor and the receiving woman never learn each other's identity; the whole process is kept about as impersonal as is a transfusion received from a blood bank. And the donor selection process takes into account the husband's physical characteristics, and possibly some demographic factors. For some couples, artificial insemination is the answer to their infertility problems. But for others, especially when donor semen is used, there can be significant emotional problems, and adoption may for them be a more appropriate alternative.

Q. How can you tell you're pregnant?

A. If you were using contraception for some time before your decision to have a baby, you will probably be very conscious of the fact that you *could* become pregnant during the very first month after you stop using it. But beware. You may begin to find pregnancy symptoms that aren't there.

It is theoretically possible, of course, that you could "just know" you're pregnant the very night it happens—or within a few days after you've missed your period. Some women get early clues that they are pregnant: not only is their menstrual period late, but their breasts are fuller and more sensitive than they usually are premenstrually and might even feel vaguely tingling. Morning sickness may occur within a couple of days after the day of the expected menstrual flow, urination may become more frequent, and the desire to fall asleep in the middle of the day may be almost overwhelming.

Occasionally there is some slight staining for a day or two about the time of the missed period, a form of spotting that results from the new cell's successful attempt to break through the layers of the endometrium.

Q. When should you get a pregnancy test?

A. The evidence of a pregnancy does not really get to be impressive until your normal menstrual period is ten days to two weeks late. After that point, your condition needs some scientific confirmation.

Although it's not a good idea to go running into your physician's office the very moment you even suspect a pregnancy, it is also not wise to wait much more than a couple of weeks after missing a period before you do have a laboratory pregnancy assessment. You've probably heard about home pregnancy tests (most of which are now reasonably accurate and simple to use), or mail-order pregnancy detection services. But if you have been having unprotected sex, or actually were practicing reverse rhythm, and have passed your latest probable menstrual date by ten days, why settle for anything but the real thing?

Q. What pregnancy tests are being used today?

A. There are a number of different types of tests. Most of them can diagnose a pregnancy within about four weeks after the conception occurred—two weeks after the missed menstrual period. Experimental tests can detect pregnancy even earlier. Some of them take a couple of days to reflect their verdict; others take only a few minutes or hours. In the Ascheim Zondek procedure (A-Z tests), some of the woman's urine is injected into a laboratory animal. The animal's ovaries develop spots if the urine they received came from a pregnant woman, but twenty-four to forty-eight hours may elapse before you know for sure what the animal's reaction was. The high cost of experimental animals has led to wider use of chemical slide or tube tests which give relatively quick readings.

Q. Why is early pregnancy medical care so important?

A. On rare occasions, something goes wrong in the days immediately following fertilization. In about one out of every three hundred pregnancies, the fertilized egg implants somewhere other than in the uterus. This could be the ovary, the abdominal cavity, or even the cervix, but in 95 percent of the cases, the misplaced zygote settles in the lining of the Fallopian tube, and the condition is diagnosed as an *ectopic* (or tubal) pregnancy. Perhaps the tube was abnormal in some way and its inner lining didn't do a good enough job in pushing the egg toward its intended destination. Whatever the cause, an ectopic pregnancy presents a serious risk to the woman if it is not found early. The oviducts do not have the expansion capability of the uterus—and if the growth is not stopped, the tube will burst. If you think you may be pregnant, find a gynecologist or family doctor soon. Don't take unnecessary chances by attempting to diagnose your own condition. Ask some of your friends to recommend a doctor—or if necessary, call the local medical society. Friends can probably give you a more personal evaluation—and clue you in to the facts about the physician's orientation, whether he believes in natural childbirth, anesthesia, induced labor, or the stork.

Q. What about adoption? How do you "make contact"?

A. There are two legal means of applying for an adopted child: through a municipal agency or voluntary service, or through a private, independent agent; that is, a physician, nurse, lawyer, or other professional who handles adoption. There are advantages and disadvantages in both routes.

"The cost of a private agent was so prohibitive," one adoptive mother-to-be told me, "that we decided in favor of the three- to four-year wait for a white infant. We knew from friends that the agency, as opposed to the private route, would be more hassle—more interviews, home evaluations, and general examination of our personal affairs—but we really wanted a child, and in our financial position we didn't have a choice."

This woman told me that she and her husband, when they first contacted the agency, were invited to a meeting of other prospective adoptive parents ("I thought of them all as competition") where the speaker encouraged them to consider other than the healthy white infants that so many people wanted and who were in such short supply. She and her husband then filed an application ("I'm glad we had our medical infertility records complete," she told me. "That really moved things along. We were given higher priority than those couples who had no proof that they had tried on their own"), and then they waited. ("It was worse than waiting for a guy to call for a second date.") At the time I last saw this couple, the agency had just begun a period of home study—to see if they were qualified to take on the responsibility of a child—and they were preparing for a long wait.

Some of the screening methods used by the social adoption agencies may annoy those applying. As one waiting man told me, "They ask you all about your sex life—then call in the middle of a Saturday afternoon to say they're coming over, just when you are settling down with your fourth beer and a football game. I felt I was constantly on call to put on a show." The stringency of the screening techniques is largely reflective of the sincere desire of the placement bureaus to ensure that the prospective parents really want a child—and that they can handle one, both emotionally and financially. But the recent high demand and low supply has given the placement staff even more control over what baby goes with which family.

Q. How can you go about adopting a "hard-to-place" child?

A. There is a shortage of adoptable babies, but there is not a shortage of adoptable children. For instance, the Adoption Resource Exchange of North America (ARENA), a program sponsored by the Child Welfare League of America, works with adoption agencies in the United States and Canada to help them find homes for hard-to-place children. Hard to place? Generally this definition covers black children of all ages (but read about the qualification on this below), children with severe physical handicaps, children of limited intellectual ability, school-age children (seven to fourteen years) of all racial and ethnic heritages, and those who are members of groups of brothers and sisters who must be placed together. Obviously it takes a special type of couple—or individual if it is a single-parent adoption—with a sense of maturity and flexibility to accept the challenges these children offer. But an increasing number of people are turning to this option and are meeting the challenge successfully.

The qualification on the availability of black children is part of considerable controversy currently surrounding this subject, particularly from the black community. A growing number of black children are being offered for adoption with the qualification that they will be placed only in black homes; agencies are having second thoughts about the motivation of some would-be adoptive parents who insist on transracial adoption.

Q. Is it true that after you adopt a child, you're more likely to become pregnant?

A. "The ink was hardly dry on the adoption papers when she found she was pregnant," goes the adage.

In the Book of Genesis, there is an example of this: "And Sarah said unto Abraham, 'Behold now, the Lord hath restrained me from bearing; go in, I pray thee, unto my hand maid; it may be that I shall be builded up through her.' "

The folklore has spread to include the statement, "If your dog has puppies, it will help." Is there any basis to this?

The answer lies in the title of a paper that appeared recently in *Psychosomatic Medicine*—"Conception after Adoption: An Open Question." In other words, we don't know. The literature in the last thirty years has presented conflicting results, and right now there is no statistical evidence that there is such a relationship. There are some biological hypotheses that suggest it could be true for some individuals. Perhaps, for instance, adoption resolves some of the conflicts that are inhibiting conception. There is evidence that emotional stress can interfere with the normal functioning of the menstrual cycle. Maybe ovulation becomes more regular when the pressure to have a baby is removed. Or possibly, some physicians feel, there is a reduction in the spasms of the Fallopian tube which might have been causing problems. One researcher has suggested that because the husband enters into a form of competition with the new intruder, his sexual demands are increased—and they have intercourse more often.

Q. Are there special problems associated with an adopted child?

A. Not necessarily. As the American Academy of Pediatrics has noted, "the risks inherent in adoption are essentially the same as those inherent in family life generally." There can be some inherited problems—but the agency or representative usually tells you as much as possible about the biological parents beforehand. There can be some emotional adjustments; for instance, dealing with those untactful types who say, "Whose fault was it you couldn't have children?" or even better, "Don't you wonder who her *real* parents are?" And, in the back of most adoptive parents' minds is the concern that the child will grow up and set out on a worldwide search for his "true heritage." Women's magazines are full of stories about "how I found my real mother." (Some states now do give an adopted child the right to know the names of his biological parents when he turns eighteen, a right that is exercised very infrequently.)

Q. What's good parenthood etiquette?

A. With respect to the general discussion of this book, it is the ability to be comfortable with your decision to have a child and also to respect other people's right not to. For you, parenthood may be great, but different people have different ideas, and those who choose not to have children do not appreciate the oh-you're-missing-so-much routine. (And *please* don't bore them with pictures of your "little darlings.")

For Nonparents

Q. Should you expect questions and unsolicited advice from friends and family when they hear of your decision?

A. But of course! "It's easier to be a radical than a childless wife," one confirmed nonparent complained to me. "People wouldn't think of telling you how to vote or conduct your sex life, but they feel free to criticize you for not having a baby. Being childless by choice is more of a stigma than being divorced."

When mature, responsible adults make decisions to do something—whether it is to go on for professional training in graduate school, take a new job, buy or sell a house—they might be questioned as to why they are doing it. They are making a positive move toward some goal, are generally aware of the motivational forces that are operative, and can freely discuss their action. They have rational reasons for their behavior. Rarely would these same people be questioned about why they *weren't* going to graduate school, why they *weren't* changing jobs, or why they *weren't* buying a house.

However, the opposite is often true in the parenthood department. Rarely are couples asked *why* they are having children. But those who choose to remain child-free or to stop at one are constantly bombarded with queries and accusations. Pressures in this direction appear to be abating as more publicity is given to the option of remaining child-free or stopping at one or two, but you probably still will get some comments, subtle and otherwise.

When you get a question about why you're not having children, first figure out why the person is asking you. Is he or she just curious? Trying to start a fight with you? Attempting to convert you? Or, if the people who ask are parents, can you detect some feeling that they are perhaps unsure about whether or not they made the right decision for themselves? (Keep a grain of salt handy: people who have children have a vested interest in parenthood, just as married people stick up for marriage, and singles stick up for the swinging single life.) In most cases the question is rhetorical anyway—or can be satisfied by a simple "because we thought about it and realized that not having children was best for us," or "at this point we are not ready for children." Only in the minority of cases will you really have to go much further than that—unless you want to.

Of course, if you meet some of the common arguments against nonparenthood, you should be prepared. "You're selfish!" is a favorite. Perhaps you could point out, as Oscar Wilde did, that "selfishness is not living as one wishes to live; it is asking others to live as one wishes to live." Or you might say that you do not feel in yourself the commitment that having a child requires. For you, having a child would be selfish. "But it's natural!" (This one is subtitled, "You're going against all the biological instincts.") If you are in the mood for quotations, you could quote John Stuart Mill, who said, "Everything which is usual appears natural," and remind them that if you did everything that came naturally, you'd end up in jail.

Then there's always, "Oh, I feel so sorry for you!" You might meet this by explaining that, for you, the decision to remain child-free is a positive one, not a negative one requiring condolences. "You're going to be sorry later . . . ," you might hear, or "Your husband will change his mind when he is forty-four and he'll leave you for another woman," or "Your wife will wake up one morning and be very frustrated and make life miserable for you." You might calmly

254 / A Baby? . . . Maybe

explain that none of us can predict the future, but that from your point of view, if there is something to be sorry about later, at least no third person will be involved.

Two final standbys are, "Don't you like children?" (In other words, "Are you a monster or something?") And, "You're just the type who should be having children." To the first question you might answer that it is possible to be very fond of children and still want to make a contribution to them and the rest of the world by assuming a role other than parent. As for the second, you might discuss why you feel you are not the parent type and how you feel that you can make better contributions to society without reproducing your gene pool.

Parenthood is a very emotional issue. If you are challenged about not having children, the least risky and most constructive route is to defend your position without undermining the challenger's.

Q. What do you tell your parents?

A. "How did you tell your parents?" I asked one young husband who, with his wife, had decided in favor of nonparenthood.

"I have to go back somewhat to answer that question. The day before we were married, my mother pulled me aside and told me the facts of life. I was thirty-two, so I guess she figured it was time to tell me. She told me to 'go easy' on the wedding night because women were 'fragile.' I decided to nod agreeably and not make a scene about her getting involved in my private life. The day after the wedding, my parents came to the airport to see us off for Barbados, and she again pulled me aside to ask 'how things went.' I was furious. And I told her it was none of her expletive deleted business. From then on, she has never once asked us a question about our private lives. What would I advise other couples to tell their parents? The same thing. It's none of their business. Of course there are nicer ways of putting that message, but that's basically it."

There *are* nice ways of discussing this delicate subject. Reflect on the reason why your parents want grandchildren. Take into account their feelings, too. It is your decision, and they should understand that, but they have needs too. Perhaps you can help them meet those needs in other ways, by looking into foster grandparent programs in your neighborhood or in some other way getting them involved with young people. Now consider some possible ploys that may get you off the hook.

First, you can delay ("Oh, well, someday maybe. We're not quite ready yet"), or as *Glamour* magazine once suggested in its sticky-problem-of-the-month section, tell them, "You're too young to be grandparents."

Second, you can meet the situation straight on: "We've thought it through, and we feel that for us it is the best decision. We've considered all sides of the issue—and it wasn't an easy decision to make. But that's how we see it." (Here you risk being told to see an ophthalmologist.)

Third, there is the cop-out for cowards: flip a coin to determine who is going to take the sterility rap and then tell your parents of your "plight." They may even feel sorry for you—and they certainly will stop bugging you until they give some thought to the adoption question. And if you ever change your mind and have a child—well, miracles do happen.

Q. What are some of the pitfalls some nonparents face?

A. One is committing yourself publicly to a decision not to have children. Let me give you an example.

In the March 1974 issue of *Esquire*, there was an article on child-free living, and a picture that carried the title "Home, Sweet, Kidless Home." Among others, the photo featured Ike Hill (of the Chicago Bears) and his wife, Sandra, an attorney, as one of five couples who had chosen to be child-free. "People are planning more, planning their futures," the article stated. Ike was quoted as saying, "I'd like to be more financially secure," and Sandra, "Children demand sacrifices, and Ike and I enjoy each other too much to make those sacrifices." That was fine, except that five months later I saw the announcement of their first child. (Ellen Peck of NON subsequently gave them the Responsible Parents of the Year Award).

NON associates have explained to me that there is no hard feeling when a member does decide to become a parent. Indeed, a number of active NON members, including the executive director, do have children. But why commit yourself? Why say you're definitely not going to have children? Why paint yourself into a corner when there's no reason to do so? If you do change your mind, you may feel uncomfortable. Or worse, you may convince yourself that because of your prior commitment, you *can't* change your mind. That's the first "beware of "— don't get overly and prematurely enthusiastic about nonparenthood.

Here are some additional bits of nonparenthood etiquette. People who have children are *aware* of the freedom that goes with being child-free. It's not necessary to say, "Oh, yes, we ran off to London that weekend, and to Rome the next. It's so delightful to be able to get up every morning and peacefully read *The New York Times* leisurely over a second cup of coffee. We have the most *wonderful* life—every night is Saturday night . . ." The great majority of married people in this country *do* have children. And although you have the option not to, that doesn't mean you should think less of or even subtly denigrate someone who does choose parenthood. Nonparents often complain that couples with children are total bores, talking about their children day and night, insisting you look at the latest photograph of this one and that one. But there is such a thing as a child-free bore who in a supercilious way conveys the opinion that a career in market research is on a higher level than parenthood, or who takes every opportunity to criticize parents on the way they are handling their jobs.

Finally, it's always worth keeping in mind that the cause of nonparenthood is a civil liberties issue only; that is, those who choose to remain childless should not be stigmatized in any way. It's a personal matter. *But nonparenthood itself is not a social goal,* not something you should be trying to sell them.

Society obviously must improve its approach to make decisions about parenthood really free ones. Until individuals fully accept other people's decisions in this area (and feel less unsure of their own) probably the best rule to follow is to resolve the question the way that seems best for you—and then tread softly.

If you have further questions on any of the topics in this Appendix, consider following up some of the references listed on the next pages.

Suggestions for Further Reading

Biology of Reproduction, Birth Control, Pregnancy Planning, Infertility, and Sex Predetermination

American Medical Association. *Human Sexuality*. Chicago: American Medical Association, 1972.

Anderson, Alan J. "Will My Baby Be Normal?" *The New York Times Magazine*, 8 September 1974.

"Antenatal Diagnosis and Down's Syndrome." National Institute of Child Health and Human Development, DHEW Publication no. (NIH) 74–538, 1973.

Bernard, Will. "Your Legal Rights When Birth Control Fails." *Woman's Day*, 17 July 1979.

Boston Children's Medical Center. *Pregnancy, Birth and the Newborn Baby*. New York: Delacorte Press, 1972.

Brant, H., and Brant, M. *Dictionary of Pregnancy, Childbirth and Contraception*. London: Mayflower, 1971.

Brody, Jane. "Survey Finds Boy Preferred as the First-Born, Girls as Second." *The New York Times*, 4 May 1974.

Brown, Fred., and Kempton, Rudolf. *Sex Questions and Answers*, 2nd edition. New York: McGraw-Hill, 1970.

Brozan, Nadine. "Women Who Waited: Starting a Family After the Age of 30." *The New York Times*, 23 September 1977.

Bumpass, Larry, and Westoff, Charles. *The Later Years of Childbearing*. Princeton, N.J.: Princeton University Press, 1970.

Bylinsky, Gene. "What Science Can Do about Hereditary Problems." *Fortune*, September 1974.

Calderone, Mary. *Manual of Family Planning and Contraceptive Practice*. Baltimore: Williams and Wilkins, 1970.

Campbell, Arthur. "Three Generations of Parents." *Family Planning Perspectives* 5 (1973):106.

Carter, Betsy. "Baby Talk." *Newsweek*, 8 August 1977.

Clark, Matt, with Dan Shapiro. "Fertility Rites." *Newsweek*, 11 October 1976.

Clark, Nancy Hughes. "Birth Defects: How to Prevent Them." *Harper's Bazaar*, July 1977.

257

Cole, William. "The Right to Be Well-Born." U.S. Department of HEW, National Institute of Child Health and Human Development, Public Health Service, Bethesda, Md., undated.

Coombs, Lolagene C. "How Many Children Do Couples Really Want?" *Family Planning Perspectives*, September/October 1978.

David, Henry P., and Johnson, Raymond L. "Forum: Population Planning" ("Fertility Regulation in Early Childbearing Years: Psychosocial and Psychoeconomic Aspects"). *Preventive Medicine*, March 1977.

Demarest, Robert, and Sciarra, John. *Conception, Birth and Contraception*. New York: McGraw-Hill, 1969.

Evans, Ginny, with Judith G. Hall, M.D. "The Older the Sperm . . . " *Ms.*, January 1976.

Evans, Olive. "Married, Working, 30 Years Old—Is There Room for a Child?" *The New York Times*, 6 June 1973.

Fabe, Marilyn, and Wikler, Norma. *Up Against the Clock*. New York: Random House, 1979.

"Facts About Mongolism for Women Over 35." National Institute of Child Health and Human Development, DHEW publication no. (NIH) 74–536, 1973.

Feldman, David M. *Birth Control in Jewish Law*. New York: New York University Press, 1968.

Fielding, Waldo L. *Pregnancy: The Best State of the Union*. New York: Thomas Y. Crowell Company, 1971.

Flaste, Richard. "A Baby? Now or Later? Or Maybe Never?" *The New York Times*, 7 May 1976.

Fleishman, N., and Dixon, P. *Vasectomy, Sex and Parenthood*. New York: Doubleday, 1973.

Galton, Lawrence. "Decisions, Decisions, Decisions." *The New York Times Magazine*, 30 June 1974.

Glass, R., and Kase, N. *Woman's Choice*. New York: Basic Books, 1970.

Hafez, E.S., and Evans, T.N. *Human Reproduction*. New York: Harper and Row, 1973.

Havemann, Ernest. *Birth Control*. New York: Time–Life Books, 1967.

Helitzer, F. "Do You Want a Boy or Girl?" *Princeton Alumni Weekly* 21 May 1974.

Insel, Paul M., and Roth, Walton T. *Core Concepts in Health*, 2nd edition, chapter 8. Palo Alto, Calif.: Mayfield Publishing Co., 1979.

Joël, K. *Fertility Disturbances in Men and Women*. New York: Karger, 1971.

Kaatz, Pam. "My Search for a Child." *Redbook*, June 1975.

Kahn, H., and Wiener, A. "The Next Thirty Years." *Daedalus*, Summer 1967.

Kane, Leslie. "Baby Boom on the Way as Wives Near 30 Start to Panic." *The National Star*, 22 November 1977.

Kapel, Saul. "Parenthood Is Life's Most Fateful Decision" (syndicated column). *New York Daily News*, 8 July 1976.

Kaufman, S. A. *New Hope for the Childless Couple: The Causes and Treatment of Infertility*. New York: Simon and Schuster, 1970.

Knepp, T. *Human Reproduction: Health and Hygiene*. London: Carbondale and Edwardsville, 1967.

Kramer, Rita. "A Fresh Look at the Only Child." *The New York Times Magazine*, 15 October 1972.

Leboyer, F. *Birth Without Violence*. New York: Alfred A. Knopf, 1975.

Lednicer, D. *Contraception: The Chemical Control of Fertility*. New York: M. Dekker, 1969.

Lieberman, E. James. "The Case for Small Families." *The New York Times Magazine*, 8 March 1970.

———— . "A Doctor Forecasts Determining of Sex of Child in Advance." *The New York Times,* 27 November 1968.

Macleod, J. S. "How to Hold a Wife: A Bridegroom's Guide." *Village Voice,* 11 February 1971, p. 5.

Maine, Deborah. "Does Abortion Affect Later Pregnancies?" *Family Planning Perspectives,* March /April 1979.

Masters, William, and Johnson, Virginia. *Human Sexual Response.* Boston: Little, Brown & Co., 1966.

McCauley, Carole Spearin. *Pregnancy After 35.* New York: E. P. Dutton & Co., 1976.

McNamara, Helen. "Doctor, Am I Too Old to Have a Baby?" *Good Housekeeping,* January 1977.

Milinaire, Caterine. *Birth.* New York: Harmony Books, 1974.

Miller, M. A., and Leavell, L. *Anatomy and Physiology.* New York: Macmillan Co., 1972.

"More Than One-Third of U.S. Children Will Live in One-Parent Homes as Result of Broken Marriage." *Family Planning Perspectives* (Digest), March /April 1979.

Morton, Marcia C. *Pregnancy Notebook.* New York: Workman Publishing Co., 1972.

"Planning Your Pregnancy." Family Planning Program, Office of Health Affairs, Office of Economic Opportunity, July 1970.

"Please God Let Us Have a Baby!" Fertility Research Foundation, 1973.

Price, Jane. *You're Not Too Old to Have a Baby.* New York: Penguin Books, 1977.

Roberts, F. *Breast Feeding.* Bristol, England: John Wright & Sons, 1968.

Rossman, Isadore. "Two Children by Choice: Why Smaller Families Must Become the New American Ideal." *Parents' Magazine,* May 1970.

Rudel, H., et al. *Birth Control.* New York: Macmillan Co., 1973.

Sachs, Sylvia. "To Parent Or Not, That Is the Question." *Pittsburgh Press,* 6 January 1976.

Salk, Lee. "Parents After 40." *Harper's Bazaar,* August 1975.

Schrier, Jack J. "It's a Girl! It's a Boy! It's a Father for the First Time at Age 47!" *The New York Times,* 3 June 1979.

SerVaas, Cory. "Medical Mailbox" (re: male fertility). *The Saturday Evening Post,* September 1975.

Simons, G. L. *A History of Sex.* London: NEL Books, 1970.

———— . *Sex and Superstition.* London: Abelard–Schuman, 1973.

"Sound Off to the Editor: Limiting the Family Size." *American Baby,* May 1973.

Sussman, Marvin B. "The Family Today." *Children Today,* March/April, 1978.

Understanding. Ortho Pharmaceutical Corporation. Raritan, N.J., undated.

"U.S. Family Is Changing: Nearly Half of All 1977 Babies Will Spend Some Part of Childhood with One Parent Only." *Family Planning Perspectives* (Digest), January/February 1978.

"U.S. Women Marrying Later, Having Babies Later, Spacing Them Further Apart Than in Earlier Years." *Family Planning Perspectives,* September/October 1978.

Volpe, E. P. *Human Heredity and Birth Defects.* New York: Pegasus, 1971.

Warner, M. *Modern Fertility Guide: Practical Advice for the Childless Couple.* New York: Funk and Wagnalls, 1968.

Westoff, Charles F., and McCarthy, James. "Population Attitudes and Fertility." *Family Planning Perspectives,* March /April 1979.

Westoff, Leslie A. "Sterilization." *The New York Times Magazine,* 29 September 1974.

Westoff, Leslie A., and Westoff, Charles F. *From Now to Zero.* Boston: Little, Brown & Co., 1968.

Whelan, Elizabeth M. *Boy or Girl?: The Sex Selection Technique That Makes All Others Obsolete.* New York: Bobbs-Merrill, 1977.

———— . "Can You Control Your Baby's Sex?" *Modern Bride,* June/July 1974.

_____ . "Parenthood: If 'Yes,' When?" *Bride Magazine*, August/September 1974.

_____ . "Pregnancy Basics." *Vogue*, Spring/Summer 1979.

_____ . *The Pregnancy Experience*. New York: W. W. Norton, 1978.

Whelan, Elizabeth M., and Quadland, M. C. *Human Reproduction and Family Planning: A Programmed Text*. Palo Alto, Calif.: Syntex Laboratories, 1973.

Whitbread, Jane. "Birth Control: A Drug That Lasts Three Months." *McCall's*, May 1975.

"Will the Child Be Normal? Ask Mother." *Science News*, 1 October 1977.

Psychology of Parenthood; Economics of Having Children

Anthony, E. James, and Benedek, Therese. *Parenthood: Its Psychology and Psychopathology*. Boston: Little, Brown & Co., 1970.

Benedek, Therese, "Parenthood as a Developmental Phase." *Journal of the American Psychoanalytic Association* 7 (1959): 389.

Blaine, G. *Are Parents Bad for Children?* New York: Coward, McCann & Geoghegan, 1973.

Blood, R. O. *Marriage*. New York: Free Press of Glencoe, 1962.

Blumenfield, Samuel L. "Motherhood: A Proud Profession." *Vital Speeches*, 15 August 1977.

Bombeck, Erma. "Parents Closet Poll Is Revealing." Syndicated column in Clarksville (Tenn.) *Leaf-Chronicle*, 2 October 1979.

Boston Women's Health Book Collective. *Our Bodies, Ourselves*. New York: Simon and Schuster, 1973.

_____ . *Ourselves and Our Children*. New York: Random House, 1978.

Bricklin, Barry, and Bricklin, Patricia. *Strong Family, Strong Child*. New York: Delacorte Press, 1970.

Chapman, J. *The Feminine Mind and Body*. London. Vision Press, 1967.

Chasseguet-Smirgel, J. *Female Sexuality: New Psychoanalytic Views*. Ann Arbor, Mich.: University of Michigan Press, 1970.

Colman, Arthur, and Colman, Libby. *Pregnancy: The Psychological Experience*. New York: Herder and Herder, 1971.

Cooper, L. "Predispositions toward Parenthood: A Comparison of Male and Female Students." *Sociology Research* 42 (1957):31.

Corman, Avery. "The Beginning of the End of Sex: The First Baby." *Cosmopolitan*, October 1974.

Curley, Jayme, et al. *The Balancing Act: A Career and a Baby*, Edited by Sydelle Kramer. Chicago: Chicago Review Press /Swallow Press, 1976.

Curtis, Jean. *Working Mothers*. Garden City, N.Y.: Doubleday & Co., 1976.

de Beauvoir, Simone. *The Second Sex*. New York: Alfred A. Knopf, 1971.

De Rosis, Helen. *Parent Power/Child Power*. New York: The Bobbs-Merrill Company, 1974.

Deutsch, Helene. *The Psychology of Women*. 2 vols. New York: Grune and Stratton, 1945.

Dodson, Fitzhugh. *How to Father*. New York: Signet, 1975.

Drabble, Margaret. "Midway Through Motherhood." *Parents' Magazine*, April 1974.

_____ . "All My Love (signed) Mama." *The New York Times Magazine*, 4 August 1973.

Dunn, H. P. "Quality v. Quantity in Children," letter to the Editor. *British Medical Journal,* 19 November 1977.

Erikson, Erik H. *Identity, Youth and Crisis.* New York: William Norton, 1968.

———— . *Childhood and Society.* New York: W. W. Norton, 1950.

Evans, R. I. *Dialogue with Erik Erikson.* New York: Harper and Row, 1967.

Fallaci, Oriana. *Letter to a Child Never Born.* New York: Simon and Schuster, 1976.

"The Fathering Instinct: Working Fathers." *Ms.,* May 1974.

Fawcett, James T. *Psychology and Population.* New York: The Population Council, 1970.

Finder, Alan. "Children?—A Choice, Not a Duty." *The Sunday (Bergen, N.J.) Record,* 26 September 1976.

Finn, J. "The Birth of a Father." *Parents' Magazine,* May 1974.

Fletchner, R. *Instinct in Man.* New York: International University Press, 1957.

Flynn, L. "Society and Motherhood." *Speaking Out.* SIECUS Sex Information and Council of the United States Report, September 1974.

Ford, C. S., and Beach, F. *Patterns of Sexual Behavior.* New York: Harper and Brothers, 1952.

Francke, Linda Bird. "The Myth of the Liberated Housewife." *Harper's Bazaar,* February 1977.

Freud, Sigmund. *Psychopathology of Everyday Life.* New York: Macmillan Co., 1941.

———— . *An Outline of Psychoanalysis.* New York: W. W. Norton, 1949.

Glickman, Beatrice Marden, and Springer, Nesha Bass. *Who Cares for the Baby?: Choices in Child Care.* New York: Schocken Books, 1978.

Goldman, G. D., and Milman, D. S. *Modern Woman: Her Psychology and Sexuality.* Springfield, Ill.: Charles C. Thomas Company, 1969.

Gordon, Sol. "What Makes a Good Father." *Harper's Bazaar,* July 1975.

Gould, Robert. "The Wrong Reasons to Have Children." *The New York Times Magazine,* 3 May 1970.

Griffin, Susan. "On Wanting to Be the Mother I Wanted." *Ms.,* January 1977.

Grossman, J. *Life with Family: A Perspective on Parenthood.* New York: Appleton-Century-Crofts, 1948.

Group for the Advancement of Psychiatry. *The Joys and Sorrows of Parenthood.* New York: Charles Scribner's Sons, 1973.

Guss, Rosemary and Coleman, Diane. "If They Had It To Do Over Again—*Good Housekeeping* Readers *Would* Have Children." *Good Housekeeping,* October 1976.

Hern, Warren. "Is Pregnancy Really Normal?" *Family Planning Perspectives* 8 (1973):5.

Hollingworth, Leta S. "Social Devices for Impelling Women to Bear and Rear Children." *American Journal of Sociology* 22 (1916):19.

Horney, Karen. *Feminine Psychology.* New York: W. W. Norton and Company, 1967.

"How Do You Really Feel About Having Children?" *Redbook,* September 1977.

Howell, Mary. "Employed Mothers and Their Families." *Pediatrics* 52 (1973):252.

"In Praise of Fatherhood: Its Responsibilities and Joys." *Parents' Magazine,* May 1974.

Klopfer, P. H. "Mother Love: What Turns It On?" *American Scientist* 59 (1971):404.

Kole, Jane. "Mothers and Daughters: 8 Successful Women Discuss Motherhood." *Harper's Bazaar,* October 1976.

Kurtz, Irma. "A New Life in My Life." *Cosmopolitan,* December, 1975.

Lake, Alice. "Three for the Seesaw: How a First Baby Changes a Marriage." *Redbook,* April 1974.

Landers, Ann. "If You Had It To Do Over Again Would You Have Children?" *Good Housekeeping,* June 1976.

Lebowitz, Fran. "Children: Pro or Con?" (The Lebowitz Report). *Mademoiselle*, November 1976.

Lehfeldt, H., and Guze, H. "Psychological Factors in Contraceptive Failure." *Fertility and Sterility* 17 (1966):110.

Leonard, John. "The Fathering Instinct." *Ms.*, May 1974.

Lublin, Joanne S. "Questions a Woman Asks Herself." *The Wall Street Journal*, 2 January 1976.

Mayo, T. J. "The High Cost of Parenthood." *This Week*, 27 September 1976.

McBride, Angela. "Why Do You Really Want a Baby?" *Glamour*, October 1973.

————. *The Growth and Development of Mothers*. New York: Harper and Row, 1973.

McGrath, Nancy and Chip. "Why a Baby?" *The New York Times Magazine*, 26 May 1975.

Mead, Margaret. "Trial Parenthood." *Redbook*, June 1974.

————. *Male and Female*. New York: William Morrow and Company, 1949.

Mead, Margaret, and Heyman, Ken. *Family*. New York: Macmillan Co., 1965.

"Measuring the Quality of Life in America: A New Frontier for Social Science." *Institute for Social Research*, Summer 1974.

Millett, Kate. *Sexual Politics*. New York: Doubleday, 1970.

Morris, Bernadine. "Finding Someone Responsible to Care for the Children." *The New York Times*, 7 January 1974.

Morrone, Wenda Wardell. "Motherhood . . . How Much Chance for Personal Growth?" *Glamour*, December 1974.

Nye, F. I., and Hoffman, L. W. *The Employed Mother in America*. Chicago: Rand McNally, 1965.

"$1,500 Price Tag for Today's Baby." *Perspective*, The Blue Cross Magazine. 2nd quarter, 1970.

Peck, Ellen, and Granzig, William. *The Parent Test: How to Measure and Develop Your Talent for Parenthood*. New York: G. P. Putnam's Sons, 1978.

Perutz, Kathrin. "Why Have Children?" *PHB* (Polaroid Company), September 1974.

Pogrebin, Letty Cottin. "Motherhood." *Ms.*, May 1973.

Porter, Sylvia. "What It Costs Now to Have a Baby." *Ladies' Home Journal*, July 1970.

Price, Jane. *How to Have a Child and Keep Your Job*. New York: St. Martin's Press, 1979.

"The Pros and Cons of Parenthood." *Ebony*, July 1977.

Reed, Ritchie H., and McIntosh, Susan. "Costs of Children." *Economic Aspects of Population Changes*, Research Reports, vol. 2, Commission on Population Growth and the American Future.

Rheingold, Joseph C. *The Fear of Being a Woman*. New York: Grune and Stratton, 1964.

Rhodes, P. *Woman: A Biological Study of the Female Role in Twentieth Century Society*. London: Corgi Books, 1969.

Rich, Adrienne. *Of Woman Born: Motherhood as Experience and Institution*. New York: W. W. Norton, 1976.

Richardson, S., and Guttmacher, Alan F. *Childbearing: Its Social and Psychological Aspects*. Baltimore: Williams and Wilkins, 1967.

Rodgers, Mary Augusta. "A Working Mother's Tough Decision: Taking Time Out from a Career to Be with Her Baby." *Woman's Day*, 17 July 1979.

Russell, Dora. *Children: Why Do We Have Them?* New York: Harper and Brothers, 1933.

Safran, Claire. "What 80,000 Women Can Tell You About Your Biggest Decision—Having a Baby." *Redbook*, May 1978.

Salk, Lee. *Preparing for Parenthood.* New York: David McKay Co., 1974.

Scott, Loretta. "Family: The Case for Kids." *Syracuse (N.Y.) New Times,* 21 December 1975.

Sherman, J. *On the Psychology of Women.* Springfield, Ill.: Charles C. Thomas, 1971.

Silberman, Arlene. "If I Had My Kids to Raise Over Again." *Woman's Day,* 17 July 1979.

Spock, Benjamin. "How Much Should a First Baby Change a Marriage?" *Redbook,* March 1976.

Stannard, Una. "Adam's Rib, or the Woman Within." *Trans-Action,* November/December 1970.

Susman, Edward. "I Was a Mother for Six Months." *Good Housekeeping,* July 1977.

"Turning Baby 'Maybe' Into a Firm Decision." *Baltimore Sun,* 20 August 1976.

Vahanian, T., and Olds, S. "Will Your Children Break . . . or Make . . . Your Marriage?" *Parents' Magazine,* August 1974.

"What Life Is Like with 12 Children . . . Two . . . None." *U.S. News and World Report,* 4 October 1976.

Whelan, Elizabeth M. "How Much It Costs to Have a Baby." *Glamour,* November 1974.

———. *The Pregnancy Experience: A Psychological Guide for Expectant Parents.* New York: W. W. Norton, 1978.

———. "Should a Career Woman Have Children?" *Harper's Bazaar,* February 1977.

"Women's Attitudes on Working Studied." *The New York Times,* 24 April 1971.

Wyse, Lois. "Parenting: You Learn, Too." *Vogue,* December 1977.

Nonparenthood

Albert, E. "The Unmothered Women." In *The Challenge to Women.* Edited by S. Farber and R. Wilson. New York: Basic Books, 1966.

Ayling, Jean. *The Retreat from Parenthood.* London: Kegan Paul, Trench, Trubner & Company, 1930.

Balchin, Nigel. "Children Are a Waste of Time." *Saturday Evening Post,* 9 October 1965.

Bombeck, Erma. "At Wit's End" (syndicated column on nonmothers). Clarksville (Tenn.) *Leaf-Chronicle,* 13 May 1979.

Bush, Sherida. "NON—Making the Case for Childlessness." *Psychology Today,* November 1977.

Buxton, Bonnie. "Why We Have No Children." *American Home,* January 1976.

"Down with Kids." *Time,* 3 July 1973.

Gaylin, Jody. "Choosing a Life Without Children." *Psychology Today,* November 1977.

Greene, Gael. "I Could Be Happy Without Children. Maybe Forever." *McCall's,* April 1974.

———. "A Vote Against Motherhood." *Saturday Evening Post,* 26 January 1963.

Grosswirth, Marvin. "Kids . . . Who Needs 'Em?" *Science Digest,* October 1976.

Haskell, Molly. "Yes We Have No Bambinos." *Viva,* March 1975.

Kamien, Marcia. "We'll Never Have Kids!" *Woman's Day,* 9 January 1978.

Kramer, Rita. "The No-Child Family." *The New York Times Magazine,* 24 December 1972.

McLaughlin, Mary. "Parents Who Wouldn't Do It Again." *McCall's,* November 1975.

Michels, Lynnell. "Why We Don't Want Children." *Redbook,* January 1970.
"Miss Stephanie Mills Vs. Motherhood." *Look,* 21 April 1970.
Peck, Ellen. *The Baby Trap.* New York: Bernard Geis Associates, 1971.
Peck, Ellen, and Senderowitz, Judith. *Pronatalism: The Myth of Mom and Apple Pie.* New York: Thomas Y. Crowell and Company, 1974.
Radl, Shirley. *Mother's Day Is Over.* New York: Charterhouse, 1972.
Rollin, Betty. "Motherhood: Who Needs It?" *Look,* 22 September 1970.
Safran, Cl ire. "Motherhood Is Not My Game." *Today's Health,* May 1975.
Silka, Linua, and Kiesler, Sara. "Couples Who Choose to Remain Childless." *Family Planning Perspectives,* January/February 1977.
Silverman, Anna, and Silverman, Arnold. *The Case Against Having Children.* New York: David McKay, 1971.
Simon, John. "Why I'm Childless." *Harper's Magazine,* May 1975.
Veevers, Jean E. "Voluntary Childlessness: A Neglected Area of Family Study." *The Family Coordinator* 22 (1973):199.
──────. "Voluntarily Childless Wives: An Exploratory Study," *Mental Health Digest* 5 (1973)(October):8.
──────. "The Social Meaning of Parenthood," *Psychiatry* 36 (1973):291.
──────. "Childlessness and Age at First Marriage." *Social Biology* 18 (1971):292.
Willis, Ellen. "To Be or Not to Be a Mother." *Ms.,* October 1974.
Wills, Garry. "What? What? Are Young Americans Afraid to Have Kids?" *Esquire,* March 1974.

Adoption

"Adopting a Child Today." *Changing Times,* April 1977.
"Adoption Shortage Called Acute." *McCall's,* September 1971, p. 41.
Berman, C. *We Take This Child.* New York: Doubleday and Company, 1974.
Dywasuk, C. T. *Adoption: Is It for You?* New York: Harper and Row, 1973.
Klemesrud, J. "Adoption Costs Soar as Births Decline." *New York Times,* 20 February 1973.
Klibanoff, S., and Klibanoff, E. *Let's Talk about Adoption.* Boston: Little, Brown & Co., 1973.
"On Adoption: Things You Should Know about Adopting a Child if You're Single." *Mademoiselle,* November 1972.

Second Child

Belmont, Lillian; Stein, Zena; and Zybert, Patricia. "Child Spacing and Birth Order: Effect on Intellectual Ability in Two-Child Families." *Science,* 1 December 1978.
Franklin, Peter Eston. "Second Time." *American Baby,* March 1970.
Freeman, Hugh, and Freeman, Joan. "Does Birth Order Affect Your Child's Chances?" *American Baby,* December 1970.
Jimenez, Sherry Lynn Mims, and Jones, Linda Corson. "Pregnancy: The Second Time Around." *American Baby,* August 1979.
Kaufman, Sherwin A. "What To Tell the Children Before the Baby Comes." *Parents' Magazine,* September 1978.

King, Karen. "Is Two-Under-Two Right for You?" *Parents' Magazine and Better Family Living,* January 1973.

Ramos, Suzanne. "Introducing the Second Baby." *American Baby,* March 1972.

Roesch, Roberta. "Should You Have Another Baby?" *The Reader's Digest,* May 1971.

Roiphe, Anne. "Why Have More Than One?" *The New York Times Magazine,* 5 June 1977.

"The Second Baby." *American Baby,* March 1976.

Index